EAST ASIA

HISTORY, POLITICS, SOCIOLOGY, CULTURE

Edited by
Edward Beauchamp
University of Hawaii

T0386511

A ROUTLEDGE SERIES

EAST ASIA: HISTORY, POLITICS, SOCIOLOGY, CULTURE
EDWARD BEAUCHAMP, *General Editor*

ENGINEERING THE STATE
*The Huai River and Reconstruction
in Nationalist China,
1927–1937*
David A. Pietz

JAPANESE DIRECT INVESTMENT IN CHINA
*Locational Determinants and
Characteristics*
John F. Cassidy

SHOKO-KEN
A Late Medieval Daime Sukiya *Style
Japanese Tea-House*
Robin Noel Walker

FROM TRANSITION TO POWER
ALTERNATION
Democracy in South Korea, 1987–1997
Carl J. Saxer

HISTORY OF JAPANESE POLICIES
IN EDUCATION AID TO
DEVELOPING COUNTRIES,
1950s–1990s
*The Role of the Subgovernmental
Processes*
Takao Kamibeppu

A POLITICAL ECONOMY ANALYSIS OF
CHINA'S CIVIL AVIATION INDUSTRY
Mark Dougan

THE BIBLE AND THE GUN
Christianity in South China, 1860–1900
Joseph Tse-Hei Lee

AN AMERICAN EDITOR IN EARLY
REVOLUTIONARY CHINA
John William Powell and the
China Weekly/Monthly Review
Neil L. O'Brien

BETWEEN SACRIFICE AND DESIRE
*National Identity and the Governing
of Femininity in Vietnam*
Ashley Pettus

NEW CULTURE IN A NEW WORLD
*The May Fourth Movement and the
Chinese Diaspora in Singapore,
1919–1932*
David L. Kenley

ALLIANCE IN ANXIETY
*Détente and the Sino-American-
Japanese Triangle*
Go Ito

STATE AND SOCIETY IN CHINA'S
DEMOCRATIC TRANSITION
*Confucianism, Leninism, and
Economic Development*
Xiaoqin Guo

IN SEARCH OF AN IDENTITY
*The Politics of History as a School
Subject in Hong Kong, 1960s–2002*
Edward Vickers

PITFALL OR PANACEA
*The Irony of US Power
in Occupied Japan, 1945–1952*
Yoneyuki Sugita

THE RENAISSANCE OF TAKEFU
*How People and the Local Past
Changed the Civic Life of a
Regional Japanese Town*
Guven Peter Witteveen

THE PROSPECTS FOR A REGIONAL
HUMAN RIGHTS MECHANISM IN
EAST ASIA
Hidetoshi Hashimoto

AMERICAN WOMEN MISSIONARIES AT
KOBE COLLEGE, 1873–1909
New Dimensions in Gender
Noriko Kawamura Ishii

A PATH TOWARD GENDER EQUALITY
State Feminism in Japan
Yoshie Kobayashi

JAPAN'S FOREIGN POLICY MATURATION
A Quest for Normalcy

Kevin J. Cooney

ROUTLEDGE
NEW YORK & LONDON

Published in 2002 by
Routledge
711 Third Avenue, New York, NY 10017(US)

Published in Great Britain by
Routledge
2 Park Square, Milton Park, Abingdon, Oxon OX14 4RN (UK)

First issued in paperback 2013

Routledge is an imprint of the Taylor & Francis Group, an informa business

Library of Congress Cataloging-in-Publication Data

Cooney, Kevin J.
    Japan's foreign policy maturation : a quest for normalcy / Kevin J.
Cooney.
        p. cm. — (East Asia: history, politics, sociology & culture)
    Includes bibliographical references.
    ISBN 0-415-93516-4 (HB)
    ISBN 978-0-415-86494-7 (Paperback)

    1.Japan—Foreign relations—1945–1989. 2. japan—Officials and
employees—Interviews. I.Title. II. East Asia (New York, N.Y.)
DS889.5.C66 2002
327.52'009'045—dc21   2002020839

To My Family
Everything I do, I do for you,
my family whom I love.

CONTENTS

LIST OF FIGURES   xi
ACCRONYMS AND TERMS   xiii
ACKNOWLEDGMENTS   xv

1 THE STORY TO BE TOLD AND THE PUZZLE TO BE SOLVED   3
   Introduction   3
   The Catalyst for Change   4
   The Research Question   6
   The Literature   8
   — Foreign Policy Restructuring   8
   — Hermann's Model   11
   — Japanese Foreign Policy   11
   The Research—Elite Interviewing   13
   — Reliability and Validity   15
   — The Variables   16
   Objectives and Expected Significance of the Book   18
   Outline of the Book   19

2 THE STORY OF JAPAN'S "ABNORMAL" FOREIGN POLICY UNDER ARTICLE NINE   23
   Historical Background   25
   Japanese Foreign and Security Policy 1952-1990   31
   — The Yoshida Doctrine   33
   The Gulf War and Japanese Foreign Policy   35
   The Peace Keeping Operations Law (PKO)   37
   — Legal Issues   37

— International Politics and the PKO   39
— The Political Debate   40
   1. The Kaifu Bill and Why it Failed   40
   2. The Miyazawa PKO Bill   41
— Cambodia, Mozambique, and the Golan Heights   42
Towards a Security Council Seat and Beyond   43

3 REALISM AND FOREIGN POLICY RESTRUCTURING IN JAPAN   57
Japanese Limitations   58
Foreign Policy Restructuring   62
The Research Model   68
The Research Tool   77
The Field Research   83
Overview of the Results of the Field Research   86
— Old verses New   88

4 JAPAN'S SECURITY OPTIONS   103
Japan's National Security   105
Abandonment   108
Japan's Options   111
— Option #1: China   113
— Option #2: Russia   115
— Option #3: Multilateral Options including ASEAN/ARF   115
— Option #4: South Korea   116
— Option #5: North Korea   118
— Option #6: Unilateral Options or Go It Alone   118
— United Nations   119
Conclusion   119

5 HOW JAPAN VIEWS ITS PLACE IN THE WORLD AND THE "MYTH" OF *GAIATSU*   135
Adjusting to the Post-Cold War World   136
Gaiatsu   139
The "Myth" of *Gaiatsu*   140
What is Japan Doing?   145
— China   145
— Multilateral Efforts   146
— The United Nations   148
— The United States   149
— The Koreas   150
Conclusion   151

6 WHERE IS JAPAN GOING?   159
   Future Sources of Foreign Policy   159
     — The Diet   160
   The SDF in Japanese Foreign Policy   162
   Constitutional Reform   163
   World Leadership   165
   Japan's Limitations   166
   Japanese Hegemony?   166
   Japan's Future   168
   Suggestions for Foreign Policy Normalization   170
   Implications for Hermann's Model: What have we learned?   171
   Pragmatic Realism   172
   Further Research   175
   Concluding Remarks   175

APPENDICES   185
   A. Government/Diet Member Interview Questions
   B. Academic/Journalist Interview Questions
   C. Introduction Used for the Field Interviews   187
   D. Partial List of Elites Interviewed   193
                                                                           199
BIBLIOGRAPHY   201

INDEX   205

                                                                           223

LIST OF FIGURES

1:1   The mediating role of the decision processes between
change agents and degree of policy change.   12

1:2   Variables.   17

3:1   A diagram illustrating why a nation practicing Realism
might choose other options for Realist reasons.   65

3:2   The mediating role of the decision processes between
change agents and degree of policy change.   74

3:3   Hermann's Model plus External Pressure.   75

3:4   Hermann's Model plus Intervening Variables.   76

3:5   The "Interflux of Change" as it effects Hermann's Model
of Foreign Policy Restructuring.   90

4:1   Security Threats to Japan as Named by Foreign Policy Elites.   109

4:2   Japan's Options: Pluses and Minuses.   120

4:3   How Should We Perceive East Asian Security?.   122

5:1   Top Foreign Policy Concerns as Named by Foreign Policy Elites.   138

5:2   Hermann's Model plus External Pressure.   140

6:1   Hermann's Model plus Intervening Variables (a).   173

6:2   Hermann's Model plus Intervening Variables (b).   173

6:3   Hermann's Model plus Intervening Variables (c).   173

ACRONYMS AND TERMS

APEC   Asia-Pacific Economic Cooperation

ASDF   Air Self Defense Forces.

ASEAN   Association of Southeast Asian Nations

ARF   ASEAN Regional Forum

"Comfort Women"   Women forced into sexual slavery by the Imperial
                        Japanese Military to "service" Japanese troops serving
                        in the front lines. Many of these women who survived
                        the war are requesting compensation from the
                        Japanese government for what they suffered.

CPJ   Communist Party of Japan

Diet   The Japanese Parliament.

DMZ   The *Demilitarized Zone* separates North and South
Korea.

DPJ   Democratic Party of Japan.

Gaiatsu   Foreign Pressure, and in particular American pressure.

Gaijin: Foreigner.

GSDF	Ground Self Defense Forces.
GNP	Gross National Product.
ICBM	Intercontinental Ballistic Missiles.
Japan Passing	The concept that Japan is being ignored and passed by the other great powers.
JCP	Japan Communist Party
JDA	Japan Defense Agency
katakana	The Japanese syllabary for rendering foreign words in Japanese.
KEDO:	Korean Energy Development Organization
kenpou	The Japanese constitution.
kiretsu	Monopolistic Japanese business cartels.
LDP	Liberal Democratic Party.
manga	Japanese comic books read by both children and adults.
Meiji Era	Meaning "enlightened rule". Named for the Emperor Meiji it lasted from 1868-1912. During this period Japan modernized faster than any nation had ever modernized and became a major military power.
MOFA	Ministry of Foreign Affairs.
NCO	Non Commissioned Officer.
NPR	National Police Reserves (predecessor to the SDF 1950-52).
NSF	National Safety Forces (predecessor to the SDF 1952-54).

nemawashi	A Japanese term for the consensus building process.
ODA	Official Development Assistance.
on	indebtedness.
Oxwalk tactics	The tactic used by the SDP during the passage of the PKO Law. The SDP Diet members walked as slowly as possible in protest to cast their ballots thus delaying the final outcome.
PKO	Peace Keeping Operations
PKF	Peace Keeping Forces
ROK	Republic of Korea (South Korea)
Sangin	Upper house of the Japanese Diet; The House of Councillors.
SCAP	Supreme Command/Commander Allied forces-Pacific.
SDF	Self Defense Forces.
SDP	Social Democratic Party.
SDPJ	Social Democratic Party of Japan the predecessor to the current SDP.
SLOC	Sea Lines Of Communication.
Shugin:	The lower house of the Japanese Diet, The House of Representatives.
TMD	Theater Missile Defense system.
wa	harmony.
WTO	World Trade Organization.

ACKNOWLEDGMENTS

I n the writing of this book I owe thanks to so many people. My first thanks goes to Routledge Publishers for accepting it for publication and to Edward Beauchamp and Farideh Koohi-Kamali for their work in editing this book. In the research phase I am indebted to all the Japanese officials who granted me time out of their very busy schedules to see me and permit me to interview them. I am especially indebted to Councillor Kei Hata who granted me an interview without a reference and helped me gain access to other Diet members. I am also grateful to Tsuneo Akaha of the Monterey Institute who introduced me to several people in MOFA and the JDA. My research assistant, Yoko Takagi, deserves special thanks for her help in setting up the initial interviews and working so hard to make the field research a success. Thanks are also due to my *senpai* Donald Thompson for his help and my former students Rudi and Yuko Azali for their work in answering phone calls and setting up interviews. Thank you also to both the Takagi family and the Sakurai family for opening their homes to a foreigner and permitting me to stay with you during my time in Japan.

I am also deeply indebted to my professors and colleagues here at Arizona State University for all their help and advice. I want to thank Dr. Michael Mitchell for his help and friendship. I am grateful to Dr. Kim Kahn for all her help in helping me prepare the questionnaires for the field work and for all she taught me about research methods. Special thanks goes to Dr. Stephen Walker and Dr. Peter McDonough for reading and commenting on this book. I have learned a great deal from both of you and I value your friendship.

I also am grateful to many of my colleagues in my department who helped in so many ways. I am especially grateful for the scholarly support and friendship of John Linantud, Elaine Jordan, Tong Ge, Matthew Stevenson, and Mike Yawn without whose support I would not have made it this far. I am especially grateful to Dr. Seng Tan, my colleague, brother in Christ, and dearest friend. Seng has helped me through some of my most difficult times both personally and academically. His friendship went above and beyond the call of duty by reading and commenting on all the drafts and revisions of this book. I am a richer person because of his advice and friendship. Thank you.

I owe one of my greatest debts of gratitude to my mentor, Dr. Sheldon Simon. Dr. Simon has been both a friend and councillor to me. He is one of the finest examples of a gentleman and a scholar that I have ever known. I hope to follow his example of kindness and integrity throughout my personal and professional life. Furthermore, he and his wife Sharlynn opened their home and hearts to both my wife and myself on many occasions. We will always remember your kindness and our Thanksgivings with you. Thank you.

Further thanks are due to my friends and family, both near and far. Thank you to Mark and Barbra Rentz, Brad and Ayako Tritle, Wayne and Lisa Rich, Shaun and Shelly Orchard and family, Dan McCoy, and all our friends in the International Students Club. You are the best. Thank you also to my Japanese family in Japan for all your support and love, *honto ni arigato gozaimashita*. I also want to thank my family for all of their love and support throughout the years. I especially owe the deepest debt of gratitude to Jerry and Arliss Cooney, my father and mother, for all the time, effort, and money they put into raising me to follow Christ and contributing to my education.

My penultimate words of thanks go to the woman who made this all possible, my wife Atsuko. This is your book too. Without your love, support, and kindness this never would have been possible. You are the reason that I get up in the morning; I am so proud that I married you. Thank you for all your unending love, patience, and encouragement. The future has yet to be written for us but as long as we are together I know that we will be happy. I Love You! Last of all I want to thank God from whom all good things come and for his blessing our lives with our daughter Aiyana Khrysti and a new soon to be born little one. Thank you one and all.

Kevin J. Cooney,
November 17, 2001

JAPAN'S FOREIGN POLICY MATURATION

THE STORY TO BE TOLD AND THE PUZZLE TO BE SOLVED

... the political organism is always experiencing both continuities and change, and thus is always in motion, slipping behind, moving ahead, holding fast, or otherwise adjusting and changing in response to internal developments and external circumstances.— James N. Rosenau[1]

INTRODUCTION

Japan, as a nation, is in the midst of change. Much of this change has been brought about by the end of the Cold War. This change is evidenced by the fact that Japan is sending troops overseas for the first time since the end of the second world war and is very anxious to demonstrate that it can make a "human" contribution to the world community in spite of its constitutional limitations. It is also attempting to step out of the larger shadow of the U.S. and take its place alongside the U.S. and the other great powers. At the same time Japan is coming to terms with the fact that in spite of its great economic strength it is fully vulnerable to both international and domestic economic turbulence and its own structural problems. It is additionally coming to terms with the idea that as a major power on the world stage it can be a target much as the U.S. is. An instance of this is the Peruvian embassy hostage incident in December 1997.

This book will argue that Japan is in the midst of a maturation process in which it is seeking to present itself as a great power. The book also argues that there is a process underway in the Diet (legislature) to take power from the powerful bureaucracies in Japan and transfer it to the elected legislative leadership of the Diet. Additionally, significant political elements in Japan are seeking to escape the constitutional constraints imposed by Article Nine of the constitution, which is the most important barrier to Japan's becoming a normal nation.

This book is thus a narrative about political leaders in Japan and this author's quest to understand shifts and changes in their foreign policy. It is, moreover, an account and exploration of the people in leadership positions and the way they view the world. It is also the story of the Japanese foreign policy leadership based on the author's conversations and interviews with them. The basic thesis of this book is that people make policy while institutions administer. It is for this reason that people, or agents if you will, will be the primary focus of this book. This will be a study of the human element in politics and specifically foreign policy. It is for this reason that the conclusions of this book will primarily be based on trends in observed behavior and attitudes rather than statistical data or institutional analysis. The study of structure or institutions will be secondary.

To put this succinctly, this book will be an empirical examination of changes in Japanese foreign policy brought on by the end of the Cold War and a study of what the Japanese political leadership feels that Japan's role in the world should be. Japan is a major player and its growing power on the world scene and changes in its foreign policy frequently impact the rest of the world. Furthermore, the study of change in Japan provides an excellent case study of a major power engaged in foreign policy change during an extended period of peace.

THE CATALYST FOR CHANGE

As in Virgil's phrase "a new order for the ages" so the "New World Order" rang in the end of the Cold War, and as in Virgil's Roman Empire, the post Cold War world of *Pax Americana* has witnessed wars and uprisings on all fronts. For Japan, the simple world it knew during the Cold War had become complex. Choices were no longer clear. Decisions became difficult and complex.

It is said that some nations live by the sword and perish by the sword. In Japan's case, since World War II it has lived by the dove of pacifism and must now choose whether to let its role in the world dwindle or perish by its self imposed pacifism[2] or take up the sword and risk the casualties and enemies it has avoided since the end of World War II.

Japan is not alone in feeling the effects of the sudden and unpredicted end to the Cold War. The end of the Cold War brought about many profound changes in the foreign policies of many nations. The bi-polar conflict that had governed the post World War II era ended in such a way that no nation was fully prepared to deal with a world turned upside down. The U.S./Soviet conflict left, nevertheless, a residue of structures, institutions, and policies that continue to shape and govern the foreign affairs of many nations in the so called "New World Order". One of the nations whose foreign policy has been greatly affected by the ending of the Cold War is Japan. This was due in many ways to the uniqueness[3] of Japanese Foreign Policy and its constitutional restraints.

During the occupation of Japan by the United States after the Second World War, the Occupation Government headed by General Douglas MacArthur wrote and gave Japan its post war constitution. This constitution has been called "The Japanese Peace Constitution." The key foreign policy peculiarity of Japan's constitution is article nine of Chapter II: The Renunciation of War. It states:

> "Aspiring sincerely to an international peace based on justice and order, the Japanese people forever renounce war as a sovereign right of the nation and the threat or use of force as a means of settling international disputes.
>
> In order to accomplish the aim of the preceding paragraph, land, sea, and air forces, as well as other war potential, will never be maintained. The right of belligerency of the state will not be recognized."[4]

Article Nine was written shortly before the onset of the Cold War and is fundamental to the understanding of Japanese post-war foreign policy. As a result of the onset of the Cold War, Japan was pressured by the U.S. into establishing the Self Defense Forces (SDF) which were to have *defensive* capabilities only and to provide a domestic defense against foreign invasion. The lynchpin of this arrangement is the U.S./Japan Security Treaty which promises U.S. support if Japan is ever attacked, thus negating the need for Japanese force projection (offensive) capabilities.

The long term effect of Article Nine was that Japan had a constitutional excuse <u>not</u> to act as a "normal" nation in international affairs. The primary architect of Japan's foreign policy under Article Nine was then Prime Minister Shigeru Yoshida.[5] His foreign policy strategy/agenda became known as the Yoshida Doctrine. Japanese foreign policy during much of the Cold War was based on this Yoshida Doctrine which permitted Japan to focus on economic development while depending on the U.S. for its international security. The great benefit of this was that Japan did not have to spend much of its GNP on defense and national security related needs. The cornerstone of the Yoshida Doctrine was the Japan/U.S. Security Treaty in which the U.S. guaranteed Japanese security. Japanese foreign policy, in turn, was largely based on loyalty to and support for the United States.

This worked well until the end of the Cold War and the Gulf War that followed. The Gulf War took Japan, politically, by surprise; "like a bolt out of the blue."[6] Iraq's invasion of Kuwait on August 2, 1990 and the subsequent war had a major impact on the politics of Japan.[7] Japan was forced to face the true reality of its economic superpower status for the first time in a major international crisis. Initially Japan sprinted out of the blocks at the start of the crisis only to stumble and be left dazed and bewildered when it realized that the Cold War was over and the rules had changed. Japan was asked to participate at a level that was commensurate to its economic status in the world and Japan was not prepared to do this. Japan's "checkbook" diplomacy, in which it contributed financially to international actions by the US and the UN but never made a "human" contribution by putting its soldiers in harms way, caused it to be severely criticized abroad. The Yoshida Doctrine that had served it so well was in desperate need of revision.

At the core of the problem was the old constitutional question of Article Nine. Could Japan send troops overseas even if they were under United Nations command? Japan was not ready to answer this question, but the world was waiting for an answer. Japan was still in the middle of trying to come to terms with the end of the Cold War and its impact on US/Japanese relations and the Japan/United States Security Treaty. Japan was searching to find its new place in the world when the Gulf War forced Japan to make some hard choices. These choices, though inadequate in the eyes of many, started a debate within Japan that has forced it to attempt to reconcile its economic superpower status and its constitutional obligations.

As a result of the external pressures brought on by the Gulf War and its aftermath, the Japanese Diet passed on June 15, 1992 *The Law Concerning Cooperation in U.N. Peacekeeping and Other Operations* (otherwise known as the PKO Law) which went into effect on August 10th of that same year. This law marked the most significant change in Japan's post-war foreign/military policy since the creation of the Self Defense Forces (SDF) in the 1950s, and marked a fundamental shift in the course of Japanese foreign policy.

THE RESEARCH QUESTION

Japan's constitution renounces war and prohibits the maintenance of military forces. There has been some commentary on this situation in legal and military circles, but little has been done in the area of political analysis. The questions that are being asked are: "What is Japan's new role in the world?", "What accounts for the gradual change in the role of the SDF?", "What are the driving forces domestically behind these changes?", and "What is Japan's long term foreign policy agenda?"

This book will look at the causes and implications of foreign policy changes in Japan since the end of the Cold War. The author recognizes that, restructuring is **not** fundamentally changing Japanese foreign policy. This is because Japan is not fundamentally changing its loyalties, rather it is working to establish a fuller partnership with the U.S. Under the constraints imposed by Cold War interpretations of Article Nine, Japan limited its foreign policy under the Yoshida Doctrine. In the post Cold War era Japan is seeking to enlarge its foreign policy role to that of a normal nation. At the same time, these changes in Japanese foreign policy are not merely incremental course corrections, but major shifts in national policy. Japan is undergoing a period of foreign policy maturation in which Tokyo is stepping out of the larger shadow of the U.S. and taking its own place as a more equal and normal partner in the international arena. This study of Japanese foreign policy maturation is based on the foreign policy change literature which can be applied to Japan. It looks at foreign policy change from three different levels of analysis.[8] These levels are: the international system level, the individual level,[9] and the state level. The importance of the choice of these levels of analysis is that Japan operates as a major player within the international system, but it is Japanese societal values and their influence which dictate Japan's state to state relations. The first level of analysis used is the international system within the theoretical framework of Neorealism.

The end of the Cold War brought about many changes in the international system. The bipolar world was replaced with a multipolar one (or a unipolar one according to many traditional Realists) that presented new opportunities for Japan as well as many other nations. The book will look at these changes in the international system from a Japanese foreign policy point of view. The idea being to show how Japan is reacting and adapting to changes in the international system and the opportunities that these changes present.

The second level of analysis that will be used is the Individual/Societal level. This will look at the rise of new values and ideas in Japan's younger generation of leadership which matured after the Second World War and contrast them to the attitudes of Japan's older generation of leaders that lived through the war. This section employs existing survey data, field interviews with Japanese elites conducted during the summer of 1998, and secondary literature to assess changes in the attitudes and values within Japanese society as they relate to foreign policy and the role of the armed forces. It also looks at the formation of foreign policy within the major political parties as reflective of these societal dynamics.

The third level of analysis is the State. This level looks at and determines whether Japanese foreign policy is undergoing a maturation process or is merely a continuation of its current policy. By "maturation" I ask whether Japan is directing its foreign policy to act as a "normal nation" with interests independent of its ally, the U.S. In other words, is Japan really trying to step out of the larger U.S. shadow and its Yoshida Doctrine based foreign policy and act as an independent player? The State level also examines Japan's larger role in the world *vis-à-vis* other states. It particularly looks at its role in the world political economy and regional security. The security issue offers a range of questions and possibilities for Japan such as whether it will attempt to establish an independent naval presence in East Asia and whether the nations of East Asia will accept a larger Japanese role. There is also the link between its economic dominance and a possible future regional security role through Asia-Pacific Economic Cooperation forum (APEC) and Association of Southeast Asian Nations (ASEAN) Regional Forum (ARF).[10]

THE LITERATURE

The primary literatures for this research include foreign policy change and Japanese foreign policy. First we will look at the restructuring literature to be followed by the literature on Japanese foreign policy making. As previously mentioned, even though I acknowledge that Japan is not changing its basic foreign policy, that policy is undergoing a maturation process for which the foreign policy restructuring literature provides an explanation. Some nations from their own perspective, such as China, see Japan as restructuring. Other nations see simply minor course corrections.

The concept of foreign policy maturation helps deal with this problem of perspective by giving us a different angle to study. Since the Gulf War, there has been a fundamental change in Japanese foreign policy as evidenced by its dispatch of SDF troops overseas under U.N. command; but there has been no reorientation of foreign allegiance which is typically the basis for defining foreign policy restructuring.[11] The key to understanding the Japan case is that under Article Nine Japan has not been behaving as a "normal" nation. The changes exemplified by the PKO Law demonstrate that Japan is attempting to change its foreign policy so that it can take its place among normal nations.

FOREIGN POLICY RESTRUCTURING

The literature involving foreign policy restructuring began in the 1980s with James N. Rosenau. This was followed by the works of Kal Holsti, Kjell Goldmann and Charles Hermann in the mid to late 1980s. These efforts are important but are in no way conclusive; and they uniformly issue invitations for more scholarly work on the issue of foreign policy restructuring.

The seminal work is James Rosenau's *The Study of Political Adaptation* published in 1981. This book is a set of essays written and published throughout the 1970s on the subject. The basic argument that Rosenau makes is that:

> . . . our understanding of politics can better be deepened and broadened by treating political phenomena as forms of human adaptation....the political organism is always experiencing both continuities and change, and thus is always in motion, slipping behind, moving ahead, holding fast, or otherwise adjusting and changing in response to internal developments and external circumstances.

Therefore,

> ... to analyze how the adjustments are made, the changes sustained,
> and the continuities preserved is to engage in the study of political
> adaption.[12]

What Rosenau specifically does is to postulate that foreign policy is essentially a mechanism for a nation to adapt to or deal with changes in the world
around it.

Rosenau's work was furthered by Kal Holsti in his book *Why Nations
Realign: Foreign Policy Restructuring in the Postwar World* (1982). This book
takes the form of a collection of essays by Holsti and others looking primarily at examples of foreign policy change in the Third World and small states.
Foreign policy change in the First World is acknowledged by Holsti as being
difficult to handle, but cases of change are examined from Canada and
France. There is the beginning of a theoretical element of foreign policy
change in this work. Rosenau described what he saw as happening to nations
when they made changes in foreign policy, but Holsi begins to theorize as to
what is happening when nations adjust their foreign policy. Thirteen types of
foreign policy restructuring are identified by Holsti as possible for a nation
state to make over time. These thirteen types are subsumed into four ideal
kinds of foreign policies. They are isolation, self-reliance, dependence and
nonalignment-diversification.[13] The framework of his model focuses on the
roles of external factors, domestic factors, background historical and cultural
factors, and factors within the policy making process itself.

What Holsti regrettably concludes is that we can not explain from a foreign policy point of view why some states restructure and others do not
when faced with similar circumstances. In spite of this Holsti was able to give
us an understanding of certain conditions that would predispose a state to
change its foreign policy. Holsti also found that it was easier for a nation to
declare its intent to change foreign policy than to implement the announced
change. This last aspect of change has an interesting application to the
Japanese case in that some current aspirations for change are not being
implemented due to both overt and covert international opposition. This
study provides an excellent opportunity to examine the factors that can prevent foreign policy change at the state level. On the other hand Holsti's work
deals almost exclusively with threat based change rather than situation or
environment based change as would be more applicable to the Japanese
case. It is for this reason the book does not rely primarily on the model developed by Holsti for foreign policy restructuring.

Kjell Goldmann in his 1988 book *Change and Stability in Foreign Policy:
The Problems and Possibilities of Détente*, looks at the patterns of political
action to understand the process of détente. He looks at the pressures for
change and the pressures on the other hand for continuation of previous
policies.[14] Goldmann lays out a "theoretical sketch" for the stabilization of

foreign policy which demonstrates whether a foreign policy will continue or change. His strength is in the cataloging of ways in which foreign policy can undergo change, and in which stability could be undermined. The application of Goldmann's "theoretical sketch" to this inquiry is limited in that the research does not look into the stabilization of Japanese foreign policy. Rather, the book examines change and the causes of change in Japanese foreign policy since the end of the Cold War.

Charles Hermann's 1990 presidential address to the International Studies Association is particularly useful in that it looks at redirection of foreign policy incrementally. The title of his address/paper is *Changing Course: When Governments Choose to Redirect Foreign Policy*. It is Hermann's model that is used for this research. The reason for this is that Hermann's model, more than Holsti or Goldmann, allows for the continual change in foreign policy that is always happening, as noted by Rosenau. Furthermore Hermann says, "Change is a pervasive quality of governmental foreign policy."[15] Hermann investigates the study of foreign policy change and finds that the "decision making process itself can obstruct or facilitate change."[16] Thus there is the argument that change always exists in foreign policy and that the study of foreign policy and the study of foreign policy restructuring are one and the same. Hermann however, disagrees with this argument and this author concurs that there is a difference. This difference requires a close examination of change in the decision making process which is one element of this discourse.

According to Hermann, "Changes that mark a reversal, or at least, a profound redirection of a country's foreign policy are of special interest because of the demands their adoption pose on the initiating government and its domestic constituents and because of their potentially powerful consequences for other countries."[17] Wars may begin or end because of foreign policy changes. It is for this reason some conclude that due to the effort needed to change foreign policy, regime change may be the only way to facilitate this. However, as Hermann points out, when we reflect on this we find cases where the same government that started a foreign policy was the one responsible for its reversal or replacement.

The question that Hermann is asking in general and that I am asking with respect to Japan is, "Under what circumstances do these kinds of changes occur in which an existing government recognizes that its current course is seriously inadequate, mistaken, or no longer applicable? What are the conditions under which self-correcting change may arise?"[18] The answers to these questions can and will have significant impact on the study of foreign policy. This not only because foreign policy changes are for the better (because they often are not), but rather for the consequences they generate and pose for the country's people and institutions as well as other countries.

HERMANN'S MODEL

Hermann is concerned with the fundamental redirection of a nation's foreign policy. Hermann deals with this through a four level graduated description of foreign policy change. The four involve increasing level of change: (1) Adjustment Changes, (2) Program Changes, (3) Problem/Goal Changes, and (4) International Orientation changes. This last change involves a basic shift in the international actors' roles and activities in which not just one policy but many are simultaneously changed. This typically but not always involves a shift in alignment with other nations or a major shift in the role that it plays within an alignment.

The conditions for change based on Hermann's research into different academic disciplines beyond political science like political psychology, psychology, sociology, education, and others are fourfold. First, domestic political systems may affect foreign policy. For example, a) issues become a centerpiece in the struggle for political power; b) the attitudes and beliefs of a dominant domestic constituency undergo a profound change; and c) a realignment occurs of the essential constituency of a regime, or a revolution or other transformation takes place.[19] The second is bureaucratic decision making. The third is cybernetics and the fourth is learning.

Hermann further develops his model by selecting from his review of the literature two things necessary to effect change in a domestic political system's foreign policy. They are: first, that there must be change in that system and, second, that systemic change must trigger a change in the government's foreign policy.[20] The agents of change are labeled as leader driven, bureaucratic advocacy, domestic restructuring, and external shock.[21] The interaction of these with the decision making process can be seen in figure 1:1. Of course there is likely to be interplay between these agents of foreign policy change.

The rest of Hermann's article deals with the various phases of foreign policy decision making and will be examined more closely in chapter three of this book. Next we will quickly look at the various sources about Japanese domestic and foreign policy that will provide the foundation for my analysis of the recent changes in Japanese foreign policy. These works relate to the foreign policy change literature and Hermann's model in that they examine unique cultural factors and Japanese attitudes toward foreign policy. They also give us a greater understanding of the various agents of change at work in the creation of Japanese foreign policy.

JAPANESE FOREIGN POLICY

Gerald L. Curtis, a leading expert on Japan, is the author of several books on Japan. In his book *The Japanese Way of Politics* (1988), he provides much of the foundation for the study of the Japanese political system. Curtis explores

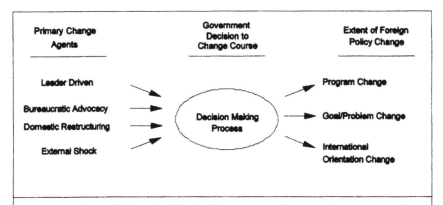

Primary Change Agents	Government Decision to Change Course	Extent of Foreign Policy Change
Leader Driven		Program Change
Bureaucratic Advocacy	Decision Making Process	Goal/Problem Change
Domestic Restructuring		
External Shock		International Orientation Change

Figure 1:1   The mediating role of the decision processes between change agents and degree of policy change . (Hermann, 13)

the foundations of the Japanese postwar political system and the establish-ment of the Liberal Democratic Party (LDP). He also looks at the main oppo-sition party, the Socialists, and their role in perpetual opposition. The inter-action of these two parties is explored in the context of Japanese political decision making. Finally, Curtis looks at the changing nature of the Japanese voter which has accelerated rapidly since the book was published.

A second and more recent book by Curtis is an edited volume called *Japan's Foreign Policy after the Cold War: Coping with Change* (1993). This vol-ume was the first work to look at Japan's post cold war options. It analyzes Japan's diplomatic style, economic needs, security concerns, relations with its neighbors, and most importantly looks at Japan and the new multilateralism. It provides state of the art thinking on Japanese foreign policy making.

Curtis also provides in his edited 1994 book *The United States, Japan, and Asia* a collection of papers exploring the current status of Japan in relation to the U.S. and the rest of Asia. This work provides an excellent analysis that is salient background for this research proposal. Military concerns such as the stability of the U.S./Japan Security Treaty and how the differing regional pow-ers and groupings, such as China and ASEAN, view it are examined in detail. More importantly the current and ongoing economic tensions between the U.S. and Japan are examined with an eye towards the future role of Japan in the world.

Reinhard Drifte, another leading expert on Japanese foreign policy, take a look toward the future of Japanese foreign policy in his 1998 book *Japan's Foreign Policy for the 21st Century: From Economic Superpower to What Power?* Professor Drifte sees Japan as increasingly willing to act as a major power, having come to terms with the end of the Cold War. He sees Japan's position in the world having increased to the point that even non-action by the

Japanese government can have a major effect on other nations.[22] Furthermore, Japan is seen as having not yet fully established its "ideological, intellectual and moral leadership" resulting in a 'leadership by stealth'.[23]

Sampson and Walker (1987) provide a basic examination of cultural norms that govern Japanese politics. This survey and its comparison with France's political workings highlights the central thesis of this book, which is that Japan is changing the direction of its foreign policy and that of its role in the world. Gaenslen in his 1992 paper on Decision-Making Groups further explores the theoretical application of group decision making which is very valuable in the case of Japan in that nearly all decisions of consequence are made by groups. This group dynamic is an especially interesting application for Hermann's model.

Probably the most important recent work on the role of Japanese domestic political power is Karel van Wolferen's book *The Enigma of Japanese Power* (1993). Van Wolferen systematically takes apart almost every area of Japanese political and public life in his search for the core of Japanese power. Van Wolferen's conclusion is that the main source of Japanese power is in the bureaucracy rather than in democratic institutions such as the Diet and to a lesser extent the Prime Minister's Office. While *The Enigma of Japanese Power* may have overstated the power of the bureaucracy, it is also the first scholarly work to assess the significance of the Japanese bureaucracy in detail.[24] While van Wolferen focuses on bureaucratic power, this book gains from the book's views about the interface of that power and the people, and the Diet and the potential application of bureaucratic power as a major agent of change. This book further argues that foreign policy making power is slowly shifting away from the Ministry of Foreign Affairs (MOFA) to the Diet.

Several works by such scholars as Takashi Inoguchi, Warren Hunsburger, and Yoichi Funabashi among others further the book's study of Japan's foreign policy agenda. Overall the available secondary literature provides good background for this book. The history of Japanese foreign policy is covered in detail along with an informative and useful discussion of Japanese decision making norms. What is lacking is any empirically based study of why the PKO law was passed over the strong objections of the opposition and how the law relates to future Japanese foreign policy objectives. This book partially fills this gap in the literature by examining the intentions and opinions of relevant members of the Japanese Diet and the Foreign Ministry. It is hoped that these will provide the reader with an opportunity to glimpse the direction and future goals of Japanese foreign policy.

THE RESEARCH —ELITE INTERVIEWING

The empirical core of this book is a series of fifty-six elite field interviews conducted during the summer of 1998 with Japanese Diet members of both houses, Foreign Ministry officials, members of the Japanese press, Cabinet officials, and Defense Agency officials. Since there are 512 members in the lower House of Representatives and 252 members in the upper House of Counselors the interviews concentrated on Japanese members who focus on foreign policy or sit on foreign relations or defense related committees in the Diet. Even a random sampling of the Diet would be so large as to be unwieldy. Interviews with Diet members possessing expertise in foreign policy from every major party were conducted. Foreign Ministry officials who dealt and deal with the PKO law and its implications were also interviewed.

Japanese politicians often confide in members of the press corp in exchange for their silence on an issue until the matter is resolved. Once the issue is resolved the reporters are free to chronicle the events that transpired from their knowledge gained from first hand interviews. Given this unique relationship between the Japanese press and politicians two interviews were conducted with members of the press corp specializing in foreign policy. Defense Ministry officials were also interviewed to gauge their reactions to changes in Japanese foreign policy.[25]

Access to these elites was gained through initial letters of introduction and email contacts. Once the first contacts were made the initial interviewees gave the author access or references to other elites thus establishing the network of elites that were interviewed. More on details the interview methods and their reliability will be discussed in later chapters.

The interviews were in Japanese or in English as required for the comfort of the interviewee. The interviewee was also given the opportunity to remain anonymous if he or she so chose. This helped elicit more frank and honest answers rather than party/government positions. Any comments by those who chose to remain anonymous are cited as being anonymous.

Two separate but similar questionnaires were constructed for the interviews in both Japanese and English. One was designed for Diet members and the other for government officials and academics.[26] A special set of open ended questions was designed to probe the Diet members for the reasons they supported or opposed the PKO Law and their personal thoughts on the future direction of Japanese foreign policy. One question probed the individual member's feeling on the need for this change in policy by asking the question, "Why do you feel that the government felt it necessary for Japan to pass the PKO Law?" This was asked to get at the government's explanation to Diet members asked to pass the PKO Law and the differing perspectives on this by political party. This was followed by a question asking whether the member agreed or disagreed at the time and why.

A follow-on question asked the Diet members if they would change their vote now if they could and if so, why. This was to check for any realignment or change of opinion. The questions thus give us both past and present perspectives.

The second set of questions reflected Hermann's change paradigm by looking for the primary change agents and the extent of foreign policy change that they bring about. Some of the questions were: What the interviewee believes the goals of Japanese foreign policy should be?, What needs to be done to achieve these goals?, What are the obstacles to these goals?, How should Japan deal with these obstacles?, How does this fit with Article Nine?, What role, if any, should Japan seek in international security fora?, How will Japan deal with its history in East Asia if it does take on a larger role? What could or would be the domestic consequences of this larger role?, Who or what groups are pushing for foreign policy change?, and What are the forces outside of Japan that are pushing for change? The questions were designed to build on each other. For example: Where do you feel that Japan is going in the future with its foreign policy?, Do you feel this is the right direction?, Why or why not?, If not, where would you like to see it go in the future?

RELIABILITY AND VALIDITY

Research based on elite interviews means that the validity of the results is dependent on the integrity of the answers given by the interviewees. Internal validity will only be a problem with the translations from Japanese and the codification of the results. Most of the interviews were recorded[27] and the translations were cross checked with others in order to control for this potential problem. The criterion-related or predictive validity of the interviews that can be applied to the direction of Japanese foreign policy in general is reasonably strong. As Japanese society revolves around consensus so does decision making. Even with a highly controversial issue, the Diet still had to forge a majority consensus to pass the PKO law. The Foreign Ministry for all its power still needs the Diet to change or reinterpret constitutional law. Thus the opinions of the Diet members, ministry officials, and the press do matter and will matter in any future foreign policy legislation.

The main threat to validity is history. If there are any events that happened before, during, or after the survey relating to the PKO or Japanese national security and in particular if these events are bad (ie. a squad of Japanese soldiers is killed while participating on a U.N. peacekeeping mission) the results could look dramatically different than they were in this study.[28] These types of problems are impossible to control for; and one needs to be aware of and acknowledge them. An example of this was the nuclear tests by India the week before the interviews started, the Pakistani test during the interview period, and the North Korean missile test over Japan following the interviews.[29]

The main threat to reliability is that the answers given would not be the same answers that would be given to a Japanese scholar. The reasoning behind this is that the Japanese as a whole tend to be very private about what they consider to be internal matters. Consultation and research yielded no definite conclusion concerning what type of answer would be given to a *gai-jin*[30] studying Japanese foreign policy making. Conventional wisdom was that it is likely that the survey would result in true answers and possibly even clearer answers than a Japanese would receive under similar circumstances.[31] The actual interview experience seemed to uphold this hypothesis and several illustrations of this are given in the chapter dealing directly with the results of the interviews.

THE VARIABLES

The end of the Cold War and the Persian Gulf War are seen as the initial independent variables for Japan's foreign policy maturation as they are watershed events which clearly demonstrated the need for change in Japanese foreign policy. The PKO Law was the first major effort to deal with the realization that change was needed in Japanese Foreign Policy in the aftermath of the Persian Gulf War. The PKO Law is thus a dependent variable representing the change brought about by these independent variables. After its enactment, the PKO Law can be seen as a new independent variable for foreign policy change accounting for the changes in the role of the SDF on UN peacekeeping missions. The reason for this is that the PKO Law permitted Japan to send troops overseas for the first time since World War II. This new ability took Japan a giant step forward in its quest to be a normal nation.

Furthermore, one can see the end of the Cold War as an independent variable accounting for the dependent variable of the September 1997 revision of the U.S./Japan Defense Guidelines. These guidelines spell out major changes in Japanese foreign/security policy *vis-à-vis* the U.S. and bring this book up to date with recent foreign policy changes. For example, Japan will now in the event of a crisis or war provide ports and airports for U.S. forces. It will also provide minesweeping and receive refugees from war zones into Japan as needed. This change is not with out opposition. The Japanese Maritime SDF was to be given the right to enforce any U.N. embargo on the open sea by boarding ships to inspect their cargos; however the bill authorizing this was withdrawn from consideration in the Diet under heavy criticism and this right of boarding ships under U.N. auspices is not part of the revised Guidelines. Significantly, Japanese forces still can not enter in to combat or operate in a combat zone. However SDF forces on U.N. peacekeeping missions can now act in self-defense as units rather than as individuals. How a combat zone is defined in any future conflict, like the Korean peninsula, will also mark a significant foreign policy challenge for Japan. The interaction between the different variables is illustrated in figure 1:2.

This being said, the principal independent variable for this book is the PKO Law since it marks such a significant change in what had been Japanese foreign policy. A secondary independent variable is the end of the Cold War as it is the primary event that created the need for change in Japanese foreign policy. The principal dependent variable is foreign policy change. The elite interviews combined with the research in secondary sources measure the direction of foreign policy change. Further dependent variables are support for and attitudes toward foreign policy changes. The elite interviews along with existing poll data expose attitudes toward the quantity of and level of support for change in Japanese foreign policy among elites and the general public.

The elite interviews revealed a dichotomy based on party affiliation with some overlap based on members who have switched parties or simply changed their opinions. The study found a majority that supported the PKO law on varying grounds relating to Japan's role in the world. The far right wing in Japanese politics strongly supported it on the grounds that it is time

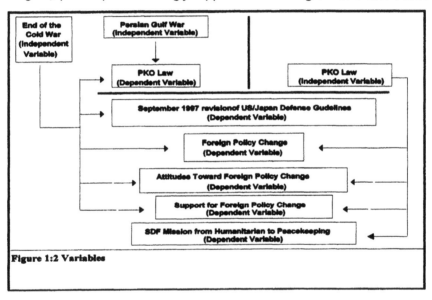

Figure 1:2 Variables

that Japan asserted a more active military role. Others of a less radical bent welcomed it with softer language than the far right, but with the same desire to get the proverbial "monkey" of World War II and Article Nine off their backs. Still others saw it simply as a chance for Japan to give to the world by helping the U.N. There seemed to be a consensus on the direction Japanese foreign policy should take, even though the reasons for that consensus differed.

A strong minority, coming mostly from the Socialist Party and other leftist groups, opposed Japan's continued participation in peacekeeping and more active role in world affairs for two reasons. The first being Japan's past role as military aggressor. They feel that elements within Japan desire to see the country become a power in the world so that it could again be a military power. The other grounds for rejection of the PKO Law are based on the simple principle that it violates the "pacifist constitution" of Japan and that a remilitarized Japan is a step in the wrong direction. One or both of these reasons were often cited by those who oppose the PKO missions but there also seemed to be a resignation on the part of most that the future of the PKO missions were "set in stone" and that there was little hope for change or reversal of policy.

One surprise gleaned from the interviews was the apparent decline in the power of MOFA and a corresponding rise in power for the Diet to make foreign policy. It is because of this that this book, will hopefully produce a better understanding of the way foreign policy decisions are made in Japan and how Japanese foreign policy changed in the post-Cold War.

The interviews found that while there was strong bureaucratic advocacy for the PKO law, the real push for the law's passage was leader driven. The external shock of the Gulf War was primary in the push for change. The research also discovered other factors for change that Hermann's model did not cover.

Furthermore, all of these differing potential "Change Agents" (leader driven changes, bureaucratic advocacy, external shock, domestic restructuring), as Hermann calls them in his model, go into the decision making process and result in various foreign policy changes in Japan (see figure 1:1). It is the intention of this book to shed light on the strength of the various agents of change in the Japanese decision making process that results in foreign policy change. Often there are multiple agents of change at work. Each agent is trying to influence foreign policy to some extent and may vie with other agents. For example, the bureaucracy might choose to advocate small or incremental program changes. At the same time the leaders might push for an international orientation change, and domestic sources of restructuring might be advocating no change at all. The resulting change when balanced by the various strengths of the competing interests might result in a goal or problem change reflecting the strength of the leadership and the relative weakness of domestic influences for change.

In sum, the elite interviews help to clarify the Japanese process of foreign policy change and help test the utility of Hermann's model for Japan. To be useful, social science models should help us understand the real world, and this book provides an example of this.

OBJECTIVES AND EXPECTED SIGNIFICANCE OF THE BOOK

The conventional wisdom has been that Japan may be a rising hegemon which is presenting itself as a challenger to the current and declining hegemon, the United States, as well as China.[32] However, Japan's sustained economic slump has led many both inside and outside of Japan to question the idea that Japan is capable of being a hegemon. Some have even mockingly asked the question, "Is Japan number one or number twenty-three?" Given Japan's potential to pull itself out of its own economic slump and its position as the second largest economy in the world the question that should be asked is: "Does Japan desire to be a hegemon?" And if so, are the recent changes in its foreign policy a sign of this or merely a reaction to the end of the Cold War by implementing a "goal/problem change." Or are the recent changes a sign that Japan is radically changing its foreign policy, an "international orientation change." In other words there are three possibilities. The first is that Japan wants to become a hegemon. The second is that Japan does not want to take a more significant role in the world and is merely trying to raise its standing in the world by attempting to provide humanitarian assistance through the U.N. The third is that Japan is trying to become a more important or larger player/partner with the U.S. without hegemonic aspirations. The following chapters explore these alternatives.

The objective of this study has been to submit the changes in Japanese foreign policy to empirical inquiry to see what elites and the Japanese public believe their country's global security role should be. The significance of this study is twofold in that it contributes to a better understanding of Japan's foreign policy and secondly, that the nature and causes of foreign policy change can now be better understood. It studies the opinions of some of the most influential Japanese politicians and bureaucrats through a series of elite interviews as well as public opinion surveys and applies these findings to explain the current and future direction of Japanese foreign policy. It will also hopefully stimulate further research, so that scholars can continue to study Japanese foreign policy decision making methods and contribute, in a wider sense, to our understanding of foreign policy change in general.

OUTLINE OF THE BOOK

In order to provide the context of Japanese foreign policy for the book chapter two looks at the history of Japan's postwar foreign policy and its implications for current foreign policy. The third chapter looks at the theoretical framework for the research in detail in light of international relations theory and the foreign policy change literature. This chapter attempts to clarify and theoretically further Hermann's model. It will also describe in detail the field research methods used. The fourth chapter looks at Japan's state to state relations with an eye on national security and regional security. Special attention will be paid to Japan's security and alliance options within East Asia. The fifth chapter examines Japan's place in the international system and address the question of Japanese hegemony. It also examines the domestic societal level Japanese attitudes towards foreign policy with a focus on what this author calls the "Myth" of *Gaiatsu*. Extensive use of existing survey data is used in both chapters four and five along with the results of the interviews conducted by the author in the field. The sixth chapter and final chapter attempts to be predictive as to the future direction of Japanese foreign policy as described in the fourth and fifth chapters and draws the conclusions of the book and details the needs for future research.

NOTES

[1] James N. Rosenau, *The Study of Political Adaptation: Essays on the Analysis of World Politics*, New York: Nichols Publishing, 1981, pp. 1–2.

[2] Japan's pacifist constitution was externally imposed on it during the occupation by General MacAurthor and the allies at the end of World War II, but as will be argued in chapter 2 the Japanese people have adopted it as their own, and the constitution reflects the democratic will of the people.

[3] The term "uniqueness" is used here in the sense that all nations have unique foreign policies. It in no way should be construed to mean that the author subscribes to the argument or theory of "Japanese uniqueness" that has been put forth by many conservative revisionists in Japan.

[4] *The Constitution of Japan, Law and Contemporary Problems*, Spring, 1990: 200–214.

[5] For the purposes of this book all Japanese names will be written in the Western style of given name followed by the family name rather than the Japanese style which requires the family name to be listed first.

[6] Takashi Inoguchi, "Japan's Response to the Gulf Crisis: An Analytic Overview," *Journal of Japanese Studies*, 17:2 (1991): 257.

[7] Jiro Yamaguchi, "The Gulf War and the Transformation of Japanese Constitutional Politics," *Journal of Japanese Studies*, 18:1 (1992): 155.

[8] The concept of levels-of-analysis was introduced to International Relations theory by Kenneth N. Waltz in his book *Man, the State, and War: A Theoretical Analysis*. New York: Columbia University Press, 1954, 1959.

[9] The individual level seen as influenced by the society and it is societal influences on the individual level that will be examined in the book.

[10] I do not intend to introduce the concept of regionalism here as a level of analysis. Japan tends to deal with the individual ASEAN members in the same way a major state would deal with a minor state, but it deals with the unit of ASEAN as it would a "major" state in the international system.

[11] Holsti defines foreign policy restructuring as "the dramatic, wholesale alteration of a nation's pattern of external relations." Kal J. Holsti, ed. *Why Nations Realign: Foreign Policy Restructuring in the Postwar World*, London: George Allen and Unwin, 1982: ix.

[12] Rosenau, pp. 1–2.

[13] Holsti, pp. 4–7.

[14] Kjell Goldmann, *Change and Stability in Foreign Policy: The Problems and Possibilities of Détente*, Princeton: Princeton University Press, 1988, 3–4.

[15] Charles F. Hermann, *Changing Course: When Governments Choose to Redirect Foreign Policy, International Studies Quarterly* (1990) 34, 3.

[16] Ibid., 13.

[17] Ibid., 4.

[18] Ibid., 5.
[19] Ibid., 7.
[20] Ibid., 10–11.
[21] Ibid., 11.
[22] Reinhard Drifte, *Japan's Foreign Policy for the 21st Century: From Economic Superpower to What Power?* (Oxford: St. Antony's Press, 1998), 1–2.
[23] Ibid., 14.
[24] As a measure of the significance of this book, the Japanese edition of van Wolferen's book was effectively banned by the Japanese Government (Bureaucracy) as being too revealing for the Japanese public in general to read.
[25] A list of all those interviewed is provided in Appendix D.
[26] Appendix A and B contain the text of both questionnaires in both English and Japanese.
[27] Two of the interviewees asked that I not record them and the tape recorder failed during two other interviews.
[28] The point here being that politicians will change their opinions like the wind when there is a popular need for it. It has been long argued that if Japanese troops were to receive significant casualties while on a PKO mission, support for the PKO in the general populace could evaporate and thus the politicians would stop supporting the PKO.
[29] Several interviewees were contacted after the North Korean test to measure their reactions to this significant event. The results are reported on later in the book.
[30] *Gaijin* is most often translated as "foreigner", but literally means "outsider" and it carries a connotation with it that can be considered derogatory at times.
[31] The rationale for this stems from Japanese attitudes toward their language. They view their language as being very difficult (and rightly so) especially for foreigners. They thus tend to be more frank in English or when talking to a foreigner because they can always claim to have been misquoted or translated if their comments come back to haunt them.
[32] For more on this view that Japan is an up and coming hegemon see Paul Kennedy's book *The Rise and Fall of the Great Powers: Economic Change and Military conflict from 1500–2000*, New York: Random House, 1987.

CHAPTER 2

THE STORY OF JAPAN'S "ABNORMAL" FOREIGN POLICY UNDER ARTICLE NINE

. . . land, sea, and air forces, as well as other war potential, will never be maintained. — Article Nine, The Constitution of Japan[1]

The Japanese Diet passed on June 15, 1992 *The Law Concerning Cooperation in U.N. Peacekeeping and Other Operations* (otherwise known as the PKO Law) and it went into effect on August 10th of that same year. This law marked the most significant change in Japan's post-war foreign and security policies since the creation of the Self Defense Forces (SDF) in the 1950s. Japan's constitution renounces war and, when interpreted narrowly or at face value, would seem to prohibit the maintenance of any military forces. The sending of SDF troops overseas was an extremely controversial change in policy for the Japanese government.

During the occupation of Japan by the United States after the Second World War, the Occupation Government headed by General Douglas MacArthur in concert with the Japanese Cabinet, rewrote and revised Japan's constitution. This post-war constitution has been called, "the Japanese Peace Constitution." This is based on Article Nine of Chapter II: The Renunciation of War. This article states:

"Aspiring sincerely to an international peace based on justice and order, the Japanese people forever renounce war as a sovereign right of the nation and the threat or use of force as a means of settling international disputes.

In order to accomplish the aim of the preceding paragraph, land, sea, and air forces, as well as other war potential, will never be maintained. The right of belligerency of the state will not be recognized."[2]

Article Nine was written before the onset of the Cold War. As a result of the Cold War, Japan was pressured by the U.S. into establishing the Self Defense Forces (SDF) which were to have *defensive* capabilities only. The lynch pin of this arrangement is the U.S./Japan Security Treaty which promises U.S. support if Japan is ever attacked, thus negating the need for Japanese force projection (offensive) capabilities. The parties of the left wing in Japanese politics have never accepted this arrangement as constitutional and it has been part of their party platforms to dissolve the SDF if and when they came to power.[3]

Japanese politics in general tends to be governed by consensus. This consensus in Japanese politics is a result of cultural norms. The Japanese view of the role of the nation is clearly demonstrated by Walker and Sampson in their comparative study of Japan and France.[4] The Japanese basic organizational motif is the group. Consensus within the group is primary within most areas of Japanese life. All sides of an issue spend extensive time in a process called *nemawashi* which serves the purpose of building consensus within the group at an early stage as to not break the harmony (*wa*), indebtedness (*on*), and the dependency on and concern for other people (*amae*).[5] This institutional group harmony within the Diet[6] was broken with the passing of the Peacekeeping Operations Law (PKO Law) by the LDP over the strenuous objections of the principal opposition party, the SDP.[7]

The very fact that this challenge to the *wa* happened is a significant sign of a major change in the direction of Japanese politics. The LDP obviously felt that the passing of the PKO law was more important to Japan than the maintenance of the general harmony within the Diet. The opposition felt that to support this law would be detrimental to Japan and to the integrity of the constitution. The result is two differing attitudes as to the correct direction that Japan should take in the coming years and the role of its foreign policy on the world scene. The LDP policy towards the United Nations and peacekeeping is now a priority in Japanese foreign policy and has been enlarged to include a campaign for a permanent seat on the U.N. Security Council. Japan has, since World War II, not posed a threat to the region through military power. The possibility that Japan could rearm itself offensively very quickly if the US/Japan Security Treaty ever fails is of concern to Japan's Asian neighbors.[8] Japan has even been called a virtual nuclear power because of the general consensus that Japan has the technology and resources to develop, produce, and deploy nuclear weapons in a relatively short period of time.[9] The questions being asked, by those who study Japan, are these, "Where is Japan, as a nation, headed in relation to its role in the world?" And how will its U.N. role be perceived by its neighbors?

Japan's neighbors, China and South Korea in particular, have voiced concern over Japan's new, more activist approach to foreign policy and more significantly there are a large number of internal domestic questions as well. The *New York Times* noted in an editorial that: "Japan is slowly overcoming decades of reticence about building and using military forces. This change in attitude carries important implications for Asia and the United States."[10] Some, like Professor Kazuo Ota of Rakuno Gakuen University,[11] are wondering if there is a clear, coherent, and definite agenda to Japan's Foreign Policy or if it is merely a reflection of the norms of the foreign policy of democratic states.[12] Will Japanese foreign policy swing to domestic demands? How important are domestic concerns to the formation of Japanese Foreign Policy? Will domestic fears of war and militarism prevent Japan from becoming a hegemon? Critics have alleged that the PKO law is just a pretext for securing the legitimacy of the SDF by invoking the name of the United Nations and capturing Japan a place in superpower diplomacy.[13] There is a strong fear that Japan will repeat the mistakes of its past if the government is permitted to use the SDF as a tool in its foreign policy.[14] The *New York Times* recently wrote: "...in recent months, Tokyo has shown a new willingness to stand up to North Korean bullying, deflect criticism from China and involve itself in regional defense arrangements."[15]

This chapter will look into the these questions within the larger issue of whether Article Nine violates the sovereignty of Japan and prevents Japan from acting as a sovereign nation (or as a normal nation). I first examine the historical background of the Japanese "Peace" Constitution and Article Nine. Next Japan's Cold War foreign policy will be addressed. Thirdly, the Gulf War and its impact on Japanese Foreign Policy will be examined. Fourthly, the political and legal issues surrounding the PKO law will be studied. Last of all the Japanese quest for a Permanent Security Council seat will be assessed along with probable future trends and objectives in Japanese foreign policy. It is here that the potential for Japan's role as a world leader will be stressed in particular.

HISTORICAL BACKGROUND

In the closing days of World War II the Allied leaders met in the Berlin suburb of Potsdam from which they issued the Potsdam Declaration. This declaration set forth the terms for the surrender of Japan. The primary purpose of this "was to eliminate the authority and influence of the old order that had misled the Japanese people into a war of conquest, with a view toward establishing a new order of peace, security, and justice."[16] The Allied policy declared,

> The ultimate objectives of the United States in regard to Japan, to which policies in the initial period must conform, are
>   (a) To insure that Japan will not again become a menace to the United States or to the peace and security of the world.
>   (b) To bring about the eventual establishment of a peaceful and responsible government [which] should conform as closely as may be

to principles of democratic self-government but *it is not the responsibility of the Allied Powers to impose upon Japan any form of government not supported by the freely expressed will of its people.*[17]

It is important to note that the Potsdam Declaration wanted popular reforms that would last beyond the occupation. The Allies though, were determined to destroy Japan's dominant "military establishment with a new constitution that imposed a new relationship between the people and their leaders."[18] Many historians consider the ability of the military to control the Cabinet to be the major defect of the Meiji Constitution.[19] General MacArthur believed that it should be the Japanese themselves who should come up with the constitutional reforms of the Meiji Era Constitution, but he put a high priority on the reform of the constitution (called the *kenpou* in Japanese) by requesting that the government draft a revised constitution.[20] This push for the revision of the *kenpou* seems to reflect the belief that if power was placed in the hands of the people Japan would no longer be a threat. The idea behind this being that democracies do not fight each other.[21] The will of the people is the primary factor in an democratization effort. John Mensing commenting on Japan's occupation and democratization writes: "...(the evidence) clearly shows how democratization, or the promise of it, was embraced by the Japanese people as a benefit for themselves, as something that many people aspired to, or quickly recognized as something they desired."[22]

The first draft of the revised *kenpou* that was presented to the occupation authorities was totally unacceptable to General MacArthur and his staff in that it contained only cosmetic changes of no real substance or changes to the old order. The requirements of the Potsdam Declaration would not have been fulfilled under this draft.[23] General MacArthur then ordered his staff to draft a model constitution for the Japanese government to follow.

It is in this model draft that Article Nine first appeared. The exact origin of Article Nine is unknown and may never be known.[24] Many have incorrectly assumed that it came from General MacArthur and the victorious Allied powers. It is virtually certain that it came neither from official Washington sources nor from internal political debate from within Japan, but rather it came from less official sources.[25]

The importance of the origin of Article Nine centers around the question of whether it violates Japanese sovereignty and prevents it from acting as a truly sovereign nation. If Article Nine is of Japanese origin it then is not a violation of Japan's sovereignty because it represents a feeling that emerged from Japanese representatives even if it came under the occupation. On the other hand, if its origin is with the United States and the victorious Allied powers or General MacArthur, then it does violate Japanese sovereignty in the sense that Japan is not and was not able to determine its own destiny as any truly sovereign nation has the right to do. This does not mean that Article

Nine should automatically be revoked. If it has gained the support of the majority, then its current status reflects the will of the people.

This would seem to be the case given the current interpretation by the government and courts of Japan.[26] This author would also argue, based on the evidence presented by the late Colonel Charles Kades a member of the Government Section of General MacArthur's staff and Kenzo Takayanagi the distinguished Chairman of Japan's Commission on the Constitution, that the origin of Article Nine is Japanese. Kades makes a strong case and Takayanagi's research concurs, that Article Nine was suggested to General MacArthur by then Prime Minister Shidehara during a private meeting. Takayanagi wrote:

> Shidehara behaved as if Article 9 were proposed by MacArthur, although he never clearly said so. If he had said that the proposal was his and not MacArthur's, it might have been rejected by the Cabinet. Shidehara was diplomatic enough to know this. So Cabinet Members who attended the meeting, including Yoshida and Ashida thought that the proposal was made by MacArthur and not by Shidehara. After this [Cabinet] meeting, Shidehara told a number of his close friends that 'Article 9 did not come from abroad' and that it was his own proposal. Neither Yoshida or Ashida was aware that the original proposal was made by Shidehara. They thought, as I did at the time, that it was imposed by the Allied Powers. These events account for the difference between Ashida's public statement at the plenary session and his private opinion in his pamphlet, and Yoshida's written memorandum sent to the Commission on the Constitution which denied that the article was Shidehara's.[27]

Kades goes even further by noting the possibility that Article Nine may have had its origin with the Emperor himself and Shidehara merely passed on the Emperor's idea.[28]

Major General Frank Sackton, USA, (Ret.), then Col. Frank Sackton, who was one of MacArthur's chief aids during the occupation and was also present in SCAP headquarters during the writing of the *kenpou* has a contradictory opinion to Col. Kades on this issue. In an interview, General Sackton[29] stated that he felt that it must have been MacArthur that had written Article Nine because it fit MacArthur's personality to do something that had never been tried before, like taking away a state's right to wage war. Gen. Sackton disputed the idea that the Emperor could or would have come up with such a radical idea that would potentially undermine Japanese power in the future. Furthermore, Gen. Sackton stated that he doubted that Shidehara could have come up with such a radical idea by himself because he lacked the intellect for such an original idea.[30] This is possible, but in hindsight Article Nine is arguably the most significant element of the *kenpou*. However with foresight its significance would have been very difficult to predict. Problems with the limitations imposed on Japan by Article Nine cropped up as early as 1950 with the Korean War. The US wanted to rearm Japan and it could not because it failed to adequately foresee the Cold War when it permitted Japan to have Article Nine as part of its constitution.

It is important to note that during the occupation the Japanese leadership wanted to limit the damage to elite political institutions as much as possible. At the same time the Allied leadership, grateful that they had been spared the need for a invasion of the Japanese home islands, feared losing control of occupied Japan to a popular uprising if they instituted radical changes that upset the populace.[31] It is for this reason that the SCAP under MacArthur desired to keep the Emperor system. They feared that if they abolished the emperor system the people would revolt. At the same time they wanted to strip the elites of their power and place it in the hands of the people. In many ways they were attempting to play the people against the elites.

Japanese leaders on the other hand feared that SCAP was planning to abolish the imperial throne, knowing that the people were fairly ambivalent towards the imperial system after Japan's surrender. This is a classic case of both sides not knowing the intentions and fears of the other. Had they known the American fears, the Japanese leadership might not have been as willing to make the proposals and concessions that they did.[32] They are unlikely to have proposed Article Nine to MacArthur. It is more likely that it was the result of a maverick individual (like Shidehara or a person close to him who gave him the idea) or small group than any consensus within the Japanese leadership. At the same time it is strange that if MacArthur did author Article Nine that he did not mention such a radical idea to anyone before proposing it, but given MacArthur's personality[33] it is not unthinkable that he couldn have come up with the idea. The occupation government did a similar thing to the people of Japan that Article Nine does to the nation as a whole when it took away the right to personal self defense from Japanese citizens after World War II which has also remained a part of Japanese law since then.[34]

In summary, Kades does note and Sackton agrees that no one knows for sure where Article Nine came from.[35] It was just assumed for many years that it was a U.S./MacArthur product when in reality it was not something that the victorious Allies had planned in any way.

Another argument against Article Nine is that the whole Constitution was imposed on Japan against its will. This was never the American intention at all from MacArthur's point of view as mentioned earlier. The will of the Japanese people was foremost, in this regard, in the minds of the occupation forces. They realized that unless the reforms enacted were reflective of the will of the Japanese people, then they would be useless once the Allies ended the occupation and left. For this reason MacArthur's staff emphasized very clearly to the Japanese government that this draft was not being forced on the Japanese people. Evidence of this is contained in a memorandum by Jiro

Shirasu who was present when General Courtney Whitney presented the Government Section's draft of the proposed constitution. Shirasu summarized General Whitney's remarks as follows:

a. The Japanese Government draft has been rejected as "totally unacceptable."
b. The SCAP (Supreme Commander for the Allied Powers) draft is "acceptable" to all the Allied Nations and to SCAP.
c. *This draft is not being forced on Japan.*
d. The United States believes the Japanese people *want* this draft.
e. SCAP has supported the Emperor. This draft supports the Emperor and is the only way for protecting the Emperor System from those opposing the Emperor.
f. It is better if the Japanese conservatives moved far to the left.[36]

Genkichi Hasagawa, who was also present at the meeting concurred with this in his notes when he wrote, "Whitney said neither the form nor the contents were being forced on Japan. . . . He said he believed the SCAP draft met the wishes of the Japanese people."[37]

   This last point involving the will of the Japanese people is of primary importance in understanding Article Nine and its origins. The Japanese Cabinet originally resisted the SCAP draft and Article Nine, but General MacArthur threatened to take the draft directly to the Japanese people if the Diet refused to consider it. This demonstrates how much the Allies had tapped into the popular mood of the nation. They had every confidence that the Japanese people wanted this constitution which would permit them to have a measure of control over their government that they lacked before. The Japanese people were sick and tired of the horrors of war that they had suffered and were eager to renounce war and the military.[38] Alfred Oppler who was involved in the reforms of the occupation wrote: "One only had to read the newspapers and speak to the man on the street...to realize that there were powerful movements among the people of enthusiastic support of Occupation objectives."[39]

   These occupation objectives were established in the new *Kenpou* as fundamental principles. John M. Maki of the University of Massachusetts in his introduction to *Japan's Commission on the Constitution: The Final Report* notes these components that have made the *Kenpou* an enduring constitution. They are:

1) The three basic principles of the constitution: -popular sovereignty, pacifism, and the guarantee of fundamental human rights;
2) No single crippling defect in the constitution surfaced;

3) The constitution is functioning effectively in practice as a fundamental law for Japanese society based on the principles of democracy;
4) No matter what the outcome on the question of revision, one
inevitable result would be a deep scaring of the body politic;
5) No revision, whether on a large or small scale would be quick or
easy.[40]

There are probably other reasons for the constitution's stability. Probably
foremost among these reasons is that it captured the hearts and minds of the
people who were weary of war and desired peace, especially the peace that
was offered by Article Nine.[41]

Further specific support for Article Nine is shown in a newspaper poll by
the *Mainichi Shimbun* taken in May 1946. The poll found that seventy percent of those polled supported Article Nine and the renunciation of war. Only
twenty-eight percent opposed it.[42] Tesu Katayama, who would later become
Prime Minister, told a plenary session of the House of Representatives that the
reason that the Socialist Party was endorsing the new constitution was that
"sovereign power is in the hands of the people." and because of Article Nine
which "has by no means been given or dictated from outside but is an
expression of a strong current of thought which has been running in the
hearts of the Japanese people."[43]

During the Diet debate[44] on the new constitution several changes were
made to Article Nine with the consent of the SCAP. First was the total ban on
Self-Defense that would have clearly outlawed the current SDF. The second
was the Ashida Amendment which in essence opened the door for the SDF
in the future. It is important to note that the purpose of the ambiguous language in the Ashida Amendment was not clear to those who voted for it or
the new constitution.[45] Many at this time thought that Article Nine banned
the military forever. When asked why Japan had not expressly reserved the
right to self-defense, then Cabinet Minister and later Prime Minister Yoshida
said:

Of late years most wars have been waged in the name of self-defense.
This is the case of the Machurian Incident, and so is the War of
Greater East Asia. The suspicion concerning Japan today is that she is
a warlike nation, and there is no knowing when she may rearm her-
self, wage war of reprisal and threaten the peace of the world. . . . I
think that the first thing we should do today is to set right this misunderstanding...it cannot be said there is no foundation for that suspicion.[46]

It is important to note this lack of provision for self-defense because with the outbreak of the Cold War and the Korean War, the priorities of the United States and its requirements from Japan changed drastically. The United States wanted Japan to provide for its own self-defense and to ally itself with the United States against the Communist bloc. This caused a domestic debate within Japan to begin — one that is still continuing to this day over the constitutionality of this issue. General MacArthur from his command of the United Nations forces in Korea and again in his memoirs stated that he had never intended the Japanese to be without a means of self-defense.[47] But as Kades notes, what General MacArthur and those in the Occupation Forces thought was no longer as relevant as it had once been and is currently totally irrelevant. Japan is a sovereign nation and it is *its* interpretation of *its* constitution under *its* laws and courts that is relevant.[48]

Still, the San Francisco Peace treaty had yet to be signed and the United States in its role as the principal occupying power, instructed the Japanese to organize a 75,000–man National Police Reserve (NPR) in 1950 . This organization was in reality a mere disguise for a new Japanese Army according to Colonel Kolwalski of the United States Army who assisted in its organization.[49] The NPR was justified as being essential to internal security following the transfer of SCAP forces to Korea.

The signing of the San Francisco Peace Treaty in 1952 ended the occupation of Japan a decade earlier than originally planed. The United States wanted to make Japan into a Cold War ally and convinced many other nations to sign the treaty also. Japan to this date claims that the peace treaty ended all claims for reparations from the Japanese government. The treaty was a rushed effort by the US at best and the lack of an apology for its actions by the Japanese government continue to haunt Japanese foreign policy to this day.

JAPANESE FOREIGN AND SECURITY POLICY 1952–1990

In April 1952 the NPR was renamed the Japanese National Safety Forces (NSF) and were headed by Prime Minister Yoshida himself. The NSF contained both ground and maritime elements. In 1954 with the establishment of the Defense Agency Establishment Law, Japan began building the Ground Self-Defense Forces and the NPR received its third name the Self-Defense Forces or the SDF as it is known today.

Each of these incremental changes was challenged in the courts and in the public arena of debate as violating the *Kenpou* and Article Nine. The Japanese public recognized on one hand the need for self-defense due to the proximity of the Korean War. On the other hand they passionately disapproved of any military capability that could be deemed offensive in nature.[50] Pacifism had taken root in Japanese culture. Royer cites an example of this in a note by Fukui which stated:

> Pacifism represented and popularized by Article 9 rapidly developed
> into a *popular cult*. Pacifism became the object of fervent devotion
> among large numbers of Japanese. It became deeply instilled in their
> hearts incomparably faster than did any of the democratic principles
> of government also proclaimed by the new Constitution. During and
> immediately following World War II, the people of Japan experienced
> destruction, hunger and death directly, physically and personally, not
> just abstractly and intellectually. Thus, the post-war Japanese were
> emotionally devoted to the ideal of *peace at almost any cost*.[51]

In an interview Jiro Kodera advanced this argument when he described the
Japanese people as believing that peace simply exists and one need not fight
in order to have it. Kodera described the Japanese people (in general) as
being so pacifist that they largely had no concept of the work and vigilance
it take to maintain peace.[52] While this may be an overstatement, it illustrates
that pacifism is the norm in Japanese culture. Another example of the
Japanese people's devotion to the principles of pacifism contained in Article
Nine occurred when Prime Minister Hatoyama tried to gain approval for
amending the constitution in 1955 by calling a general election. The left and
right wings of the Socialist Party successfully united and prevented any
attempt at amending the constitution by winning over one third of the seats
in the Diet. It is important to note that the constitution has yet to be amended or revised since its original form adopted in 1947.

After this, successive governments have refrained from attempting to
amend the constitution; rather, they have reinterpreted the *Kenpou* to fit the
needs of the times. The results of this has been a greater and greater liberal-
ization of the meaning of "self-defense" capabilities and "offensive" capabilities (see the earlier quote from Prime Minister Yoshida for reference). What
was defined as offensive capability by one Cabinet may not reflect another
Cabinet's definition. An example of this would be when Director General
Kimura, who succeeded Yoshida in the Safety Ministry, was asked to name
something that would be definitely forbidden as constituting "war potential". Kimura replied that, "A jet airplane would constitute war potential."[53]
Kimura had no idea that by the 1980's the Air Self-Defense Forces would be
flying the F-15; the most advanced fighter in the United States Air Force.[54]
Times had changed and so had the interpretation of Article Nine.

Another example of this is the well know, Cabinet policy statement
of 1967 which announced the "three non-nuclear principles". Japan pledged
that it would not possess, manufacture, or permit nuclear weapons to be
brought to Japan.[55] What is not so well known is the 12 March 1959 statement that was made by Prime Minister Kishi to the House of Counselors:
"The Government intends to maintain no nuclear weapons, but speaking in
terms of legal interpretation of the Constitution there is nothing to prevent
the maintaining of the minimum amount of nuclear weapons for self-

defense."[56] A week later the Kishi Cabinet issued an official statement which said:

> In the event that an attack is waged with guided missiles and there are no other means of defense, counter attacks on enemy bases are within the scope of self-defense. With the right of self-defense retained as an independent nation, the Constitution does not mean for the nation to sit and do nothing and await its death.[57]

With each broadening/change in the interpretation of Article Nine came a new challenge to the government from the left wing political parties and from individuals often in the form of court challenges to the constitutionality of the SDF. The Japanese courts have consistently upheld the constitutionality of the SDF. Lower courts have at times ruled the SDF to be unconstitutional, but all of these decisions have been overturned by higher courts or the Supreme Court (the *Saikosaibansho* in Japanese).[58] The Japanese court system under the Meiji constitution was responsible to the executive. The new constitution tried to separate judicial and executive power, but to a large extent it has failed in reality.[59] The use of judicial review is scant and the *Saikosaibansho* has made no attempt in the last forty years to establish itself as an activist court, especially in the area of constitutional issues.[60] This has resulted in the government having nearly free reign in the area of constitutional interpretation. The conservative LDP's uninterrupted rule from 1958 to July 1993 offered consistency to this arrangement; one party was continuously interpreting Article Nine.

THE YOSHIDA DOCTRINE

One of the founders of the LDP was Prime Minister Yoshida. It was Yoshida who first discovered that Article Nine could be used in Japan's favor.[61] With the presence of United States forces and Nuclear Umbrella to protect Japan and the constitutional ban on (offensive) military forces, Japan was free to pursue rapid economic development without the added economic weight of having to maintain a standing military that would drain resources badly needed to rebuild the economy. This became known as the Yoshida Doctrine and essentially permitted Japan to have a "free ride" throughout the Cold War. Japan had only to maintain a minimal level of self-defense capability in order to please the United States and most of the time follow the United States lead in foreign policy.[62]

The key component of this arrangement is the United States/Japan Security Treaty. This treaty was first signed in 1952 and revised in 1960 amid great controversy and debate within Japan. The two versions are in essence two totally different treaties even though the 1960 version is only called a revision of the original treaty signed during the occupation. The 1952 version essentially gave the United States carte blanche access to Japan for military purposes. The 1960 version required consultation between the two nations and was much more equal in nature. The U.S./Japan Security Treaty is Japan's only formal military alliance.[63] This makes the United States Japan's only formal ally. The Treaty has taken on an increasingly vital role in the maintenance of peace within the Pacific Rim and can be compared in importance to NATO for the United States.[64]

The Security Treaty helps alleviate fears within the Pacific Rim of a remilitarized Japan, especially among nations that were occupied by Japan during the Second World War. The reasons for these fears touches on potential future problems for Japanese Foreign Policy and will be discussed later in chapter six.

It is important to note the role of the United States in the process of the formation of the SDF into its current state. U.S. pressure is a issue that runs throughout the formation of Japanese defense and security policy. Japanese politicians have been able to explain many of their bolder actions regarding the SDF by referring to pressure from the United States.[65] This "American Pressure" is called *gaiatsu*. This can literally be translated as, "pressure from the outside" and is a common term in any newspaper report on the subject.[66] Thus the official Japanese explanation for many of their defense and security policy decisions is essentially that, "the Americans made us do it."[67]

As the strain of the Cold War grew, the Americans were "making Japan do" more and more in terms of its own defense. Even with the one percent GDP limitation, the size of the Japanese economy raised the Japanese defense budget to the third largest in the world behind the United States and the former Soviet Union's, by 1990.[68] The Japanese SDF is, currently, one of the most modern and well equipped forces in the world. All of this in a nation that is not even supposed to have an army, navy, or air force when one interprets its constitution literally. The LDP managed to "amend" the constitution by reinterpretation[69] and created an armed force that exists even though it is severely limited in what it has been authorized to do.

The limitations on the SDF will be discussed in the next two sections, but the question of sovereignty arises when one mentions that the "Americans made us do it." This author would argue that if Article Nine is of Japanese origin (and the author believes that the evidence indicates that it is), then it can be said to represent the anti-militarist/anti-nationalist aspirations in Japan. The militarist/nationalist elements within Japan could be said to have been at their weakest during the occupation period. The popular imposition of constitutional reform including Article Nine, by the Allied powers, serves as a check on right wing forces in Japan. Foremost in peoples minds, in the immediate postwar period, was to prevent a repeat betrayal by military leaders. So much had been sacrificed for nothing but defeat and humiliation in the end. The left wing, which represents politically these fears of a repetition of military expansionism, has been able to use the opportunity created by Article Nine to its advantage in preventing a repeat of the mistake of World War II by inhibiting the SDF so that it can never become the war machine that the Imperial Armed Forces were. Thus, Article Nine does not represent a loss of sovereignty, but rather it is a domestic check against the potential rise of militarism in Japan once again.

For the past forty-five years, Japan has in essence attempted to live within the spirit of Article Nine. The choices that it has made regarding the SDF, reflect the choices of a sovereign nation. The United States might have influenced these decisions but in the end, they were the decisions of a popularly elected government on what it believed was best for Japan. With the end of the Cold War many things changed for Japan. The next section will look at how the Gulf War shaped changes in Japan.

THE GULF WAR AND JAPANESE FOREIGN POLICY

The Gulf War took Japan, politically, by surprise; "like a bolt out of the blue."[70] Iraq's invasion of Kuwait on 2 August 1990 and the war had a major impact on the politics of Japan.[71] Japan was forced to face the reality of its economic superpower status for the first time in an international crisis. Japan sprinted out of the blocks at the start of the crisis only to stumble and be left dazed and bewildered when it realized that the Cold War was over and the rules had changed. Japan was asked to participate at a level that was equal to its economic status in the world and Japan was not ready to do this. Japan's checkbook diplomacy caused it to be severely criticized abroad. The Yoshida Doctrine that had served it so well was in need of revision.

At the core of the problem was the old constitutional question of Article Nine. Could Japan send troops overseas even if they were under United Nations command? Japan was not ready to answer this question although the world was waiting for an answer. Japan was still in the middle of trying to come to terms with the end of the Cold War and its impact on the Japan/United States Security treaty. Japan was searching to find its place in the world when the Gulf War forced Japan to make some hard choices. These choices though inadequate in the eyes of many started a debate within Japan that has made it come to better terms with its economic superpower status and its constitutional obligations. How Japan reacted to the Gulf crisis is important in order to understand the debate within Japan on this issue.

Japan's historical relations with the Middle East before late in this century were almost nonexistent. Japan's first major encounter with the Middle East was the 1973 oil crisis and the OPEC oil embargo. Its second encounter was the 1980 oil crisis. Neither of these crises affected Japan militarily. The Gulf crisis was different in that Japan was expected to be a full fledged partner in the war efforts.[72] The Japanese government did not want to do this. Rather it wanted to contribute in other ways, primarily financial.

It is to Japan's credit that it was unusually swift in responding to the invasion of Kuwait by initiating its own economic embargo against Iraq even before the United Nations. This is in contrast to the way Japan stumbled through almost every other issue that it dealt with during the Gulf War.[73]

The first stumble that Japan made was when the United States called on its Allies to support and contribute to the Gulf Crisis/War effort in any way possible. Japan initially pledged 400 million dollars to the effort. This was raised a few days later to 4 billion dollars, but not before the damage was done. The question was, "Why not $4 billion in the first place?"[74] Japan was perceived as being stingy. Japan had more at stake with the potential loss of oil imports than most other western nations yet it was perceived to be willing to make only a small contribution. The final financial contribution pledged by Japan toward the Gulf effort was 13 billion dollars, but the earlier image remained.

In the meantime, President George H. W. Bush was using his now famous style of telephone diplomacy to raise a multinational force. Japan was asked to contribute. Before the Gulf Crisis no Japanese politician had ever voiced the idea of SDF serving overseas.[75] Now it was receiving *gaiatsu* from the United States and the international community to send troops to the Gulf. Japan needed to make a "human" contribution not just a financial one to the maintenance of international order.[76] If other nations were sending their men and women to fight and possibly die in a foreign war, then it was reasonable that Japan should as a nation that benefitted more than most from Persian Gulf Oil.

The problem was Article Nine and domestic opposition to involvment, both in the Diet and in the public in general. It would be a very difficult decision for the government to make. No matter what the choice there would be opposition to face. Prime Minister Kaifu[77] was basically faced with three choices:

1. Recognize the constitutional prohibition against sending troops abroad imposed by Article 9 and refuse to participate militarily in the Gulf.
2. Make sending troops abroad for U.N. purposes legal by enacting a constitutional amendment.
3. Make sending troops abroad for U.N. purposes legal by extra-constitutional means; that is, amending the SDF law or enacting a new deployment authorization law.[78]

Kaifu chose the third option. On the 27th of September 1990, Prime Minister Kaifu announced a plan to send a "United Nations Peace Cooperation Team" to Saudi Arabia. This team would be made up of "civil service personnel and members of the Self-Defense Forces."[79] Its purpose was to sidestep Article Nine by creating a non-SDF contingent to send to the Gulf. What it could not do was sidestep popular opposition. On the day the proposal was submitted to the Diet, 23,000 people gathered in protest.[80] The Bill was forced to be withdrawn from the Diet in November of that year, but it served as a forerunner to the PKO Law which was passed two years later.

Japan in the end was only able to send minesweepers to the Gulf conflict after the fighting had ended. This was done by reinterpreting the *kenpou* to permit the Maritime Self-Defense Forces to protect Japanese (and in reality other) shipping in the Gulf from mines sown by the Iraqis. This small flotilla performed very well in Japan's first overseas military venture since the end of World War II.[81] The seeds were sown though, for changes Japan's security and defense policies.

THE PEACEKEEPING OPERATIONS LAW (PKO)

The Gulf War/Crisis made Japan rethink its defense and security policies. This rethinking led to two Bills being brought before the Diet. The first was the Kaifu Bill which failed and the second was the bill brought by his successor Kiichi Miyazawa. Both bills generated an intense debate that is still going on. This debate, domestically and internationally, asks what Japan can and should do in maintaining international order and stability. Aside from the constitutionality of the SDF, are the fears of a rearmed Japan justified? Even the Socialists (SDP) who traditionally pledged to dismantle the SDF when they were part of the coalition Hosokawa government in 1993 and 1994 and when their leader Tomiichi Murayama became Prime Minister in the summer of 1994, did not push for a dismantling or even a scaling back of the SDF. Rather they moved to formally accept it as legitimate.

Legal Issues

The legal issues that surround this debate center on how far one can stretch the interpretation of Article Nine's ban on military forces. They also address Japan's legal obligations to the United Nations. Japan in the 1950's had a stated United Nations centered diplomacy upon which it wished to base its foreign policy. The problem is that the United Nations Charter requires members to be:

1) "a peace loving state,"
2) "accept the obligations contained in the present Charter," and
3) to be "able and willing to carry out these obligations."[82]

Of importance to this discussion is the requirement to "carry out these obligations." This is due to the fact that two of these obligations are:

1) "All Members shall give the United Nations *every assistance* in any
action it takes in accordance with the present Charter."
2) "the Members of the United Nations *agree to accept and carry out*
the decisions of the Security council in accordance with the present
Charter."[83]

Japan's constitution runs into direct conflict with this when it comes to military peacekeeping and enforcement of United Nations Resolutions. In the
past Japanese Cabinets have said that they could not participate in United
Nations' Peacekeeping or Peacemaking efforts. After the Gulf War this all
changed. The conservative LDP actively sought to legalize Japanese participation in United Nations Peacekeeping efforts.

To accomplish this without violating the constitution, the PKO law needed to guarantee that the SDF peace-keepers sent from Japan would not be
involved in any situation that would require the use of force. The ban on the
use of force even includes the ability to participate if United Nations peace-
keepers come under fire. This does not though, include shooting back if the
SDF troops come directly under fire during a United Nations Peacekeeping
effort because this is a "use of weapons" in self-defense is therefore justifi-
able.[84] To achieve this goal five conditions were sent down in the PKO Bill to
minimize the chances of the SDF becoming involved in a conflict that would
require the use of force. They are:

1) Agreement on a cease-fire shall have been reached among the parties to the conflict.
2) The parties to the conflict, including territorial State(s), shall have
given their consent to the deployment of peace-keeping forces and
Japan's participation in such forces.
3) The peace-keeping forces shall strictly maintain impartiality, not
favoring any party to the conflict.
4) Should any of the above guideline requirements cease to be satisfied, the Government of Japan may withdraw its contingent.
5) The use of weapons shall be limited to the minimal necessary to protect personnel's lives, etc.[85]

This policy has its strong critics who say that the legalization of SDF participation in United Nations peacekeeping is nothing less than an attempt to
mobilize the SDF on the international stage. Making contributions to the
international community is not the primary objective but rather a secondary
one.[86] The primary objective is rather to finally shake off the constraints of
Article Nine by making the SDF a fait accompli on the world stage. These critics represent the fears of those within Japan who feel that Japan has not
learned from its past and is attempting to travel down the road to militarism
again. The natural tendency of Japan has been to revert back as much as pos-

sible, under the restraints of the new constitution, to the old Meiji constitutional style of governing.[87] This has been strongly evidenced in the development of politics in Japan during the post-war era.

The left wing of Japanese politics, which has spent most of the last forty years out of power, worries about the desire of the right wing to control the SDF if it gains status as a military again. Thus at the core of this issue is whether civilian control of the SDF can be maintained during peace-keeping operations[88] and whether Article Nine will be rendered null and void. One possible way of dealing with this is by the placing of SDF troops solely under United Nations command and control during all stages of peace-keeping operations. It can be argued that Article Nine can remain in effect and Japan/the SDF can participate in United Nations Peace-Keeping Operations if under United Nations command.[89] Thus Japan can contribute but does not have to exercise power over its contribution. This would be the best course for Japan to follow with respect to inter-Asian relations and domestic politics. Any attempt to revoke Article Nine for the purpose of greater participation would bring instability and friction to all of the above with unpredictable consequences.

Many critics of government attempts to weaken the constitutional controls on the development of armed forces see Article Nine as a check on the Japanese political system. This check was not intended by its framers, is a product of practices within the Japanese political system. Article Nine prevents conservative forces within Japan from establishing a military power base. The ability of the left to prevent the revocation of Article Nine prevents conservative forces from the total domination of Japanese politics The majority of these critics come from within Japan but many are also from without; which brings us to the next debate.

INTERNATIONAL POLITICS AND THE PKO

Western nations do not fear Japan militarily, but many Asian nations are concerned based on their own past experience. Western nations would prefer that Japan be an active player in the world scene; while many inside of Japan and Asia feel that Japan is not ready for this. With regard to Japan, the world can basically be divided into those who believe that Japan has something to offer the international community and those who do not or rather those who trust Japan and those who do not.[90] Japan's aggression during the 1930's and early 1940's left deep scars in many of the Pacific Rim Asian nations.

China is a prime example of this. When LDP General Secretary Obuchi Keizou visited China in August of 1991 seeking understanding for the PKO Bill, Chinese Communist Party General Secretary Jiang Zemin indirectly voiced his concern by calling on Japan to educate its people about the enormous harm the Japanese military caused China.[91] Prime Minister Kiichi Miyazawa met a similar reception in January 1992 during a visit to Seoul.

South Korean President Roh Tae Woo said that while he understood the reasons behind the PKO Law, many nations would like to see Japan focus on economic contributions and non-military assistance. The Philippines has also
expressed concern that the PKO legislation would nudge Japan toward militarism.[92]

Of those that supported Japan's efforts to legalize the overseas deployment of the SDF for peace-keeping, the most prominent in Asia was
Cambodian Premier Hun Sen. Cambodia wanted SDF participation in UNTAC
(United Nations Transitional Authority-Cambodia) under United Nations control. This was the only case of outspoken support for Japan within Asia with
the exception of Malaysia and Thailand.[93] Japan has been urged to make a
"human" contribution to world peace and stability and because of its past
history is having to proceed very cautiously as to not upset its Asian neighbors. Singapore's Senior Minister and former Prime Minister Lee Kwan Yew
expressed the feelings of Asians and condensed the international debate on
this issue when he spoke at a February 1992 business seminar in Kyoto. He
said, "...unlike the Germans, Japan has not been open and frank about the
atrocities and horrors committed in World War II. By avoiding talk about it,
the victims suspect and fear that Japan does not think these acts were wrong,
and that there is no genuine Japanese change of heart."[94]

THE POLITICAL DEBATE

The Japanese government's first attempt under Prime Minister Toshiki Kaifu
to legalize the sending of troops on United Nations' Peace-keeping activities
failed miserably both in the Diet and with the public. The second attempt a
year and a half later under the new Prime Minister Kiichi Miyazawa was able
to pass the Diet, but it took the actual deployment of SDF troops to begin
the process of public acceptance of the SDF's new role.

THE KAIFU BILL AND WHY IT FAILED

Against the backdrop of heavy *gaiatsu* from the United States, the first peace-
keeping bill was presented in September of 1990. The Kaifu Bill, as it is now
called, was basically doomed from the start. There were so many questions
about it, Did it violate the constitution? Does it permit the SDF to exist? Can
the SDF be sent abroad? Will the SDF be able to use force?[95] These questions
and others made the Bill extremely unpopular. Only 12.2% of the population
supported the bill wilh over 66% of the population opposing it.[96]

Prime Minister Kaifu made four major mistakes in trying to make a
human contribution to the Gulf Crisis.[97] The first was that he miscalculated
how strong the popular opposition would be to the Bill. The Japanese people in general, based on their severe experience in World War II, wanted
nothing to do with sending their sons to any kind of armed conflict. Kaifu

during his questioning on the Bill before the Diet was at times at a loss to explain what the SDF would do in certain situations. The government also made several flip-flops on their policy positions. This was perceived as waffling and further alienated those who opposed the Bill.

The second major reason was that Kaifu was overly hasty in submitting a bill of this magnitude. He broke the conventional practice of making decisions based on broad consensus. He was attacked for this by both the opposition and his own party for this. Japanese decision making takes time and is quite unlike the presidential system in the United States where decisions can be made quickly.

Kaifu's third mistake was to base his position on cooperation with the United States. Kaifu and the Foreign Ministry seemed to be focusing only on pleasing the United States. This gave the appearance of being a puppet of the Americans. The problem was that American soldiers were ready to defend international justice (and oil) with their lives and all Japan had was its checkbook.

The fourth major reason the Kaifu Bill failed was that the Prime Minister failed to provide firm guidance. If it had been explained well and clearly to the nation and the Diet it might have been able to garner support. As it was it was destined to fail. It was withdrawn from consideration in November of 1990 without ever having been voted on.

THE MIYAZAWA PKO BILL

In December 1991,the new Prime Minister Kiichi Miyazawa, submitted a revised PKO Bill to the Diet. This time the consensus of the Diet was not ignored. The LDP needed support from one or two of the opposition parties to get the PKO bill through the House of Counselors where they did not control the majority. The LDP was able to secure an alliance with the DSP (Democratic Socialist Party) and Komeito (Clean Government) parties. The Socialists on the other hand were doing all that they could to stop the Bill. The government made sure that the final version of the Bill did not require future Diet approval for PKO missions.[98]

The Bill was railroaded through the House of Representatives as the opposition tried to stall the vote. In July 1992 the Bill was introduced into the Upper House. The opposition tried every maneuver that they could to stall the vote. In the end they resorted to the "ox walk" tactic, which delayed the vote for several days and was shown in the international media.[99] The bill passed in the end and became law a few days later when it was passed again by the Lower House.

The final law was a compromise, and it has many flaws which will make life difficult for the SDF. It is though a dramatic change for Japan and one that was debated (but not at the same intensity) again in July 1995 when the law came up for the required three year review. The final draft of the law has ten basic provisions; which are:

1) The Prime Minister does not need Diet approval to send the SDF to take part in activities such as transportation, communication, construction, international humanitarian assistance, election supervision, administration and police functions;

2) SDF participation in activities such as monitoring cease-fires, supervising the disarmament or withdrawal of troops, patrolling a buffer zone, defining a cease-fire line and assisting in the exchange of prisoners is frozen until separate legislation is passed authorizing such activities;

3) When the freeze is lifted, the Prime Minister must receive Diet approval each time he wishes to send the SDF to engage in activities outlined in point 2, which clearly carry the risk of armed confrontation and shots being fired in anger;

4) Local conditions must be conducive to the success of the peacekeeping operation: a cease-fire must be in place and the parties involved must accede to the participation of the SDF;

5) The peacekeeping operation must be politically neutral, It cannot be at the service of any party to the dispute;

6) When the government wishes to extend a peacekeeping operation beyond a two-year limit, it must seek Diet approval again;

7) No more than 2,000 personnel will take part in either type of peacekeeping operation;

8) In unavoidable situations, personnel on peacekeeping missions can only use small arms to defend themselves "within a rational limit dictated by circumstances";

9) The government must review the entire law within three years;

10) Without Diet approval, the government can use SDF trucks, ships and planes for humanitarian purposes in connection with a peacekeeping operation, such as refugee evacuation. It can also sell goods to the UN necessary for peacekeeping operations at lower than market levels, or it can donate these goods outright.[100]

CAMBODIA, MOZAMBIQUE, AND THE GOLAN HEIGHTS

Japan's first two United Nations Peace Keeping assignments were to Cambodia and Mozambique respectively. An ongoing mission to the Golan Height is currently in opperation. In Cambodia the SDF worked for UNTAC and earned high praise as a professional force.[101] During the time that Japan was in Cambodia two Japanese were killed. One was a civilian worker and the other was a policeman. There were fears at the time that this would lead to calls for the withdrawal of Japanese peace-keepers. It generally did not. In fact general public support started to grow from this as it began to better understand the nature of peace-keeping.

The operation in Mozambique also went well and there was no loss of life. Japan is prepared for future peace-keeping roles but only those that fit their rules. One such mission is the current ongoing one to the Golan Heights. An example of the rules that Japan has placed on its SDF forces is that officers and NCOs (until recently) were not permitted to order their troops to fire or not to fire under Japanese law. This rule effectively negated the SDF troops from acting as a unit in a combat situation, thus destroying their effectiveness. The reality of the situation was that the commanders in the field ordered their troops to fire only when ordered to do so. The field commanders took full responsibility if an incident occurred for violating Japanese law. The field commanders were told by their superiors that they would be protected as much as possible but that they might have to take "the fall" if the incident caused a backlash.[102] No incident ever took place and in the Spring of 1999 the Japanese Diet amended the law to permit its troops to act as a normal military unit for self-defense.

It is important to note that the government decided that the SDF would only participate in "peace-keeping operations" and not "United Nations-authorized" forces such as the coalition deployed for the Gulf War or UNITAF in Somalia.[103] In spite of all the restrictions the SDF have thus begun their transformation from being defensive forces within the Japan/United States Security Treaty system to a nation that is sharing the tasks of guaranteeing international security.[104] Japan has come a long way towards normality as a nation with the PKO law, but it still has a ways to go if it chooses to stay on the same path that it has been traveling.

TOWARDS A SECURITY COUNCIL SEAT AND BEYOND

The Gulf War gave Japan the excuse to do what had been unthinkable since the end of the Second World War; send troops overseas. Japan has now expanded this newfound freedom into a desire for a permanent United Nations Security Council seat. Japan has sat on the Security Council as a temporary member six times.[105] To gain a permanent seat, the Charter of the United Nations would need to be amended and the support of all five current permanent members gained. Of these five only the United States has currently expressed open support for the election of Japan to this elite group, but numerous regular members of the United Nations have expressed support for Japan.

The fact that Japan is being considered for this position is testimony to Japan's economic power and influence internationally. Domestically on the other hand, power and influence are split. Japan is a very divided country. Some political observers have called it "divided politics" or "cultural politics"[106] The divide was strong in the post-war years, but has weakened in recent years. There are two basic platforms. The right-wing policy platform which has stressed:

1) Alliance with the United States, greater expenditure and role for [the] Self-Defense Forces, and anti-communism;
2) National identity, traditional morality, and the emperor;
3) Production, efficiency, and innovation;
4) Protection and subsidies to socially weak sectors.

And the left-wing policy platform which has stressed:

1) Neutrality or non-alignment, light defense posture, and anti-hegemony nationalism;
2) Civil freedom, egalitarian norms, and democracy;
3) A better working and living environment and protection of consumers;
4) Social welfare, education, and public expenditure.[107]

This basic political divide has been undergoing dramatic changes since the end of the Cold War as the political parties search for new ground. The Lower House election of July 1993 shattered the LDP's long hold on power. The next election will be under the new reformed electoral system. This election promises to reshape Japan's political landscape. What this new shape will be is anyone's guess.

What direction the next government will go in foreign policy is also open for speculation. Japanese hawks and nationalists like Ichiro Ozawa and Shintaro Ishihara are clearly committed to making Japan as powerful and as assertive a nation as possible on the world stage. They seek glory and power for Japan though probably not through foreign conquests as in the past.[108] If those with like-minded opinions are elected, then Japan will take on a whole new look on the world stage.

This brings us to another question: is Japan to be feared? It can be expected that combined with Western pressure and the softening of public opinion against *all* military action that the principles of pacifism, which have begun to erode, will continue to erode. While the remilitarization of Japan is probably not likely to occur, it is important that we not ignore the possibility. As several commentators have noted, it is possible that the Japanese know their own national psyche better than we do, and it would be important to listen to them.[109] An example of Japanese fears of the military outlook of some members of the SDF is given by Yoshitaka Sasaki. He recounts:

"A telling dinner conversation of a few years ago between admirals of the Maritime Self-Defense Force and the U.S. Navy exposed the thinking of members of Japan's military circle. According to well-informed sources, the U.S. admiral proposed that Japan build a large hospital ship. Why not dispatch the ship off the coasts of areas around the world stricken by natural disasters or armed conflicts and have doctors trained at the National Defense Medical College treat those affected, he suggested. The Japanese admiral instantly retorted: If we had the money, we would build an aircraft carrier.[110]

Until Japan's economic crisis of the last ten years, many both inside Japan and internationally saw (and still see) Japan as a potential future hegemon to replace the declining United States. A disturbing side effect of this is how renewed military conflict between the United States and Japan is often portrayed in the Japanese media and in *manga* or comics that are read by so many Japanese.[111] Given the current frictitous nature of U.S./Japanese relations, if the current Japan/United States Security Treaty was abandoned, there is the possibility of hostile Cold War like conflict developing between the United States and Japan. Both sides are capable of demonizing the other in trade disputes that have strong nationalistic undercurrents.[112] Posturing by both sides may leave no room for either to back down or compromise.

It is not in Japan's (or the United States) best interest to see conflict of this nature arise. Neither is it in the interest of Japan to see a premature hegemonic decline of the United States in the near future.[113] Japan depends too much on the *Pax Americana* or the U.S. hegemonic stability that the United States currently provides. Japan is in much the same position as it was before World War II. Japan imports raw materials and exports finished products. If this flow is interrupted there is little that Japan can do about it by itself, except to appeal to the United States.

Japan's economy can easily suffer economically from international instability. Japan is especially vulnerable to the loss of Middle Eastern oil since it imports over ninety percent of its oil needs. This vulnerability is in many ways no different than the sanctions that Japan faced before the Pearl Harbor attack in World War II. U.S. sanctions in 1941, cutting off oil to Japan, were causing its economic collapse and undermining if not destroying its military efforts in China.[114] The same vulnerability exists today; Japan needs open SLOCs. Japan furthermore has one major potential adversary in East Asia — China. China may develop the capability to threaten or interrupt Japan's trade. Japanese national security needs and economic needs can thus be said to be synonymous. Japan is in no way ready to take on the role of a hegemon *at this time*. It still, in the foreseeable future, needs and desires that the U.S. continue to be engaged in East Asia as a protector of East Asian stability and its own economic well-being. The risk of going it alone outweighs the benefits of being totally independent from the influence of U.S. hegemony.

There are many questions that can be asked about the debate over what Japan can, should, and will do. Questions like: Why all the debate? Why all the fuss about Japan doing what any normal sovereign nation should be able to do any time it wants to, that is contributing to global security through the United Nations? In the end it all really comes down to the one question that many, both inside and outside of Japan ask, Has Japan learned from the results of World War II and what has it learned? Can Japan be trusted to act as a civilized nation and not resort to militarism again? The answer to this last question is probably "yes", but there are obviously doubts about this inside Japan.

There are also concerns about this abroad. Much of this concern comes from the failure of Japan to come to terms with World War II. Japan needs to deal with this and accept the facts of its history. This will be difficult to do given the Japanese reluctance to admit that mistakes were made by their ancestors and the fact that many of the current leaders served in the Second World War and had friends and loved ones who died during the war. There is a generational issue here. To admit that Japan was wrong would be to admit that the Japanese who died during the war died in vain. Thus confronting the past will cause severe embarrassment to them and loss of face. This is compounded by the need to admit to wrongs committed against Korea and China, whose people many conservative Japanese feel are racially inferior to Japanese.[115] Japan has yet to make amends with its neighbors who suffered horrendously under the heel of Japanese military occupation during World War II.

Furthermore, Japan needs to come to terms with its own people, especially its children, about the events that transpired during the war. Germany has done penance for the crimes of the Nazis during World War II teaching their young people so that history will not be repeated. All German school children are taught about the Nazi past. In Japan little is taught about Japanese imperialism.[116] Thus the youth of Japan do not know of the past. Thus, the fear of its Asian neighbors.[117]

In essence Japan needs to apologize. Not necessarily to the United States, but to Asian nations. The United States was attacked by Japan and in the ensuing war defeated and occupied Japan. Anything that the United States needed from Japan in the form of an apology should have been achieved during the occupation. Furthermore, the United States does not place a strong cultural significance on apologies. This is not so with the nations of Asia which Japan invaded. Culturally Asia needs an apology because the East Asian nations better understand the cultural significance of an apology for Japan. Without an admission of guilt there can be no forgiveness for the past and without forgiveness Japan will never have credibility as a normal nation. The Japanese government's use of the SDF will continue to have strong opposition both at home and abroad. James Auer, director of the Center for U.S.-Japan Studies at Vanderbilt University and an expert on U.S.-Japan foreign policy and defense issues, feels that, "Until Japan truly comes to grips with its global responsibilities, it will continue to find itself unable to obtain the prestige of a permanent Security Council Nation."[118]

The absence of a national apology for its actions in the Second World War is hindering Japan's foreign policy. Many in Japan's foreign policy community seem to have an "ostrich with its head in the ground" mentality about the need for an apology. Director General Ryozo Kato of the Foreign Policy Bureau of the Ministry of Foreign Affairs (MOFA) is typical. He said, in the context of discussing Iris Chang's recent book *The Rape of Nanking*, that, "If we can just hold off (apologizing) for ten to twenty more years, every one who lived through it (World War II) will be gone and it will all be forgotten."[119] This was said at the same time that the former Yugoslavs were killing each other in a centuries old conflict that no one can remember who started but that each side wants to end on its own terms. If Japan lets the generation that committed and suffered the atrocities of World War II to die off with no apology, then future apologies will ring hollow to succeeding generations.

It is interesting to note that younger Japanese politicians tend[120] to desire that Japan apologize now rather than later so that they can get the proverbial "monkey" off their backs. They see the lack of an apology as a hindrance to Japanese foreign policy goals. Politicians who feel this way include Councillors Kei Hata and Ichita Yamamoto.[121] The older generation see a sincere apology as anathema even if it is better for current foreign policy and for future generations for them to apologize to those who survived the atrocities of Japan's invasion of Asia. The reason that it is better for the World War II generation to apologize, rather than future generations, is that if the generation who suffered under the Japanese can forgive those who committed the atrocities then it will be much more difficult for future generations to hold Japan responsible for actions that the victims themselves forgave.

It is important for Japan, if it wants to claim any moral leadership, to offer a sincere apology. Not the kind of "apology" that was issued on 6 June 1995 in Tokyo by the Diet. This Diet resolution used the word *hansei* which means "reflection" or "remorse" like a school kid might say about forgetting to do his/her homework. Neither the word nor the resolution gives any indication of who is responsible or should be sorry. Words like *Kokai* and *Shazai* which mean "remorse and regret" and "Apology" respectively were not used.[122] Only 230 Diet members out of 511 voted for this resolution which was a political compromise forced through the Diet by Prime Minister Tomoiichi Murayama. The resolution does not express the acceptance of responsibility that is needed by Japan's World War II enemies. Japan did apologize in the Fall of 1998 to South Korea for actions taken during its long occupation of the Korean Peninsula. This apology came out of the necessity to work with South Korea as an ally in dealing with North Korea as a "rogue" state.

In conclusion, Japan is a sovereign nation that must make its own decisions that carry their own consequences. Japan is searching for respect among nations. To achieve the ends of those within Japan who wish to see Japan take a leadership role the very thing they do not want to remember must be dealt with. Japan as Germany must deal with its history if Japan wants to reclaim its sovereignty in the minds of others. The hardest thing about this is that the need to humble itself about its past and apologize. Japan is very good at getting what it wants politically because of its general far sightedness. If this far sightedness is put together with the needs of the community of nations, then Japan may receive the respect it seeks.

Japan is caught between the West on one hand that expects it to show leadership and East Asia which objects to its leadership. Japan needs to show the world that it is willing to learn from its past and apply those lessons to the future. Japan is not likely to become a superpower but it is more likely to be a great power. The PKO is just the beginning for Japan. Many people fear the PKO Law because they are not confident that their will is reflected in their democratic institutions. The Japanese government needs to bring their people into the decision making process if they really want to be a sovereign nation that is united in purpose.

The need to bring the Japanese people into the decision making process is based on the fact of bureaucratic control by MOFA of the foreign policy making process which has limited the role of the elected Diet in directing foreign policy. Foreign policy decisions in a democratic society should reflect the will of the people or their elected representatives, not an unelected elite serving in MOFA. MOFA controls much of the decision making process due to a general lack of interest by Diet members in foreign affairs. However, interest in foreign policy is developing with a new younger generation of Diet members who are taking a more active "hands on" approach to foreign policy. The next several chapters will look at this trend among others in order to explore what is happening in Japan and its prospects for the future in East Asia and the world.

NOTES

[1] *The Constitution of Japan, Law and Contemporary Problems*, Spring, 1990: 200–214 (emphasis added).

[2] Ibid.

[3] The Liberal Democratic Party (LDP), a center/right wing party ruled Japan continuously from 1958 until July of 1993 when it was ousted by a center/left coalition. The uninterrupted reign of the LDP permitted the SDF to exist and grow throughout the Cold War period. Only since July 1993 when the largest of the center/left wing parties, the Socialists (SDP), joined in a center/left coalition government and later when they defected to join the center/right wing LDP in another coalition government, have the Socialists accepted the legitimacy of the SDF. Several of the Socialists whom this author interviewed expressed strong displeasure at their party's willingness to accept the SDF as legitimate under the constitution in order to gain power. At the same time they demonstrated a realization that the SDF will not go away. However, the Communist Party of Japan (CPJ) still views the SDF as illegitimate.

[4] Martin W. Sampson III and Steven G. Walker, *Cultural Norms and National Roles: A Comparison of Japan and France*, in Stephen G. Walker, ed., *Role Theory and*

Foreign Policy Analysis. (Durham: Duke University Press, 1987), Chapter 7, P. 105–122.

[5] Ibid. P. 109.

[6] The Diet is the legislative body in Japan. It has both an upper house, the House of Counselors (*Sangin*), and a lower house, The House of Representatives (*Shugin*). The lower house is primary in that it may override a vote of the upper house by two-thirds majority. The Prime Minister and the Cabinet usually come from the lower house, but may come from either.

[7] The SDP used "oxwalk" (similar to a filibuster but considerably less elegant) tactics to slow down the inevitable and succeeded in dragging out the final vote for several days. However the SDP's tactics backfired with the Japanese public in general and proved to be a national source of embarrassment when it was broadcast internationally. The "oxwalk" led to the perception that the SDP was outdated and out of touch with reality. The July 1993 elections resulted in the SDP taking severe losses at the polls.

[8] Robert W. Tucker, *The Inequality of Nations*, (New York: Basic Books, Inc., 1977), 88.

[9] Some have begun to question Japan's status as a "virtual" nuclear power in light of the October 1999 nuclear accident and the disclosures of gross neglect within the Japanese nuclear power industry. The feeling is that Japan would have to undertake a large and long lasting "Manhattan Project" style project with a questionable prognosis for success especially in face of large scale public opposition to the idea of Japan "going" nuclear. This author disagrees with this assessment for two principle reasons. First, it assumes that Japan does not already have plans for nuclear weapons in blueprint form or other advanced form (South Africa was an example of this). Second, it assumes that a public facing a clear potential threat would not support a government attempting to protect it from this threat. An extensive discussion of Japan's nuclear potential took place on the internet list <ssj-forum@iss.u-tokyo.ac.jp> during the late Fall of 1999 following Japan's nuclear accident in October 1999.

[10] *New York Times, Japan Discovers Defense*, 26 August 1999, internet edition <http://www.nytimes.com/yr/mo/day/editorial/26thu1.html>.

[11] Kazuo Ota, Dean Rakuno Gakuen University, interview by author, 6 June 1998, Tokyo, tape recording, in author's personal possession Tempe, Arizona.

[12] The foreign policy norms being the tendency of democratic states to set foreign policy based on perceived needs rather than on agendas. The idea is that nations are merely reacting and taking action as opportunities and problems present themselves rather than pressing forward with agendas or "master plans" which would guide the nation's foreign policies.

[13] Mutsuyoshi Nishimura, *Peace-keeping Operations: Setting the Record Straight*, *Japan Echo* Volume XIX, Number 3, (Autumn 1992): 51.

[14] Ibid., 55.

[15] *New York Times, Japan Discovers Defense*, 26 August 1999, internet edition <http://www.nytimes.com/yr/mo/day/editorial/26thu1.html>.

[16] Charles L. Kades, *The American Role in Revising Japan's Imperial Constitution*, *Political Science Quarterly*, Vol. 104, Nov. 2, 1989: 217.

[17] Proclamation by Heads of Governments, United States, United Kingdom, and China, Part I (a) and (b), PR 423 as quoted by Kades, 217 (emphasis added). Note: It is important to note that these directives did *not* call for the renunciation of war or the outlawing of the maintenance of military forces by the Japanese as contained in Article Nine of the Japanese Constitution.

[18] Sandra Madsen, *The Japanese Constitution and Self-Defense Forces: Prospects for a New Japanese Military Role, Transnational Law & Contemporary Problems*, Fall 1993: v3, 553.

[19] James E. Auer, *Article Nine of Japan's Constitution: from Renunciation of Armed Force "Forever" to the Third Largest Defense Budget in the World, Law and Contemporary Problems*, Spring 1990: 173. Note: The Imperial Army and Navy under the Feudal Meiji Constitution were cabinet ministries and their ministers were required by law to be active duty officers not elected officials.

[20] Kades, 218. Note: The Meiji Era was named after the period of the reign of the Emperor Meiji (1868–1912) and the constitution of that era was in effect until the end of World War II. It centered the power structure in Japan around the upper feudal lords and the military.

[21] This awareness that democracies do not tend to fight each other predates the Democratic Peace Theory in Political Science by several decades and demonstrates an awareness by the occupation government that true democracy (whatever that may be) with power in the hands of the people was desirable and necessary to the maintenance of peace with Japan.

[22] John Mensing commenting on how Japan embraced defeat, 13 October 1999, H-Net/KIAPS List for United States and Japanese Relations, <H-US-Japan@H-Net.msu.edu>.

[23] Kades, 219–222.

[24] Kendrick F. Royer, *The Demise of the World's First Pacifist Constitution: Japanese Constitutional Interpretation and the Growth of Executive Power to Make War, Vanderbilt Journal of Transnational Law*, 1993: v26: 777.

[25] Robert B. Funk, *Japan's Constitution and U.N. Obligations in the Persian Gulf War: A Case for Non-Military Participation in U.N. Enforcement Actions, Cornell International Law Journal Vol. 25*, 1992: 369.

[26] See Royer, 782–784.

[27] As cited by Funk, 371 and Auer, 174.

[28] Kades, 224. Note: Kades gets the idea that the Emperor was the origin of Article 9 from the Imperial Rescript of January 1946 denying his divinity, The emperor proclaimed "we will construct a new Japan through thoroughly being pacific." Comment: This seem to be a reasonable deduction based on the fact that the paramount desire of many leaders, at the time, was to preserve the Emperor System and that this might give them a strong case for its preservation. This idea is also noted by Funk, 371 and McNelly, see Funk 371 note #45.

[29] General Sackton is currently serving as Professor Emeritus in the School of Public Affairs at Arizona State University.

[30] Major General Frank Sackton, United States Army (Ret.) and former aid to General Douglas MacArthur during the occupation of Japan. Interviews by the author, 19 and 24 September 1997. Tape Recording. In author's personal possession Tempe, Arizona.

31 Sackton interview.

32 American interests were often not defined well during the occupation and this lead the Americans to undercut their own democratic policies and institutions through which they had attempted to place power in the hands of the people (and out of the hands of the elite). The Japanese leadership reacted better to indecision on the part of the American occupation authorities and were able to play elements (New Dealers v. Anti-Communists) within SCAP off against each other (Sackton interview). For more information on this see Alex Gibney, *The Pacific Century: Reinventing Japan (#5)*, produced by the Pacific Basin Institute in association with KCTS/Seattle, 60 min., Jigsaw Productions, 1992, videocassette.

33 For more information on MacArthur's personality see the PBS video series: *MacArthur: An American Caesar.*

34 Professor Keichi Fujiwara, Institute of Social Science Tokyo University, interview by the author, 11 June 1998. Note: Under Japanese law citizens if attacked do not have the right to defend themselves without risking being guilty of assaulting their attacker themselves.

35 Kades, 224 and Sackton interview.

36 Ibid., 229–230 (emphasis added).

37 Ibid., 230.

38 Toshihiro Yamauchi, *Gunning for Japan's Peace Constitution*, Japan Quarterly, April-June 1992: 160.

39 Funk, 372.

40 As cited by Kades, 243.

41 The democratization of Japan after World War II was unique (from most democratization struggles) in that the Japanese *kenpou* was democracy given by a foreign occupier against the desires of Japanese elites who had no desire for real democratic reform. SCAP captured the democratic desires of the Japanese people. For an alternative look at the democratization process more typical of struggles for democratization please see: Peter McDonough, Samuel H. Barnes, and Antonio Lòpez Pina, *The Cultural Dynamics of Democratization in Spain*, Ithica, New York: Cornell University Press, 1998.

42 Funk, 372.

43 Kades, 242.

44 The new *Kenpou* was finally passed out of the Diet with only 5 members dissenting (only a simple majority was required for passage). It should be noted however that the Japanese elite have never been happy with the way the kenpo was forced upon them. Witness former Prime Minister Nakasone's comments in *The Pacific Century: Reinventing Japan* (Vol. #5) in which he asserts that it was a wrong done to Japan. Alex Gibney, *The Pacific Century: Reinventing Japan (#5)*, produced by the Pacific Basin Institute in association with KCTS/Seattle, 60 min., Jigsaw Productions, 1992, videocassette.

45 Funk, 373–375.

46 Funk, 376 and Kades, 237. "In support of Yoshida's concern about the misuse of self defense wars, Kades notes that General Tojo, who was both prime minister and Army Minister during World War II, testified that Japanese wartime efforts, including the bombing of Pearl Harbor, were not aggressive acts but self

defense." -Funk, 376 note #86. Note: the term Yoshida used, "War of Greater East Asia" is the Japanese term for what we call the Pacific theater of World War II.

[47] Percy R. Luney Jr. and Kazuyuki Takahashi, ed., *Japanese Constitutional Law* (Tokyo: University of Tokyo Press, 1993), 72–74.

[48] Auer, 176 and Kades, 225–236.

[49] Auer, 177.

[50] Royer, 782.

[51] Cited by Royer, 782 note #149 (emphasis added).

[52] Jiro Kodera, Director First International Economic Affairs Division of the Japanese Ministry of Foreign Affairs, interview by author, 20 May 1998, Tokyo, tape recording, in author's personal possession Tempe, Arizona.

[53] Auer, 177.

[54] Ibid.

[55] It is important to note that this is not a law or a constitutional provision. It is merely a policy statement that was subscribed to in 1967 by the government of the time. It has never been put into or given the status of law. Auer, 178 note #31.

[56] Auer, 178–179 as Cited from K. Masuhara, *Nihon no Boei* (Japan's Defense) 1961, at 59.

[57] Ibid.

[58] Funk, 379–383 and Royer, 782.

[59] For background on this and on the separation of Executive and Judicial powers see Madsen's article, especially Part III.

[60] Madsen, 561.

[61] Karl van Wolferen, *The Enigma of Japanese Power* (Tokyo: Charles E. Tuttle Co. Inc., 1993), 41.

[62] This minimal level gradually increased as Japan's economic power grew and the burden of the Cold War increased for the United States. In the 1970's defense spending was limited to under one percent of GDP, but in the 1980's it broke the one percent barrier for the first time since the 1960's, though it has always remained around one percent. For a more complete analysis of this issue, see Auer, 180–181.

[63] Michael W. Chinworth, ed. *Inside Japan's Defense: Technology, Economics Strategy* (Washington: Brassey's (US), Inc., 1992), 26–27.

[64] Auer, 184.

[65] Chinworth, 9.

[66] The concept of *Gaiatsu* will be extensively discussed and analyzed in chapter five.

[67] Ibid.

[68] For a complete analysis of this see Auer's complete article.

[69] Royer, 787.

[70] Takashi Inoguchi, "Japan's Response to the Gulf Crisis: An Analytic Overview," *Journal of Japanese Studies*, 17:2 (1991): 257.

[71] Jiro Yamaguchi, *The Gulf War and the Transformation of Japanese Constitutional Politics, Journal of Japanese Studies*, 18:1 (1992): 155.

[72] Inoguchi, 257–258.

[73] Ibid., 258.

[74] Ibid.

75 Royer, 790.
76 Shinichi Kitaoka, *A Green Light for Japanese Peace-keepers*, Japan Echo, Volume XIX, Number 3, (Autumn 1992): 42.
77 As Prime Minister, Kaifu led the both the Diet and the Cabinet (selected by the Prime Minister) in fulfilling executive functions. He was also the leader of the Liberal Democratic Party (LDP). Normally the Leader of the LDP is a fairly strong politician, but Kaifu was not. Kaifu was elected head of the LDP and thus Prime Minister in August 1989 after a series of scandals toppled his immediate predecessors. Kaifu was a compromise candidate in that he was squeaky clean and not likely to be touched by scandal. His faction within the LDP was small and not very influential. He was seen as a nice man, but not really suited for the problems he would face as Prime Minister during the Gulf Crisis. This was especially evident during the debate on the first PKO Bill (to be discussed later).
78 Funk, 385.
79 Ibid.
80 Ibid., 387–388.
81 Lieutenant Colonel Andrew H. N. Kim, *Japan and Peace-keeping Operations*, Military Review, (April 1994): 24–25.
82 The United Nation's Charter article 1, Paragraph 1.
83 The United Nation's Charter article 2, Paragraph 5 and 25 (emphasis added).
84 Hirofumi Iseri, *Clearing the Mist from the Peace-keeping Debate*, Japan Echo, Volume XIX, Number 3, (Autumn 1992): 45.
85 Reproduced from the unofficial translation provided by the Embassy of Japan in Washington, D. C. *Japan: Law Concerning Cooperation for United Nations Peace-keeping Operations and Other Operations*, International-Legal Materials, v32, 215–216, (3–35) as summarized by Shunji Yanai, *The Law Concerning Cooperation for United Nations Peace-Keeping Operations and Other Operations*, The Japanese Annual of International Law, Number 36 (1993): 41.
86 Yamaguchi, 167.
87 This style of governing being to centralize power with the elite rather than the people.
88 Shunji Yanai, *The Law Concerning Cooperation for United Nations Peace-Keeping Operations and Other Operations*, The Japanese Annual of International Law, Number 36 (1993): 58.
89 Madsen, 574–577.
90 Iseri, 46.
91 Ibid. Note: One of the strongest criticisms of Japan in the post-war years in the way the Japanese refuse to educate their children on the mistakes of the past and World War II. An example of this is that of a Japanese junior high history textbook which is used in northern Japan. It contains only four pages covering the Second World War. Many Japanese teachers avoid the issue of World War II altogether by simply not finishing the text book before the end of the school year or stopping at the beginning of the twentieth century.
92 Ibid.
93 From news accounts of March 1992 in *The Japan Times* and *The Daily Yomiuri*.
94 As quoted by Yoshitaka Sasaki, *Japan's Undue International Contribution*, Japan Quarterly, (July-Sept. 1993): 261.

[95] Victor Fic, *The Japanese PKO Bill, Asian Defense Journal*, (Nov. 1992): 30.

[96] Ibid., 31.

[97] All four of the following are outlined in further detail by Atsushi Odawara, *The Kaifu Bungle, Japan Quarterly*, (Jan- March 1991): 7–12.

[98] Fic, 32–33.

[99] Note : While the public generally sympathized with the efforts to stop the PKO Bill, the "Ox Walk" tactic seamed to backfire and caused people to view it as childish and disgusting. It is considered one of the major reasons that the SDP (the largest opposition group that engineered the "Ox Walk") fared so badly in the next election.

[100] Fic., 32–33.

[101] Kim, 22–33.

[102] Interview by the author with one of the Golan Heights' commanders 5 June 1998 in Tokyo, Japan.

[103] Akiho Shibata, *Japanese Peacekeeping Legislation and Recent Developments in U.N. Operations, The Yale Journal of International Law*, v19, (1994): p346.

[104] Yamaguchi, 167.

[105] Japan served on the Security Council during the years 1958–59, 1966–1967, 1971–1972, 1975–1976, 1981–1982, and 1995–96. See Sadako Ogata, *The Changing Role of Japan in the United Nations, Journal of International Affairs*, 27 (Summer 1983): 31 note #2. Note: While Japan's public effort for a permanent seat on the Security Council has been only recent, there has been an ongoing effort since the sixties by MOFA to position Japan to gain a permanent seat.

[106] J. A. A. Stockwin , *Japan: Divided Politics in a Growth Economy*, as cited by Inoguchi, 268.

[107] Takashi Inoguchi, *Japan 1960–1980: Party Election Pledges*, as cited by Inoguchi, 268.

[108] Fic, 30. Note: Ozawa and Ishihara differ in how this should happen.

[109] Royer, 800–801 note #247.

[110] Sasaki, 264.

[111] Note: Japanese *manga* comics are read not just by children but also by adults from all walks of life.

[112] David E. Sanger, *U.S. and Japanese Told to Resolve Dispute on Trade-Blunt Warning to Both—New World Trade Chief Calls Conflict a 'Delicate Matter'—Nationalism is Cited, The New York Times*, 14 June 1995, A1. Note: Nationalism is cited as being a primary reason for the intensity of this dispute.

[113] Inoguchi, 261 and Kenji Urata, *The Peace and Security of Japan, National Lawyers Guild Practitioner*, v44, n3 (Summer 1987): 75–86.

[114] The sanctions imposed on Japan were due to Japan's war of aggression in China. Some revisionist historians in Japan have tried (in many ways successfully in Japan) to use the sanctions as an excuse to justify the surprise attack on Pearl Harbor. These historians claim that Japan's war in China was a war of liberation intended to liberate China of colonial influences. The evidence of Japanese actions clearly shows this to be false. The Chinese to this day harbor a hatred for the Japanese for the atrocities they committed in this "war of liberation". Japan's failure to recognize and take responsibility for its actions is a source of deep resentment and suspicion for most Chinese and many East Asians in general. This

legacy continues to haunt Japanese foreign policy today as actions by Japan that would appear to be normal for any other nation are greeted with suspicion by East Asian nations and China in particular. For more on Japanese atrocities during World War II please see Iris Chang's book: *The Rape of Nanking: The Forgotten Holocaust of World War II*, New York: Penguin Putnam Inc., 1997.

[115] Nicholas D. Kristof, *A Big Exception for a Nation of Apologizers*, The New York Times, 12 June 1995, A1 and A4.

[116] Some teachers do buck the system and teach World War II honestly worts and all, but they risk the Japanese adage: "The nail that sticks up gets hammered down."

[117] See the comment made by Chinese Communist Party General Secretary Jiang Zemin page 67 of this chapter and footnote #75 on the same page.

[118] Fusakazu Izumura, *Should Japan Get a Permanent Seat on the U. N. Security Council?*, Tokyo Business Today, (March 1993): 54.

[119] Ryozo Kato, Director General, Foreign Policy Bureau of the Japanese Ministry of Foreign Affairs, interview by the author, 21 May 1998, Tape Recording, In author's personal possession Tempe, Arizona.

[120] Tendencies discovered during the field research will be discussed at length in Chapter 3.

[121] Kei Hata, Member of the House of Councillors of the Japanese Diet, interview by the author, 18 May 1998, Tokyo, tape recording, in author's personal possession Tempe, Arizona and Ichita Yamamoto, Member of the House of Councillors of the Japanese Diet, interview by the author, 18 June 1998, Tokyo, tape recording, in author's personal possession Tempe, Arizona.

[122] Nicholas D. Kristof, *Japan Expresses Regret of a Sort for the War*, The New York Times, 6 June 1995, A1 and A11.

CHAPTER 3

REALISM AND FOREIGN POLICY RESTRUCTURING IN JAPAN

"We are in a period of profound change in international relations and foreign policy. — Charles F. Herman"[1]

This chapter describes Japan's adaptation to the changes brought about by the end of the Cold War through the application of Charles Hermann's model to Japan's foreign policy restructuring after the Cold War. The chapter will also describe the field research and the methods used to apply Hermann's model to the Japan case. Finally, the results and implications of the field research will be presented for the rest of the book. The overarching purpose of this chapter is to build the theoretical framework for the rest of the book. Detailed analysis of the field research and summary conclusions are saved for the final chapters.

As stated previously, Japanese foreign policy revolves around the interpretation of Article Nine of the *kenpou*. Nothing in Japanese foreign policy can be understood without a fundamental understanding of what is considered constitutional under Article Nine. Japan has managed over the years to modify its constitution through reinterpretation rather than through the more traditional method of a straight forward amendment. The *kenpou* and Article Nine have managed to establish themselves as sacrosanct, and any serious attempt to amend Article Nine is likely to result in a political uproar that the Japanese government does not want to see.[2] This is largely due to the fact that Japanese bureaucrats and politicians *tend* to be sensitive to public displeasure due to the Asian cultural desire to have a balance in the "*wa*".[3] The "*wa*" is a cultural concept of balance and harmony that is so important in many Asian cultures. Direct public conflict is not desirable. Politicians strive to maintain a balance which means the absence of open conflict. Establishing a consensus is important. Public support or rather the lack of opposition is crucial for to many Japanese politicians.[4] Nevertheless, it is important to note that while political consensus is helpful it is not always required. Witness the passage of the original PKO law. The public supported the LDP's efforts in general because the Social Democratic Party of Japan's (SDPJ)[5] "oxwalk" tactics backfired on them by causing national embarrassment when it was broadcast worldwide. The result was a solidification of Japanese public support for the LDP on this issue, regardless of personal feelings about the PKO Bill and a silencing of those who opposed the bill out of embarrassment.[6]

JAPANESE LIMITATIONS

Japan is realistic about its political power. It can not compete with the US one-on-one, period or as the British say "fullstop". Japan simply does not have the resources or the population to be a true hegemon. That is they do not have the ability or resources to both seize power and to maintain it. The same problem that plagued it during World War II is still with it today. It is a country that is poor in natural resources. This requires it to import raw materials and export finished products. Part of the problem is that Japan's population is aging at a remarkably rapid rate. By the early part of the new millennium over half of Japan's population will be over 65. Japanese live longer than any other nationality in the industrialized world. Life expectancies for men and women are 82 and 86 years respectively. Japan is already facing the severe financial task of providing retirement incomes and medical care to a growing population of retirees who are living longer and longer after retirement. The Japanese social security system is projected to run out of funds by 2010.[7] Fewer and fewer workers are supporting those on government pensions. At the same time Japan has the highest debt ratio of any developed nation. The government is deep in debt. Japan must already import foreign workers to do "dirty" jobs that Japanese will not do. This may begin to also change the social structure of Japan as Japanese intermarry with foreigners, diluting Japan's racial homogeneity. Japan has also begun to expand its industrial base overseas to partially due to the lack of workers at home.[8]

There will be a tremendous burden on the youth of Japan to support its aging population, especially when the ratio of workers to retirees is projected to reach 1:1.4 by the year 2020.[9] Japan has more citizens over the age of sixty-five than under the age of fifteen.[10] The Japanese people themselves are acutely aware of the problem. Eri Kimura (23), who works in insurance sales, is an example of how the younger generation is worried about Japan's future because of its aging population. She says, "The number of young people paying for the older generation is causing a strain on our taxes....And the number of children being born is decreasing so it's become a serious burden."[11]

Technology has given Japan the ability to be a powerful nation, but it does not give Japan the global military reach that is needed to be a hegemonic power. So many Japanese couples have only one child or are choosing not to have children that the population is expected to shrink to less than 100 million (from the 125 million today) in the next century. With so few children to grow up to serve in the armed forces, Japan like the U.S. (for different reasons), is very risk averse.[12] Japan's primary vulnerability is not to invasion, but to interruptions or the closing of the Sea Lines of Communication (SLOC). Japan must trade to survive and prosper.

Japan does not and will probably never have the resources to be a world power (in the traditional sense). Japan is much better served by working as a great power within the world community and using its economic strength as the basis of its power. Japan will continue to have conflicts with the current hegemon, the U.S., but these disputes should remain moderate in the larger scope of things.

Since World War II Japan, recognizing its own limits, has remained in the U.S. shadow through its judicious use of the Yoshida Doctrine. With the end of the Cold War and the U.S. unwillingness to permit Japan to continue to be a free rider and to use its position under U.S. hegemony to its economic advantage, Japan must decide what role and position it should have in the world. At the same time there are those within Japan on the right wing, like Ichiro Ozawa, who advocate a more independent Japan. There are even some in academia outside of Japan, like Chalmers Johnson, who advocate a more independent Japan free from the constraints of the U.S./Japan Security Treaty and the U.S. military presence that comes with it. There are also those on the left, such as the traditional old guard in the SDP and the Japan Communist Party (JCP) who desire the same thing, but they envision a more neutral or isolationist Japan rather than an activist or assertive Japan.

The obvious reality is that across the political spectrum Japan does desire a more independent/autonomous role in international security and is caught between what it desires and its constitutional restraints. Japan has extraordinary advantages because of its one way security relationship with the U.S. It is to Japan's economic benefit to stay as close to the U.S. as possible. One might even go so far as to describe Japan as being addicted to its relationship with the U.S. under the Yoshida Doctrine. An addiction like one has to say chocolate rather than drugs or alcohol. One can stop eating chocolate at any time but why stop when it tastes so good and gives one so much pleasure.

The problem for Japan is that it needs an active and in many ways more independent foreign policy. As mentioned previously, Japan has an increasing industrial presence overseas that it needs to protect. Traditionally nations have used military power or the credible threat of military intervention to protect foreign economic interests. Japan will need a more dynamic foreign policy to protect its interests for which it currently depends on the U.S. Milton Ezrati writes in *Foreign Affairs*:

> A more active foreign policy will become unavoidable as the over-
> seas expansion of Japanese industry establishes connections in the
> rest of Asia that Japan will need to secure. Though such a move goes
> against present Japanese instincts, no nation, including Japan, can
> afford to locate its production facilities abroad and not develop the
> capability to at least threaten to project power to protect those
> sources of wealth. This new security perspective will be all the more
> radical because it will run counter to Japan's long standing reliance
> on U.S. protection of Japanese interests.[13]

The problem for Japan is the constitutionality of power projection capability.
Japan depends on the U.S. to protect its interest overseas because of Article
Nine and the Yoshida Doctrine. When U.S. interests and Japanese interests
coincide this works well. As Japan and the U.S. find themselves competing
against each other for world markets, Japan will need to develop constitutionally acceptable options to protect its interests.

Part of the problem for Japan if it takes on a more independent role is
that Japan derives so many benefits from its relationship with the U.S. that
losing this relationship would cause Japan hardship even if it is somehow beneficial in the long run. Cutting itself loose from the US would force Japan to
change its foreign and security policy, but not necessarily make Japanese foreign policy any better.

The following illustration should help clarify Japan's options. The
American "father" is trying to raise the Japanese "son".[14] The father having
raised the son can set the son loose at "18" and allow the son to become
independent, or the father can continue to support, educate, and nurture the
son into a more equal relationship/partnership.

The son, on the other hand, can choose independence or continue to
permit himself to be nurtured. This raises the question of whether the son, if
he permits himself to be nurtured, will become an equal partner with the
father and a united force with the father that is stronger than either would
be alone. Alternatively, the son could remain dependent on the father and
never truly become independent.[15]

If the son chooses independence, then the son makes his own way in the
world. The son does become independent but is free to rejoin the father at
any time provided that the union/reconciliation is mutual. A historical example of this is the Anglo-American relationship in which the U.S. fought for and
won independence from the British, but during the course of two world wars
America established a "special" relationship with Britain through a common
heritage that eventually led the British to acquiesce to U.S. hegemony. This
peaceful transfer of power was historically unprecedented and in this author's
opinion represents a bond of culture/heritage that made/helped the British
see the transfer of power as something that was acceptable because it was
still "in the family".

In the U.S.-Japan relationship the situation is more abstract. There is no common language, culture, or heritage. In many ways one can hardly find two more different nations. There is however a common recent history, particularly since World War II. America gave Japan its democratic process and institutions. It also helped to promote and develop its capitalist economic system.[16] The U.S- Japan Security Treaty cemented this "adoptive" relationship where the U.S. took a willing (Yoshida Doctrine practicing) Japan under its wing and helped it to rebuild.

Japan is now at a choice point of whether it stays with the U.S. or goes its own way. The debate on this issue, within Japan, is rising. There are activist governors like former Okinawa Governor Ota and the current Tokyo Governor Shintaro Ishihara who want the U.S. military out of Japan or least its role greatly reduced.[17] The ruling LDP and MOFA are inclined to stay with the current U.S. relationship, but have failed to chart, in many ways, a coherent course for the continuation of the U.S.-Japan relationship. The September 1997 Guidelines are in many ways a temporary patch, but not a long term course change or strategy. There are very few within Japan who have articulated a long term direction for Japanese foreign policy and no one in a position of direct leadership has vocalized goals for Japan internationally over the long term (5–10 years in the future). The only prominent new goal which Japan is pursuing is its quest for a permanent seat on the U.N. Security Council.

Most of those interviewed demonstrated a clear lack of even moderate range (3–5 years) goals for the future.[18] Exceptions to this were former Defense Agency Minister Usui, Councillor Keizo Takemi, and Director General Ukeru Magosaki of the Intelligence and Analysis Bureau of MOFA who articulated specific objectives. Representative Usui's goal is to start a serious debate on foreign and security policy issues. He stated his desire to have others in leadership interviewed by this author (more on this later) because he felt that the questions asked would make others in leadership think about Japan's choices in a changing world and realize that Japan's future foreign policy was of interest to others outside of Japan.

Councillor Takemi expressed a desire to make the Diet a source of foreign policy debate. He is focusing on educating his fellow Diet members on foreign policy issues by bringing then into the foreign policy making structure through the use of committee hearings. He is also working to change the structure of the committee system in the Diet by adding sub committees to facilitate this.[19] Director General Ukeru Magosaki's paper *New Diplomatic Challenges in East Asia* (1998) is an overview of Japan's position in the Post-Cold War era and an analysis of Japan's future foreign policy options.[20]

FOREIGN POLICY RESTRUCTURING

The question is can Japan *politically* restructure its foreign policy? And if it can what form will it take? As to the question of whether Japan can restructure its foreign policy the answer is easy, "yes it can." There is a general consensus, particularly within the Diet, that Japan needs to be doing something, but the form of that "something" is a matter of debate. Some of the more charismatic Japanese political leaders have clear ideas for a more independent Japan. Examples of this are former LDP politicians such as Ichiro Ozawa and his book, *Blueprint for a New Japan: The Rethinking of a Nation*[21] or Shintaro Ishihara's *The Japan that Can say "No"*.[22] The problem is that often many of these "charismatic" foreign policy agendas concentrate on immediate gains and (in many ways) petty gratification while long term implications are not addressed.[23]

As the late former American Speaker of the House "Tip" O'Neil once said, "All politics are local" and Japan is no exception. President Clinton's 1992 campaign theme, "It's the economy, stupid!" rings true in Japan as well as in America.[24] Economic welfare and domestic needs drive voters in Japan just as they do in the United States. As one MOFA official depressingly put it, "...the voice for foreign policy change *will* come from those who emphasize domestic politics *first*. This is probably a mistake and against Japanese interests (and) it could even be a disaster for Japan."[25] The implication here is that the Japanese voter will elect political leadership that will solve Japan's domestic economic problems, regardless of their foreign policy agenda. The fear on the part of the MOFA official is that an ideologue could seize the foreign policy reigns and take Japan in an ill-conceived direction that would risk Japan's standing in the world by pursuing personal relative gains at the expense of absolute gains for the nation. An example of this could be a "nationalist" foreign policy that terminates the U.S.-Japan Security Treaty in order to assert Japanese independence forcing Japan to go it alone or to seek other possible alliances in which Japan would be the dominant player, but at the same time leave Japan internationally weaker without the hegemonic backing of the U.S.

This is not to say that Japan has ever ignored its own domestic needs. In fact under the Yoshida Doctrine Japan has, since world War II, pursued a foreign policy governed by domestic needs. Since the end of the occupation Japan has pursued a foreign policy based on Realism or "self help". Realism as described by Joseph M. Grieco:

> . . . encompasses five propsitions. First, states are the major actors in world affairs (Morganthau 1973:10; Waltz 1979:95). Second, the international environment severly penalizes states if they fail to protect their vital interests or if they pursue objectives beyond their means; hence, states are "sensitive to costs" and behave as unitary-

rational agents (Waltz 1986:331). Third, international anarchy is the principal force shaping the motives and actions of states (Waltz 1959:224–38; 1979:79–128; Hoffmann 1965:27, 54–87, 129; Aron 1973a:6–10). Fourth, states in anarchy are preoccupied with power and security, are predisposed toward conflict and competition, and often fail to cooperate even in face of common interests (Aron 1966:5; Gilpin 1986:304). Finally, international institutions affect the prospects for cooperation only marginally (Waltz 1979:115–16; Morgenthau 1973:512; Hoffmann 1973b:50).[26]

Japanese realistic foreign policy has not been the traditional power based Realism of Hans J. Morganthau.[27] Rather, Realist Japanese foreign policy has been largely based on a realistic assessment of its foreign policy limitations under Article Nine. The constitutional limitations that Article Nine places on Japan have meant that Japan has been forced to *realistically* pursue an institutionalist/neoliberalist[28] foreign policy.[29] Institutionalists would say that Japan is simply following a institutionally based foreign policy; not realism. However, the institutionalists are wrong as Grieco argues and this author concurs:

> . . . in fact, neoliberal institutionalism misconstrues the realist analysis of international anarchy and therefore it misunderstands the realist analysis of the impact of anarchy on the preferences and the actions of states. Indeed, the new liberal institutionalism fails to address a major constraint on the willingness of states to cooperate which is generated by international anarchy and which is identified by realism. As a result, the new theory's optimism about international cooperation is likely to be proven wrong.[30]

Japan has depended on U.S.-Japan Security Treaty[31] and the Untied Nations for its security needs. This institutionalist approach to it foreign policy is not based on its belief in institutionalism, but on a realistic assessment of its options, which were few.

The premise underlying this argument is that Realism *dominates or influences* all calculations going into relations between nations. This argument runs counter to the ideas of many political scientists who hold that there are more than one theoretical explanation for the behavior of nation states. As Sheldon Simon states in his 1995 paper, *International Relations Theory and Southeast Asian Security*:

> Students of international politics have debated the efficacy of alternative theories of state behavior for decades. Among the most prominent of these debates is the question of whether world politics is a zero-sum conflict in which all state-actors view one another as unmitigated competitors versus the less gloomy vision of a world in

which states can best achieve security and prosperity through cooperation rather than conflict. Put simply, advocates of the first school
see international politics as a struggle for relative gains in which the
power and the status of states are determined hierarchically. The second school disagrees, insisting that all members of the system benefit when absolute gains are achieved across the system, virtually
regardless of their distribution. Those who follow the first approach
are called realists; their more optimistic rivals take the label: neoliber-
alists. These alternative visions currently compete for the attention of
many statesmen in the post-cold war world, who are searching for
policies to secure and advance their governments' fortunes.

   While realists concede that states may be concerned in the long
run with absolute gains, they insist that immediate survival needs
take precedence and require independent military and economic
capabilities that attenuate cooperation. Neoliberals counter that
strong empirical evidence of cooperation in international politics and
the creation of institutions to facilitate cooperation show that states
do not necessarily concentrate on relative gains exclusively.

   Theoretically, under zero-sum conditions, there is no basis for
international cooperation regimes because one actor's gain is another's loss. Indeed, in the realist world, a hegemonic state determines
the structure or rules of international relations.[32]

Simon argues in his article that both realism and neoliberalism are evident in
Southeast Asian security policy. This book does not question this finding,
rather it offers an alternative hypothesis for why nations pursue an institutionalist foreign policy. An institutionalist foreign policy is a policy based on
the use of multilateral fora such as the U.N. and ARF for security rather than
traditional alliances. The book also explains why nations accept absolute
gains in cooperation with other states rather than competing over relative
gains.

   Realists argue that as the current dominant hegemon, the U.S., declines
other nations will vie for the right to be "top dog". Neoliberals argue that
states with an investment in the current hegemon's "regime" will have an
interest in preserving or in creating frameworks which will continue the rules
and regulations imposed by the reigning hegemon.[33] This second argument
by the neoliberals is seen as nothing more than an attempt by nation states
to augment their power through institutionalism. Nations are motivated by
the need for "self help", but the realities of the post-Cold War world are forcing them to pursue *relative gains* through *absolute gains*. States see the competition to be "top dog" as resulting in a net loss in terms of *relative gains* for
themselves. Part of the reasoning behind this is, as Grieco writes, "For realists, a state will focus both on its *absolute and relative gains* from cooperation,
and a state that is satisfied with a partner's compliance in a joint arrangement
might nevertheless exit from it because the partner is achieving relatively

greater gains."[34] With survival foremost on their minds nations practicing realism choose *absolute gains* over a net loss in *relative gains*. States will return to relative gains only when they are more profitable than absolute gains. With the world becoming more interdependent, nation states are less likely to find themselves pursuing *direct relative gains* when *absolute gains* offer so much more.

To illustrate this relative/absolute gains concept let us look at the case of Japan. As states are maneuvering for "top dog" status, Japan realizes that it is not in a position to be a serious contender for hegemony because of its limitations under Article Nine among other reasons. Realizing its limitations it tries to position itself for relative gains through absolute gain methods. Japan needs the stability offered by the "regime" of the current hegemon, the U.S., to continue in order to pursue relative gains. This requires that Japan pursue a neoliberal approach to its foreign policy and the resulting absolute gains. Japan's calculations tell it that *absolute gains* will give it a *greater relative gain* than if it only pursued *relative gains*. That is, the *absolute gains* from the U.S. relationship outweigh any conceivable *relative gains* from abandoning the relationship.

A nation may thus choose to pursue a purely realist path or not. It may choose to follow a liberal path because it is the rational thing to do. This is a kind of "localized rationality" on the part of Japan.[35] Part of this logic is based on the belief that people and nations must have incentives to work for goals and interests beyond their immediate selfish needs and agendas. Thus, the behavior of nations can be explained in realist terms no matter what form of policy they seem to be practicing. The circumstances in which they make a "realist" choice may reflect a view of mankind in which a nation can choose to work for the "common good" because it is in the nation's particular interest. Figure 3:1 diagrams this concept.

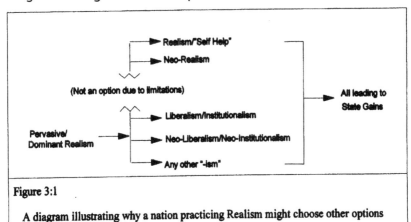

Figure 3:1

A diagram illustrating why a nation practicing Realism might choose other options for Realist reasons.

This argument adds to the ongoing debate between Grieco and Powell over the issue of relative verses absolute gains in international relations theory.[36] Neoinstitutionalists argue that states are only interested in their own gains and do not care about the gains of other states. Grieco (1993) disagrees with this and argues that nations will pursue relative gains over absolute gains *if* they can. Powell (1991) tries to marry both these schools of thought by arguing that the choice of relative or absolute gains is situational in nature. A nation will pursue relative gains from a state that it fears as a security threat. If it does not fear a state as a security threat, it will pursue absolute gains. What I am arguing, particularly in the case of Japan, is that there is simultaneous element to this process. States will pursue relative gains in any given situation even when on the surface they appear to be pursuing absolute gains. If a state does not have the option or ability to pursue a realist or neorealist strategy, it will then attempt a neoliberal strategy focused on absolute gains in economics and security. In the case of Japan its economics are strong but its security options are weak due to its limitations. It thus rationally pursues a pragmatic strategy of diplomacy in order to make relative gains in terms of intangibles such as goodwill and influence. On the surface Japan is pursuing absolute gains using a neoinstitutionalist strategy, but underneath it is seeking relative gains in the form of intangibles since it cannot make relative gains in the traditional forms of economics and security.[37]

For example, Japan needs open SLOCs. If Japan can not trade internationally it will starve. To keep the SLOCs open it must either do so by military force (which it can only do to a limited extent if at all constitutionally) or it must work with other nations through institutions to keep the SLOCs open. Japan's need to keep the SLOCs open is self centered, but it carries a benefit for other nations as well because cooperation in most cases is better than conflict. In realist terms, considering Japan's limitations, collaboration with the United States is Japan's best option. Furthermore, in realist terms security cooperation adds to Japan's power by strengthening it as a nation through goodwill and economics, thus giving it status/influence as a power which it would not have been able to achieve by military means. Japan has made a relative gain by letting other nations gain in absolute terms. In sum, this book is arguing that Japan's security policy can be explained through Realism. If one looks at Japanese options and limitations one can see a realist strategy governing Japanese foreign policy even when at first glance it appears to be an institutionalist policy (which on the surface it is).

In Japan's case, after the occupation it was forced to deal with the reality of Article Nine. Without the constitutional ability to raise an army, wage war, or threaten to wage war, Japan was forced to pursue an institutionalist foreign policy. During the Cold War Japan institutionalized its foreign policy through the U.S./Japan Security Treaty and to a lesser extent through the United Nations. Since the end of the Cold War Japan is still following an institutionalist foreign policy again with the U.S./Japan Security Treaty being the centerpiece.

At first glance the US/Japan Security Treaty is simply a "self help" effort on the part of Japan. The treaty allies Japan with the current hegemon, the U.S., by providing Japan its security guarantee. The treaty however serves other purposes for Japan. In addition to guaranteeing Japan's security it legitimizes Japan's role in East Asian security by assuring other Asian nations that the "Japanese genie" will be kept "in the bottle." Furthermore the treaty provides stabilization for East Asia as it keeps the U.S. forward deployed and engaged in the region.

However, the significance and importance of the US/Japan Security Treaty has declined (but has not been eliminated) since the end of the Cold War. Japan is not as crucial an ally to the U.S. as it was during the Cold War when America was trying to contain communism. The end of the Cold War reduced Japan's leverage vis-a-vis the U.S. because Japan was no longer seen as an essential ally in the fight against communism. Benefits from the relationship are now tipped in favor of the Japanese in that Japan's relative gains are greater than the U.S. gains even though both sides share absolute gains.[38] The full impact of this is that Japan is more vulnerable to abandonment by the U.S. if the Americans ever wished or felt it necessary to do so. This is a great fear in Japan, particularly on the right wing of Japanese politics.[39] One result of this is that Japan has been searching for new options to raise its stature and increase its power and thus its importance to the U.S. and the world in general.

Japan has been increasingly focusing on a U.N.-centric policy while at the same time participating in regional fora like ASEAN, Asia-Pacific Economic Cooperation (APEC), and the ASEAN Regional Forum (ARF)[40]. It is also championing a larger role for itself within the UN. Its high profile quest for a permanent seat on the Security Council is supplemented by the championing of its nationals for important positions within the U.N. Japan has also been accused of using its economic power to allegedly "purchase" important positions within the U.N. for Japanese. An example of this is the "checkbook" campaign that, according to an article in *Le Monde*, Japan waged on behalf of the new UNESCO head Ambassador Koichiro Matsuura.[41] In these cases, money becomes a foreign policy tool to increase Japan's political influence in international bodies.

Japanese politicians for the most part believe the revision of the *kenpou* and the removal or amending of Article Nine to be a political impossibility because of the political disruption it would cause and its dubious chances for success. At the same time, even without a wholesale revision of the *kenpou*, change is taking place in Japanese foreign policy. Four sources of this change are seen in Japan as having caused this restructuring. The first and most obvious is the end of the Cold War and the repercussions it brought to the world system. The influence of this event can not be overemphasized for its effect on Japanese foreign policy since 1990. It alone, without the other three, can be seen as a causal factor for change in Japanese foreign policy. The second is the 1994 internal rule changes within the Japanese electoral system which loosened the strangle hold that rural interests had on Japanese politics by establishing a better proportional electoral system.[42] This change resulted in changes in the type of representation and the orientations and interests of elected Diet members. Traditional style politicians began losing ground to politicians from urban Japan. The third causal factor for change is a bi-product of the second. A new younger generation of leaders is emerging in the Diet. This generation of Diet members is more likely than not to have been at least partially educated overseas and desire to see Japanese politics and policy reflect the elected leadership they have seen in other countries, rather than the bureaucratic leadership that has prevailed for so long in Japan. The fourth causal factor for change is the Persian Gulf War and the resulting criticism that Japan suffered for its role in it (or the lack of a human role in it).

This fourth causal factor produced its own result in the form of the PKO Law and continual revisions which are giving Japan a much more normal role in U.N. peacekeeping missions. Major Takashi Motomatsu, a former commander of a SDF PKO mission to the Golan Heights, describes how difficult and professionally embarrassing it was when he had to explain the exceptionalism of the SDF in a combat situation to his Polish U.N. commander in the field. The Polish officer responded by asking Major Motomatsu, "What kind of military force are you?"[43] Recent changes in the PKO Law have made such conversations less necessary, but they illustrate the problems that Japan faces when attempting to adapt its foreign policy to the realities of the post-Cold War world when Japanese still must live with the legacy of Article Nine.

THE RESEARCH MODEL

As Charles Hermann notes at the beginning of his paper, "We are in a period of profound change in international relations and foreign policy."[44] Hermann wrote this paper right after the Cold War ended and the Berlin Wall fell. Every nation was revisiting its foreign policies to reflect the disintegration of the Iron Curtain. Japan was no exception. Some nations were quicker to adapt than others. Japan was not one of these nations. It took the Persian Gulf War to wake it up to the reality of its new position in the post-Cold war world. Since that time Japan has been attempting to restructure its foreign policy to tackle the realities of a post-Cold War world while living with the one element that makes Japan unique in all the world, Article Nine.

Charles Hermann's 1990 paper, "*Changing Course: When Governments Choose to Redirect Foreign Policy,*" and the model contained in it are applied to these causal factors/independent variables of change listed in the previous section. The reason for this is that Hermann's model allows for the continual change in foreign policy that is always happening as noted by Rosenau and cited in chapter one. Furthermore Hermann notes that, "Change is a pervasive quality of governmental foreign policy."[45] Additionally, Hermann's investigation of foreign policy change finds that the "decision making process itself can obstruct or facilitate change."[46] Thus change **can** be seen as always existing in foreign policy and that the study of foreign policy and the study of foreign policy restructuring can be one and the same. Both Hermann and this book disagree with this argument and argue that there is a difference. The difference being that the study of foreign policy focuses on the continual stream of policy, the incremental adjustments that are continually being made, and the actions of decision makers. On the other hand, foreign policy restructuring focuses on the need to change policy because the old policy does not work, is not working, or has been rendered obsolete by events.[47] An important factor here is that those who are restructuring the policy are in essence the same ones who developed the policy in the first place. The change is not merely the reflection of a new government's differing ideology from the previous one's. This difference requires a close examination of change in the decision making process which is one element of this discourse.

A quick review of Hermann's argument is warranted here. According to Hermann, "Changes that mark a reversal, or at least, a profound redirection of a country's foreign policy are of special interest because of the demands their adoption pose on the initiating government and its domestic constituents and because of their potentially powerful consequences for other countries."[48] Wars or other conflicts may begin or end because of foreign policy changes. It is for this reason that there is a tendency to conclude that due to the effort needed to change foreign policy there is a need for regime change as the only way to facilitate this. But as Hermann points out when we reflect on this we find cases where the same government that initiated a foreign policy was the one responsible for its reversal or replacement.

The question that Hermann is asking in general and this book asks in relation to Japan is, "Under what circumstances do these kinds of changes occur in which an existing government recognizes that its current course is seriously inadequate, mistaken, or no longer applicable? What are the conditions under which self-correcting change may arise?"[49] In the case of Japan it was the end of the Cold War and the ensuing Persian Gulf War that began this process of change for Japan. This change continues through changes within the Diet and the make-up of its members.

Japan has not fundamentally changed its orientation vis-a-vis the rest of the world. It is still a solid democracy and the strongest democracy in Asia. It has no real intention of going head to head with the United States. It is not considering aligning itself against America and steadfastly desires to continue to have cordial relations with the U.S. What it is doing is exploring its options. With the Cold War over Japan realizes that it can no longer depend on the U.S. the way it did during the Cold War because U.S. priorities have changed and with these changes Japan's position in America's priorities.

Japan wants options in an ever changing world. It realizes that during the Cold War all of its eggs were kept in one basket and that basket was the U.S. It was a calculated gamble that Japan won. There is a saying in Japan, "Japan is always lucky." Japan was lucky, but it also does not want to press its luck. There is also a barely spoken, but very real, fear of abandonment in Japan.[50] It is worth repeating Grieco here, "For realists, a state will focus both on its absolute and relative gains from cooperation, and a state that is satisfied with a partner's compliance in a joint arrangement *might nevertheless exit from it because the partner is achieving relatively greater gains.*"[51] This last aspect of a partner exiting from a relationship is very real fear for Japan. Japan can easily be seen as getting far more from its relationship with the U.S. than the U.S. does. Japan is thus, according to Grieco and realist theory, is a *possible* candidate for abandonment by the U.S. Japan as a nation, that uses realism as its principle foreign policy framework, clearly realizes this and hence fears of abandonment.

This is a fundamental problem for Japan in that it does not want to have to go it alone. Japan is looking to expand its sphere of influence without jeopardizing its relations with the U.S.[52] Japan also realizes that the U.S. wants a more independent Japan. The U.S. would prefer to deal with Japan on a more "normal" basis. Normal meaning the same way it works with allies such as England, France, or Germany. The problem with this is again Article Nine.[53]

Japan is basically searching for a way to be "normal" while still living with Article Nine. The Yoshida Doctrine was adopted by the LDP which has ruled Japan continuously since 1958, with only a year long interruption in 1993–94. The LDP is the same party today that is making foreign policy in Japan. That is to say that the same political actor which created, adapted, and used the Yoshida Doctrine as the centerpiece of Japan's post-War foreign policy is now attempting to change it. This fits within Hermann's and the literature's definition of foreign policy restructuring. First there needs to be a change in the system and that change needs to motivate a government to change *its* foreign policy.[54] In the case of Japan the end of the Cold War and the ensuing Persian Gulf War[55] provided the change that stimulated the Japanese leadership to pursue alternatives to its Cold War foreign policy. Foreign policy changes in Japan are continuous and ongoing, but they are still driven by the same stimulus, the need for Japan to find a new role for itself in a post-Cold War world. It is to this situation in Japan that Hermann's Model is applied, as a case study, with the hope that it can teach us more about how nations restructure their foreign policy. It is also hoped that there can be an expansion of Hermann's Model (to be described later) that will give us a clearer picture of the foreign policy decision making process.

Hermann's model is concerned with the fundamental redirection of a nation's foreign policy. Defining the type of change or redirection is very important and Hermann deals with this through a four level graduated description of foreign policy change. The four involve increasing level of change: (1) Adjustment Changes, (2) Program Changes, (3) Problem/Goal Changes, and (4) International Orientation changes. This last change involves a basic shift in the international actors' roles and activities in which not just one policy but many are simultaneously changed. This typically, but not always, involves a shift in alignment with other nations or a major shift in the role that it plays within an alignment. As noted previously this is not what is happening in Japan because Japan is showing no signs of changing its loyalties vis-a-vis the west.

The first change, adjustment change, requires a change in the recipients of a foreign policy rather than a change in the foreign policy itself. This clearly does not apply to Japan. The second change, program changes, requires qualitative changes and new instruments of statecraft, although the purposes stay the same. In Japan's case this may reflect the changes since the passage of the PKO Law. But it is the third change that best describes the restructuring that Japan did after the Cold War.

The problem/goal change requires the purposes of the original policy to change. The purpose of the original Yoshida Doctrine was to support Japan's economic rebuilding by permitting it to de-emphasize its defense by relying on the US-Japan Security Treaty. At the same time it permitted Japan to deal with the constitutional limitations imposed by Article Nine. Japan found this policy unworkable in the "New World Order" that came about after the demise of the Iron Curtain. The purposes of the Yoshida Doctrine needed to be replaced with new purposes that reflected Japan's new place in the world. Japan no long needed to rebuild its economy, it is an economic giant. It desires to leave the U.S. shadow and be seen as a power unto itself. Clearly it is Hermann's second and third levels of change that are most applicable to Japan. For the purposes of this book and for the sake of consistency, foreign policy changes will be described in the same terms that Hermann uses. Program changes will be described as changes in means and goal problem/changes as changes in ends. As Hermann notes, the differences between means and ends are difficult to empirically define other that in what has already been described.[56] As Hermann writes:

> In program change, however, one would expect to find changes in the configuration of instruments, in the level of commitment, and probably in the degree of expressed affect. All these developments, plus policy statements and policy actions incompatible with prior goal or problem stipulations—if not open rejection of prior goals—accompany goal/problem changes. International reorientation

involves dramatic change in both words and deeds in multiple issue areas with respect to the actor's relationship with external entities.[57]

The conditions for change based on Hermann's research are fourfold. First, domestic political systems may affect foreign policy. For example, a) issues become a centerpiece in the struggle for political power; b) the attitudes and beliefs of a dominant domestic constituency undergo a profound change; and c) a realignment occurs of the essential constituency of a regime, or a revolution or other transformation takes place.[58] In the case of Japan, only the first two (a and b) are seen to have taken place. The LDP and the SDPJ made the PKO Law a divisive issue that shattered traditional harmony. This had an effect of changing party loyalties in the domestic constituencies of both parties. Furthermore, the pubic in Japan has grown to accept the need for Japanese troops to take part in UN PKO missions. This was caused in part by the Persian Gulf War and the effect it had as a prime time war on Japanese television. The Japanese public saw Japan as a major power that was not sending its soldiers to a major conflict being fought by its allies.

The second area is bureaucratic decision making. This area of study examines the bureaucrats who work in government agencies to see whether their roles support or oppose changes in foreign policy. It takes into account the variables of perception and personality. For Japan this is a (if not the) critical area of analysis. Japanese bureaucrats wield tremendous influence and are extremely powerful when compared to other nations. The recognition within MOFA that change was needed was a major factor in the passage of the PKO Law. It is for this reason that elites in the relevant bureaucracies, MOFA and the Japan Defense Agency (JDA), were studied intensively during the field research to be described later in this chapter.

The third area is cybernetics which is the science of communication and control[59] and deals with the agent. It attempts to monitor and examine a complex stream of variables over time. Hermann states that:

> An essential feature of [cybernetic] approaches is that the agent, attempting to pursue some standard or goal, continuously monitors a select stream of information from the environment that indicates where he is in relation to that goal and how the relation has altered across intervals of time. The agent engages in incremental self-corrective action in an effort to close on the goal or remain in close proximity to the standard. This process accounts for the association of cybernetics with the concepts of information (feedback) and control (steering).
>
> The elaboration of such a process would appear to be attractive for interpreting adjustment changes in policy. The system of control might also be extended to cover program changes as well.[60]

The area of cybernetics that Hermann notes as having the most promise for foreign policy restructuring is the part that looks closely at the fact that agents deal with the highest priorities first.[61] For example policy makers will likely focus on national survival and then move on to political survival, ideology, or personal goals. This is less enlightening in the case of Japan, but it is still important particularly when one compares the priorities of the different agents involved in the decision making process. The differing priorities of MOFA and the politicians in the Diet is fascinating as is the apparent lack (when compared to the other two) of fervor on the part of the JDA to the change process.

The fourth and final area is learning. This area is defined by nations responding not out of principle, but out of some kind of reward or punishment. Change, Hermann notes, does not always imply learning.[62] In Japan's case learning can be seen as a causal feature for change. Japan's lack of ability to make a personnel contribution to the Persian Gulf War earned it world wide condemnation and awakened Japan to the fact that its foreign policy was no longer adequate. Japan learned that the next time an international crisis occurred it needed to be better prepared to respond in an way that would be acceptable to the international community and commensurate with its status as a major economic power.

Hermann further develops his model by selecting from his review of the literature two things necessary to effect change in a domestic political system's foreign policy. They are: first, that there must be change in that system, such as the end of the Cold War, and, second, that systemic change must trigger a change in the government's foreign policy, such as the passage of the PKO law in direct response to Japan's inability to adapt quickly to the end of the Cold War.[63] Major change according to Hermann "...depends on mobilizing sufficient specialized human talents to overcome or circumvent the organizational structures and processes committed to the maintenance of existing policy."[64] It is for this reason that most studies of foreign policy change center on changes in leadership or governments. New leaders or governments are often much better able to make changes because they can change organizations.

This was not the case for Japan with the PKO Law. Existing leadership redirected Japanese foreign policy in the aftermath of the Persian Gulf War. The leaders in Japan had to form a coalition from the bureaucracy and the Diet in order to gain enough support to push the PKO Law through. The abhorrence that many Japanese elites and the public had for sending troops overseas had to be overcome. The combination of advocacy by both the leadership and the bureaucracy (MOFA) helped pass the PKO Law. These two groups were the agents of change. The agents of change, that Hermann lists, are labeled as leader driven, bureaucratic advocacy, domestic restructuring, and external shock.[65] The interaction of these with the decision making process can be seen in figure 3:2.

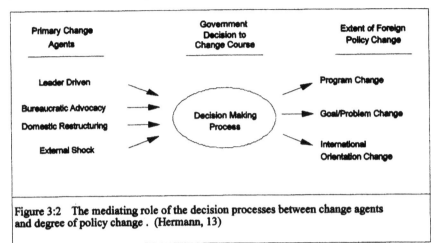

Figure 3:2   The mediating role of the decision processes between change agents and degree of policy change . (Hermann, 13)

Leader driven change is often authoritative in nature. In the case of Japan it was the strong leadership under Prime Minister Miyazawa, as opposed to the weaker leadership of Prime Minister Kaifu, that the PKO Law was passed. Without strong pressure by the party leadership on the LDP rank and file members no bill would have passed the Diet.[66]

Hermann's second change agent, bureaucratic advocacy, would seem to be a contradiction in terms. Bureaucratic groups are know for their resistance to change, but they can be open to change when it has a positive influence on their power. Especially when the advocates for change are high ranking officials within the bureaucracy itself. This was the case in Japan. As noted before, the bureaucracies in Japan are exceptionally powerful and they often write policy and present it to lawmakers. In Japan's case elites within MOFA like former Vice Foreign Minister Shunji Yanai (currently ambassador to the US) played a strong advocacy role in the writing and lobbying (behind the scenes) for the PKO bill.

The third agent of change, domestic restructuring, refers to a political segment within a society on which the regime is dependent in order to govern. If this segment loses its influence or the ability to elect members to the national body, the regime may be freed to pursue its own policies or forced to abandon policies that are no longer sustainable. In many countries this can be caused by redistricting. In the case of Japan, domestic restructuring had no effect on the passage of the PKO law, but it is having an effect on the ongoing process to adopt a post-Cold War foreign policy for Japan. The restructuring and redistricting of the Diet in 1994 for the first time since the end of the occupation, has removed much of the LDP's rural power base as apportionment has become more equitable. This has given urban voters a greater voice in national affairs resulting in a new younger generation of leadership in the Diet. (This younger generation will be discussed at the end of this chapter.)

The fourth agent of change is external shocks. This is when serious international events spur foreign policy change. The events need not be distressing events. In this case it was the Persian Gulf War in the aftermath of the Cold War that drove Japan to restructure its foreign policy. External shock is always a factor in foreign policy change but not a constant one. The test firing, by North Korea, of the Taepodong-1 missile over Japan solidified support for the Theater Missile Defense system (TMD) which is a small but significant foreign policy change for Japan.

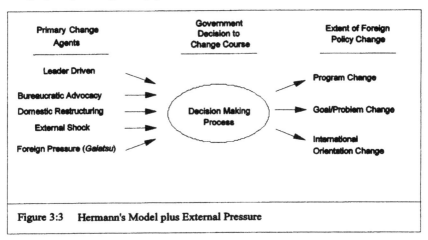

Figure 3:3   Hermann's Model plus External Pressure

It was originally hypothesized that for Japan that a fifth level of change would be: foreign pressure or *gaiatsu* in Japanese terms. This can be seen in figure 3:3. As the research progressed it became clear that this was the case. Foreign pressure plays a critical role in the foreign policy decision making process and it can be considered as a fifth agent of change. In Japan's case foreign pressure plays a special role. *Gaiatsu* is an influential factor in propagating change in Japanese foreign policy as not only an agent of change but also as a tool used by the other primary change agents to justify and "sell" their decisions to the public at large. (This use of *gaiatsu* is explored in chapter five.)

Of course there is likely to be interplay between these agents of foreign policy change. External shock can rouse a government into action and result in the agents of change interacting with each other to change policy. Sometime this change will be dramatic and sometimes it will be nonexistent as a government realizes that there is nothing that it can do. Hermann's model stops at this point, but I believe that he overlooked an important factor in his model of the restructuring process. This factor is a series of constants that intervene in the decision making process. These constants can take the form of laws, values, cultural norms, physical limitations, and the like that are unique to any particular nation. An illustration of this can be seen in figure 3:4. In the case of Japan there are the obvious limitations imposed by Article Nine. There are also the pacifist norms held by the population in general, which work to limit what Japan can do internationally.

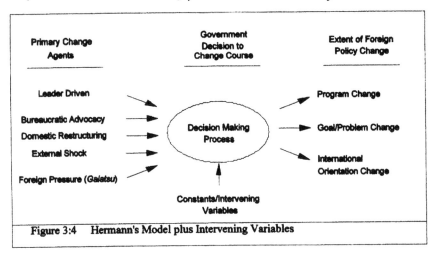

Figure 3:4   Hermann's Model plus Intervening Variables

The decision making process part of Hermann's Model could best be described as a "matrix" which contains preexisting factors which are controlled by no one or at least are virtually uncontrollable for the government trying to make the decision. It is into this matrix that the influence of the Primary change agents enters and proceeds to mix with the existing influential norms to produce some form of change or block change from occurring. If we are ever truly going to be able to understand the decision making process we need to understand not only what goes in to the decision making process, but what already exists in the process. This is because the sum of what goes in to the process *does not always equal what comes out.* A change takes place in this "matrix" which fundamentally controls the direction of foreign policy change.

In the case of Japan this can be seen in the effect of Article Nine on the decision making process. One can not understand Japanese foreign policy decisions without taking into account Article Nine. There is no logic to the results without understanding Japan's limits under Article Nine. No policy change can happen without this question being asked and answered: How does Article Nine affect this policy? Furthermore in Japan's case, pacifist attitudes that are part of the cultural norm in Japan are also part of the equation.

The rest of Hermann's research deals with the various phases of the foreign policy decision making process. The most important of these is that Hermann notes that the process is *not* linear. Decision making often takes place in cycles with pauses and is not an orderly process.[67] Hermann suggests seven stages in which developments must occur in order for major change to take place. They are:

1. Initial policy expectations.
2. External actor/environmental stimuli
3. Recognition of discrepant information
4. Postulation of a connection between problem and policy
5. Development of alternatives
6. Building authoritative consensus for choice
7. Implementation of new policy[68]

Each of these seven stages can clearly be seen and are evident in the Japanese decision to pass the PKO Law.[69]

THE RESEARCH TOOL

In order to explore the process of restructuring in Japanese foreign policy in the post-Cold War era a questionnaire was designed to probe this process. The purpose of this questionnaire was to explore through a series of personal interviews the opinions, insights, and aspirations that Japanese elites have for Japanese foreign policy. The principal tools used for the interviews were two questionnaires in both Japanese and English (For the complete text of the questionnaires please see Appendices A-D). One set of questions was designed for Diet members and government ministry officials and another set was designed for academics and journalists. The questionnaires asked basically the same questions, but from the different perspectives of those inside and outside of government.

The interview questions were based on Hermann's model and designed to invite an exploration of values on the part of the interviewee. The questions about goals imply values and values imply beliefs. The purpose was to elicit discussion about issues that elites often can not explore because so much of their public persona is devoted to meeting the expectations and assumptions of others. As diplomat and historian George F. Kennan observes in his memoirs about a particular incident in U.S.-Soviet affairs during the inter-war years:

> This episode has remained in my mind as the first of many lessons I
> was destined to receive, in the course of a diplomatic career, on one

of the most consistent and incurable traits of American statesmanship—namely, its neurotic self-consciousness and introversion, the
tendency to make statements and take actions with regard not to
their effect on the international scene to which they are ostensibly
addressed but rather to their effect on those echelons of American
opinion, congressional opinions first and foremost, to which the
respective statesmen are anxious to appeal. The question, in these
circumstances, became not: how effective is what I am doing in terms
of impact it makes on our world environment? But rather: how do I
look, in the mirror of domestic opinion, as I do it? Do I look shrewd,
determined, defiantly patriotic, imbued with the necessary vigilance
before the wiles of foreign governments? If so, this is what I do, even
though it may prove meaningless, or even counterproductive, when
applied to the realities of the external situation.[70]

What Kennan rightly observed with American diplomats can also be applied
generally to elites in democratic polities, especially in this modern age of
media in which image is everything. Elites often say what others want to hear
or what will make them look good. The questionnaire was designed to help
elites speak frankly about their genuine hopes for Japan. There also was the
possibility that the elite's fears and frustrations with Japanese foreign policy
would also be expressed. Questions that examined Japanese history helped
explore the elite's experience and conscience regarding Japan's role in the
Second World War. These were particularly useful in getting the elite to open
up. Overall the questionnaire seamed to elicit more ingenious responses from
the elites who were interviewed. Notable exceptions to this were older more
experienced elites like former Foreign Minister Yukihiko Ikeda who skillfully
controlled the interview and the direction of the answers as not to reveal too
much in the way of personal opinion.[71]

There were fourteen questions for the Diet members and government
officials and fifteen questions asked of academics and journalists. Several of
the questions had sub-parts that were designed to further probe initial
answers. Question order was carefully considered. The questions started with
the PKO issue and moved into future objectives and goals for Japanese foreign policy along with the problems that Japan faces in the immediate future.
The reason for starting with a question on the PKO Law was to bring to the
forefront of the elite's mind the fact that change had occurred in Japanese
foreign policy. This question primed them for the rest of the questionnaire.[72]

Before each interview started the author briefly introduced himself and
the purpose of his research. The interviewee was assured that the author was
not part of any media organization and that the purposes were purely academic. The interviewee was also given the opportunity to answer off the
record if he or she so wished.[73] This was done to solicit frank and honest
answers by being as forthright and honest as possible. It seemed to be appre-

ciated and served to ease the initial tension. The author also asked permission to record the interview and in only one case did this seem to be a problem. This was solved by stopping the recorder whenever anything sensitive was being said. The interviewee was asked if he had any questions and if not the first question was asked. Several of the Diet members wanted to know more about me and what my purposes were. This seemed mainly to reassure themselves that I was who I said I was. This introduction to the interview was critical to the tone and style of the interview. Those who felt that they could trust me really opened up. [74]

The first question asked why the interviewee believed that the government felt it necessary to pass the PKO law and whether they agreed with the government or not at the time and currently. This question was designed to measure the impact of the Persian Gulf War and its impact on Japanese foreign policy even though the war was not mentioned in the question. I wanted to test the effect of the war as an independent variable by not mentioning it and seeing how often it was listed as a primary factor in the government's decision to pass the PKO Law. As anticipated, nearly all of the interviewees mentioned the Persian Gulf War immediately in their answers. The follow-up questions were designed to assess political attitudes toward the PKO Law and change in attitude since the Law was passed. These questions were most significant for those who opposed the Law. The level of acceptance that was accorded the Law even by those who had opposed it was surprising. [75]

The second question asked about the differing interests that supported and opposed the PKO Law. It was expected that most would name MOFA, the parties or factions involved in lobbying for or against the Law. The purpose of this question was to explore whether there were any significant interests that were pushing or opposing the Law that had not been widely reported. As expected most named the obvious parties or party factions responsible for the passage of the PKO Law and those that opposed it. Some did however name significant individuals and their agendas. This question thus probed who were the change agents involved in the decision making process.

These two questions were asked first because they set the agenda for the rest of the interview. They subtly reminded the interviewee that change had taken place in Japanese foreign policy. [76] This led to the third question. The third question and its sub- parts asked what the respondent felt were the long term goals of Japanese foreign policy and whether they felt that these were the right long term goals. Having been reminded that change had taken place, the interviewee was now asked where he or she thought the direction of that change was going and whether that change was felt to be positive. The interviewees were permitted to ponder the implications of change in Japanese foreign policy by being asked why they felt the way they did about the changes. This aspect of question three resulted in many long pauses as clearly many of those interviewed appeared to have given little thought to why they felt the way they did about foreign policy.

The fourth question asked for the interviewee's opinion of what he or she personally thought the goal of Japanese foreign and security policy should be. This was asked in order to permit the interviewee to express his or her own agenda for foreign policy and to allow the interviewer to place the interview in the context of the respondent's own political beliefs. Follow-up questions asked what domestic and international obstacles there were to their goals and how Article Nine fit into their goals. These sub-question were partially designed to study how well the person had thought out his or her agenda particularly in light of Article Nine which is so central to Japanese foreign policy.

The fifth question asked what kind of role Japan should seek in multilateral security fora. This question was designed to test attitudes and thinking towards institutionalism on the part of Japan. This question was also used to test whether Japan saw itself in a leadership role or in a participatory role in multilateral fora. Most respondents had to be prompted with examples of multilateral fora indicating that they did not think of foreign policy in terms of multilateral efforts.

The sixth question asked the respondent to list the top three security and top three foreign policy concerns for Japan. This question was designed to test the awareness on the part of the elite of Japan's position in the world and the threats that it faces. This proved to be a very sensitive question to most because it required them to list their concerns. Many respondents asked that their answers to this question be kept off the record and even with these assurances were very careful in their answers. For example many would list **Korea** as a security threat rather than name North or South Korea specifically. Those interviewed in MOFA were inclined this way, more so than Diet members. On the other hand, some Diet member were very frank and blunt in their assessment of Japan's security threats with several listing the U.S. as Japan's number one security threat! One Diet member, Representative Eisuke Mori, was especially frank and insightful when he listed Japan's top three security threats as "the economy, the economy, and the economy."[77] His realization that Japan, *without* its economic power, would just be another country without any real global significance was extremely insightful. Japan's power and world position is directly tied to its economy. In the absence of military power and strength Japan must use its economy as the basis of its claims to power. The ten year recession in Japan has taken its toll on Japan's influence in the world.

The seventh question enquired into the September 1997 revisions of the US-Japan Defense Guidelines and their implications for Japan. This question was designed to probe the respondents' understanding of the strengths and limits of Japanese foreign policy within the context of the US-Japan Security Treaty and Article Nine. A follow-up question asked about the obstacles to the implementation of the 1997 revisions. It was hoped that this follow-up question would elicit insight into Japan's internal politics when dealing with foreign policy change as a legal issue.

The eighth question asked about the role of the SDF and the limits that should be placed on it. This question was designed to elicit attitudes toward the SDF and the desire to see Japan as a more normal nation in terms of military power. In many ways it was also a test of whether old militarist feelings would arise in the conversation thus betraying a predisposition toward a more aggressive Japan. It was also hoped that this question would explore the limits of what elites in Japan see as the potential for the SDF.

The ninth question asked about how Japan should deal with its history in East Asia if it took on a larger role in world affairs. This question was designed to get at Japanese perceptions of how they see others viewing Japan. Japan's history in East Asia is very significant for China and Korea in particular. Any action that could be interpreted as Japan taking on a more militaristic role in the world would likely be met with opposition. China has been especially vocal in opposition to Japan's PKO missions as setting a dangerous precedent. The question tested how aware Japanese elites were of how Japan is viewed by other nations. It also tested Japanese attitudes toward the other nations of East Asia.

A follow-up question asked about the domestic consequences of a larger role for Japan. Given the pacifism that took root in Japan after the second world war, it is thought that domestic opposition to Japan being more active militarily might be a major factor in Japan deciding not to pursue certain foreign policy goals. This question was designed to get at how elites viewed the domestic political situation.

The tenth question asked about domestic sources of foreign policy change. It asked about the alliances and lobbying groups within the Diet and within Japanese politics that are pushing for change. The question was designed to uncover motives and agendas for change within the Japanese political world.

The eleventh question asked essentially the same thing at the international level. Its purpose was to gain an understanding of how elites view *gaiatsu* as part of Japanese foreign policy. As stated earlier in this chapter, *gaiatsu* was thought to be a major factor in the decision making process of Japanese foreign policy. As the research progressed, however, it became clear that *gaiatsu* was not a major factor at all. Many of those interviewed were dismissive of the concept of *gaiatsu*. As one MOFA official stated, "Do you really think we would do anything that was not in our best interest?"[78] Remarkably few named the US as a source of pressure for change.

The twelfth question directly dealt with Article Nine by asking whether it should be revised in the future and what form the revisions should take. The purpose of this question was to see if there was any movement to amend the constitution and to rid Japan of the proverbial "monkey" of Article Nine. Such a move would be a radical change in Japanese foreign policy. The removal of Article Nine would normalize Japanese foreign policy and make it similar to other nations. The answers to this question split sharply along party lines with the LDP taking the forefront among those arguing for revision. (It is note-worthy that the LDP had just a few weeks before the start of the interviews convened a committee to discuss whether there was a need to create a com-mittee to plan constitutional reform.)[79]

Question number thirteen asked about the Japanese commitment to bear the costs of world order. It questioned whether Japan was ready and willing to sacrifice itself for the good of the world. The purpose behind this question was to ask whether Japan was ready to pay the price to be a world leader. Japan is often seen as motivated to act only if it furthers its own objec-tives. It has not given much indication, beyond it financial commitments through its Official Development Assistance (ODA), that it possesses the largess to be frequently involved in international situations the way the US and other western powers have.

The fourteenth question asked about the proposed revisions to the PKO Law that were before the Diet. This question brought the interview full circle and tested whether there was the resolve to push for more change. The PKO Law marked a significant change in Japanese foreign policy and the Law's revisions are the next step. The question asked about the probability of pas-sage and, when asked to Diet members, the member was asked the way he or she intended to vote on the revisions. It was hoped that with this question the interviewee could be drawn into a discussion of future changes in the PKO Law.

The fifteenth question was only asked to academics and not journalists. It simply asked the academic to place Japanese foreign policy into a theoret-ical paradigm. This was done in order to measure how Japanese intellectuals conceptualize their country's role. This question, surprisingly, resulted in the most refused answers. Most of the respondents, when asked this question, proceeded to complain about the American fixation with theory as opposed to substance. "American academics are too theoretical!" they often com-plained. The few that did answer this question placed Japan in the realist or institutionalist paradigms.[80]

At the end of each interview the interviewee was thanked and asked if they would refer or recommend someone else for an interview. Most were very helpful in this respect and some were very enthusiastic. For example, for-mer Defense Minister Hideo Usui was so excited about the questions being asked that he got on the phone himself and asked several other high ranking officials in the Diet, MOFA, and the JDA to let me interview them and set up the appointments himself! He said he wanted me to ask them my questions to get them thinking about these kind of issues as he had been trying to raise the same issues for quite awhile.[81]

One important factor of the interviews was the decision to ask the questions in person and in the field rather than to send out the questionnaire by mail. It was thought, rightly, that personal interviews would elicit better and clearer responses. Personal interviews also made more subtle observations possible that no questionnaire could capture. Many of the observations provided new insight to the research that would not have been possible otherwise. One example is the observation of the obvious difficulty that many interviewees in the Diet had at answering questions about issues that they were not accustomed to thinking about. No mail questionnaire could have captured that adequately.

THE FIELD RESEARCH

The field research, based on the questions described above, consisted of a series of fifty-six interviews conducted in country with Japanese elites from both houses of the Diet, Prime Minister's Office, the Japanese Defense Agency (JDA), the Ministry of Foreign Affairs (MOFA), and academia. The fifty-six Japanese elites were interviewed in Japan during May and June of 1998. The interviews were conducted in both Japanese and English. Those in Japanese were translated into English. It was decided that it would be best to interview, not only Diet members (though they were the primary target), but to also interview members of the relevant bureaucracies MOFA and the JDA along with journalists and academics. The rational for interviewing the Diet members was twofold. Firstly, the *kenpou* places the **ultimate** decision making power in their hands and their elected leader, the Prime Minister. Secondly, the Diet, as a result of reapportionment, is gaining significance as major source of Japanese foreign policy. Interviews were actively sought with both younger Diet members and with older more senior Diet member to gain insight into any possible generational differences between Diet members.

The rationale for interviewing the career bureaucrats in MOFA is that the ministries in Japan wield tremendous power over all aspects of their jurisdiction. An illustration of this is the fact that even academically based think tanks must seek approval of the relevant ministry in order to even operate. A foreign policy think tank must have the permission of MOFA to function under Japanese law. This power gives MOFA control over the terms of debate on an issue and more strikingly, control over what is discussed. Furthermore, MOFA has often presented policy in finished form to the Diet for its approval or "rubber stamp". The mind set of MOFA officials and their attitudes toward change were seen as potentially very important with respect to the foreign policy restructuring process in Japan.

The JDA is probably one of the politically weakest agencies in the Japanese bureaucracy because of the sensitivity to military affairs. Officials that serve in the JDA are often on loan from other ministries such as the ministry of finance. The JDA thus does not have the same internal dynamics as other bureaucracies in Japan. Because of Article Nine and the overall sensitivity in Japan to the very existence of the SDF, the JDA tends to keep a lower profile when it comes to policy advocacy.[82] The relevance of interviewing members of the JDA is important to this research in that the SDF is the organization that is charged with carrying out the PKO missions and their opinions and input into the change process is seen as significant.

Academics were interviewed as they observe Japanese politics up close everyday and their advice is often sought in matters of policy making. It is for this reason that academics with close ties to government or politicians were particularly sought; however, academics far from the centers of power were also sought out for interviews. The reason for this was to check for feelings and opinions away from the capital. As mentioned many academics in Tokyo have close ties to politicians or the various ministries. I felt that, to be proportional, I needed to interview those who looked at Tokyo politics from afar. These interviews confirmed the perspectives being given to me in Tokyo, but they also gave the added insight of how "the man on the street" felt as opposed to how the power brokers felt.

Interviews with journalists were included because Japanese journalists often have special contact with policy makers. Policymakers will often tell journalist things that they do not want published until it no longer matters. These special relationships give journalists much deeper inside stories when they finally publish them. Interviewing journalists would be a way of checking the accuracy (and honesty) of answers given by politicians. Unfortunately only one journalist was interviewed.

Overall nine interviews were conducted with MOFA officials. There were five interviews with JDA officials. Twenty interviews were conducted with Diet members. Six of the interviews were with upper house members and 14 were with lower house members. Four members of the Prime Minister's office were interviewed. Five government sponsored researchers were interviewed, and thirteen other academics were interviewed. One journalist was interviewed. One political candidate for the Diet was also interviewed (He was the son of a very senior LDP politician).

Contact with these elite was initiated by two methods. The first method, which led to most of the Diet interviews was a "cold" letter to the potential interviewee. The author simply asked the potential interviewee by letter (and email) on official university stationary for permission to conduct an interview.[83] This worked surprisingly well and led to many interviews. The second method was by referral.[84] The author was introduced to the elite by a previous interviewee or some other contact who gave permission to use his or her name as an introduction. This started a network or chain of interviews that stretched across party lines. If it had not been for time constraints the number of interviews could have easily gone over one hundred. Name dropping of previous interviewees proved to be very successful. For a partial list of those interviewed please see Appendix D.

Contact with the interviewees in Japan during the first two weeks was initially handled by an undergraduate research assistant from Grand Canyon University who was working on her own research into the Japanese political system.[85] The initial interviews were set up by phone ahead of the author's arrival in Japan. This research assistant also served as a translator for the interviews as needed.[86] A woman was hired to serve as a receptionist for incoming call backs from various government offices. This gave an air of professionalism to the process of setting up of appointments that was undoubtably helpful to the success of the field work.[87]

The interviews lasted from twenty minutes (the shortest) to three hours (the longest). Most interviews averaged forty-five minutes to an hour. With Diet members strict attention to time had to be paid due to their busy schedules, but often, as a result of the questions, the member extended the interview into their next appointment because they found the questions so fascinating (and useful to themselves?). It is interesting to note that the contact reference usually got the author the interview, but it was the quality of the questions that sustained the interview and provided the willingness on the part of the interviewees to recommend others and to let their names be used as an introduction.

There seemed to be an appeal to the questions that made the elites think about things they were not used to thinking about. There was one exception to this. A journalist was contacted for an interview on the referral of a colleague in the US. The journalist declined to be interviewed, claiming to be too busy, but said that if he were sent the questions, that they would try to answer them. Upon returning from the field research (with fifty-six interviews) a fax from this journalist was waiting which stated in very frank terms that it would be a waste of time to answer the questions as no one in Japan would take the time to answer the questions or would be willing to give me an interview!

This situation illustrates that maybe the questions that were asked in the interview are not being asked enough in Japan. The success of the field research may also demonstrate that Japanese elites are more willing to talk to foreigners than they are willing to talk to fellow Japanese about these issues. The above mentioned journalist may have felt that he had no chance to ask questions like the ones asked in the field research and assumed that a foreigner would have even less of a chance when the opposite was true. The foreigner seemed to have a better chance at gaining access than an established journalist.

In summary the interviews, given the natural tendency of political elites to guard their personal opinions carefully, gave a creative tension to the interview process. Answers to questions which challenged their values or their party's positions helped gauge an understanding with respect to the assumptions underlying those values. A deeper question is what are these elites' underlying values? This is important in that ultimate beliefs often provide the perspectives that lead to decisions. The question is then: Can ultimate values and realities be explored, maybe even realized, in ways not imagined by the current situation or under current policies? In many ways it is hoped that the answer is "yes, these values can be explored," but it will take time and the building of relationships to do this. The field research is thus a beginning of an ongoing process of attempting to understand policy makers in Japan. Encouraging to this goal is the fact that many of those interviewed agreed to be part of a long term study of Japanese politics by letting themselves be interviewed again every few years.

One immediate result of the interviews is insight into what Japan can offer the world and the UN that is more appropriate and more unique than military force. Some of the elites, especially the Socialists, tried to think outside the box of military power and the use of institutionalized violence. They welcomed the interviews as a chance to explore new ways of thinking.

Hermann's model allows for the attitudes and beliefs of a political system's constituency. These attitudes and beliefs are not so easily discovered by pollsters who look for current positions on issues. Yet some such convictions were uncovered in the interviews simply through inferences from the responses. The questions were open ended and permitted follow-up questions that helped clarify meanings. The overall picture gave insight into the way foreign policy restructures in Japan. The next section will give an overview of the results of the research and the insight that it gives us into foreign policy restructuring.

OVERVIEW OF THE RESULTS OF THE FIELD RESEARCH

The field research proved fruitful. Many insights were gained from personal contact with decision makers that could not have been gained from written questionnaire research. Personal interviews provided the author insight into the personal struggle for many of these decision makers to come up with policy. The interviews also provided insight into the process of Japanese foreign policy decision making and the obstacles to its restructuring.

The intellectual and institutional base for foreign policy making in Japan is MOFA. MOFA has some of the brightest and most intelligent people in Japan working for it.[88] It would be a grave error for any nation to underestimate MOFA. Nevertheless, a power shift is taking place in which the Diet will direct foreign policy toward great powers and issues leaving policy toward small nations and issues in the capable hands of MOFA in any given administration. Younger Diet members are looking to the Diet to be **the** source for foreign policy. While MOFA welcomes raising the profile of foreign policy issues, it will most certainly resist the erosion of its power. However, some MOFA people see this change as beneficial because the level of debate over foreign policy at the popular level has dropped to near zero in Japan.[89]

In the foreign policy change matrix there is, as in most institutions, a generational propensity for change. In MOFA it is not as evident due to the strictness of the hierarchical structure in the ministry. Change, while not anathema, does not seen to be desirable if it can be contained. This can be seen by the rote answers, to interview questions given by MOFA members. For example, when asked about the long range goals of Japanese foreign policy most MOFA officials answered "the safety and betterment of life for the Japanese people. . . ."

This is in contrast to the Diet Members who could clearly name short term goals even when they struggled to name specific long range goals. In particular newer/younger Diet members seem to chafe at the slow pace of change. They seemed to be pushing hard for change in the foreign policy decision making process. In some ways their desire is to truly reflect democratic change where the "people" or their representatives are making or at least influencing the foreign policy process on a regular basis.

Karel van Wolferen in his book *The Enigma of Japanese Power*[90] describes how Japan is basically run by bureaucrats who have an inordinate amount of influence in a country that is supposed to be a democracy. Many of the younger generation of Diet members seem to chaff at the level of control exercised by the various ministries. They wish to see Japanese foreign policy reflect the elected leadership in Japan, rather than career officials in MOFA. Many of these younger Diet member have studied overseas and have observed the foreign policy making process in other countries, especially the western democracies. They would like to see Japan have a similar foreign policy making process. The problem for Japan seems to be that most Diet members do not think enough about foreign policy, and MOFA itself fails to think originally about foreign policy. MOFA's group mind set dominates and seems to crush the individual or independent thinking. This lack of originality in thinking is stunting the maturation of Japanese foreign policy in the post-Cold War world.

It is because of the bureaucratic mentality on the part of MOFA that the largest obstacle to restructuring may be institution of MOFA itself. The legislature may attempt reform, but MOFA may choose to fight it in an attempt to preserve its power over foreign policy making. In *Structural 'Gaiatsu': international Finance and Political Change in Japan* T. J. Pempel makes the argument that institutional change is difficult without crisis.[91] While Pempel makes his argument in the area of economic reform this author would argue in foreign policy. A crises such as the Gulf War and the end of the Cold War gave Japan the push to make changes. Future restructuring will be slow in the absence of a crisis. The crisis of the Persian Gulf War pushed it to restructure, but Japan lacks a coherent plan outside a general desire not to be seen as doing nothing in future conflicts. Japan has yet to answer the question (for itself) of where foreign policy is going. With no crisis to provide impetus, Japan is drifting.

An example of the problems facing Japan as a world power is its inability to *act* as a military power alongside the U.S. Japan struggles to define the role of the SDF in peacetime as well as war time.[92] As Col. Noboru Yamaguchi said in an interview, Japanese law currently requires tanks to stop at all traffic lights even when engaged in combat (reality and common sense would dictate that the law would be ignored).[93] Japan simply has no detailed plans or contingencies for truly dealing with crises. In the event of a crisis the Japanese government would still be debating about their policy responses when other nations are acting. This lack of planning is not confined to foreign and security policy, but in other areas as well as witnessed by the Japanese government's slow response to the Kobe earthquake.

Another problem is the debate over Japan's foreign policy independence from the U.S. Because of the use of *gaiatsu* as a source for Japanese actions, many in Japan feel that Japan has given in to the US too many times.[94] Ryozo Kato, Director General, Foreign Policy Bureau of MOFA, stated that in a normal bilateral relationship each side gives in about fifty percent of the time. In the US-Japan relationship Japan gives in one hundred percent of the time; and there is a need for Japan to "win" once in a while.[95] Dissatisfied decision makers are looking for ways to "show" Japan's independence by disagreeing with the US. What they ignore is that for most of the Cold War it was America that accommodated Japan.[96] According to Kato Japan is suffering from a kind of interdependent fatigue syndrome and needs to start looking inward rather than outward.[97] Many in Japan want to see a more independent Japan vis-à-vis the U.S. The problem for Japan is that going against America is not easy when often what is good for America is often good for Japan too.[98] There seemed to be a belief on the part of many respondents that Japanese restructuring should increase the country's independence from the United States.[99] This is reminiscent of the earlier illustration in this chapter that described the US and Japan in a father/son relationship. Some just want to see Japan break away from the US and be independent for independence sake regardless of how this affects Japan in a longer time frame.

OLD VERSES NEW

Belief systems raise the question of whether the older generation in Japanese politics can change its way of doing things and invest in the future with new thinking. The younger generation in the Diet is "chomping at the bit" to raise its level of influence in the Diet. It is hindered by a seniority system that rewards seniority over competence. Climbing up in leadership was likened by one youthful Diet member to climbing a pole with a person above you and below you. The only way to move up was for someone to fall from above you. There is no chance of passing people above you.

There is clear evidence of a generational gap in the Diet.[100] The younger generation is looking for new ways while the older leadership wants to follow traditional methods. Many of the younger generation in the Diet have had foreign educations and are much more knowledgeable than the previous generation. Time is on the side of the younger generation, but the question is whether the needs of the nation for change will be met in the near future. There is a battle for influence going on in the Diet. Most of the younger generation are attempting to climb the leadership pole as quickly as possible without alienating the older members, but this is a very difficult task given Japanese societal norms which demand respect for one's elders and those in senior positions.

The youth are making an impact on Japanese foreign policy. The earlier example of Representative Hajime Funada and his actions during the debate on the PKO Bill illustrate this. They are also doing the very thing that they need to do to influence Japanese policy; they are getting re-elected. They are persuading the older generation to make some changes. The interaction between the older generation and the younger generation is the key to understanding leader driven change coming out of the Diet as a primary change agent. This interaction occurs in what I call the *"interflux[101] of change."* Change occurs not in a vacuum, but in a dynamic ever changing process. Younger Diet members are in maneuver constantly with the older generation to influence the direction of policy. There is no straight forward pattern that explains what the outcome of these maneuvers will be. The interflux of change, as it effects our theories for foreign policy restructuring and Hermann's Model is illustrated in figure 3:5 on the following page.

Part of this generational gap is due to Japan's history. Many older right wing Diet members oppose an apology of any kind to the nations of East Asia, especially China.[102] The conservative right wing in Japan is in a state of denial about Japan's image *vis-a-vis* the rest of the world. Its steadfast opposition to apologies in general and to China in particular for actions taken during World War II has led to continued mistrust of Japan and its intentions. This mistrust is a major obstacle to an independent Japanese foreign policy. A valuable lesson that these right wing elements within Japan could learn is from the positive results of Japan's apology to South Korea.

Part of the problem is that Japan in many ways still behaves as a defeated nation. People in Japan want something to be proud of and do not want to have to think about all that they have to be ashamed of. Most nations seek pride in themselves through military might/victories and/or heros. A person-hood if you will that projects the power of their nation onto themselves. An example of this for Japan would be the recent Japanese movie *Pride* that was so popular in Japan.[103]

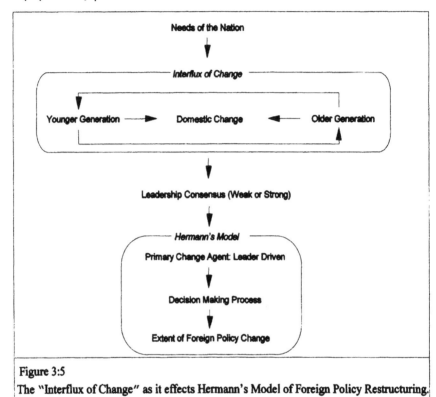

Figure 3:5
The "Interflux of Change" as it effects Hermann's Model of Foreign Policy Restructuring.

Economic power does not carry the same status as military power. The desire is to be rich *and* powerful not just *noveaux riche*. Economic power is seen as being middle "class" NOT upper class on the part of Japan's right wing. Pervasive "class' attitudes as to Japan's position in the world plague Japanese thinking. An example of this is the book by Ezra Vogel *Japan as Number One*.[104] Japan does not want to be seen as second class. First class is the only goal. Equality with others is a myth. Rank is primary. An example of how ingrained this is in Japanese society is the education system where every one must have the same opportunity, but it is test scores and class *rank* that dictates the future.

The problem with right wing aspirations for a more independent Japan is that Japan is doing well overall without having to resort to militarism. Japan is using its prestige and reputation to establish its position/role through international institutions. If it chooses to confront US hegemony outright it will win some battles at first, but in the end it will lose do to lack of resources to sustain its own hegemony.

This is not to say that Japan would not choose to pursue hegemony, but rather it is in its own best interest not to. This argument depends on the logic of Japanese leadership to foresee the misconception of pursuing hegemony.

Remember the central focus of this chapter and book: how does Japan's situation help our understanding of foreign policy restructuring and decision making and where is Japan headed as a nation? In the interviews, most respondents did not even realize what a multilateral forum was until they were shown examples (question number five). In a given situation or crisis consideration of options depends on knowing what those options are. Many in the Japanese hierarchy of foreign policy leadership failed to consider or even know of what options were available. When faced with a crisis Japanese leaders behave as realists. Their understanding of the situation is based on a world view which historically has tended to be realist in nature. They may consider other options such as neo-institutionalism, but they do it from a realist perspective. If you wed Japanese domestic conditions and international options; Japan's realism is overall very predictable. Japan will react to an external event based on its own capabilities and options as realist theory predicts.

External events thus, have the greatest potential to dictate foreign policy changes for Japan, but these external events must still filter through the matrix of domestic opinion. Witness the August 1998 testing by North Korea of the Taepodong-1 missile over Japan. Several of the Diet members who I interviewed contacted me to voice their concern and ask my opinion on the issue. The test firing of this missile also caused the Japanese public to acknowledge the North Korean threat to Japan. According to a poll taken by the *Yomiyuri Shimbun* (Newspaper) 70% of Japanese are worried about the outbreak of war and nearly 60% feel that Japan will be attacked by military force.[105] North Korea's testing of the Taepodong-1 and planned testing of the Taepodong-2 missile in August or September of 1999 (now postponed under international pressure) has led the Japanese government to purchase airborne-refueling capability for the Air Self Defense Forces (ASDF). The idea being that if a missile fell in Japan or possibly violated its airspace Japan would use the ASDF to destroy the North Korean launch site in "self defense." This new attitude marks a huge change for Japan and its interpretation of the constitution. The idea that Japan could take offensive action for defensive reasons would have been totally unthinkable several years ago. Additionally Japan is pursuing a Theater Missile Defense system (TMD) research with the US in direct response to the North Korean threat.

We see that Japan is once again restructuring its foreign policy (yet another reinterpretation of Article Nine) as a result of an external crisis.

Japanese reaction is dependent on public support or the lack of it. Japanese officials believe that the public would support a prime Minister who ordered the destruction of the North Korean launch site if a missile fell in Japan.[106] These external crises have the greatest ability to initiate change in Japanese foreign policy in the absence of an overarching policy that would otherwise focus Japan's external orientation.

Basically this chapter has argued that change takes place at two levels. At one level there are the agents of change as described in Hermann's Model. On the other there are the normative preconditions for change that govern and regulate change. These preconditions limit the change process. Without understanding these intervening variables it is difficult to understand or predict policy change.

The next chapter will examine Japan's security options in the post-Cold War world in East Asia. The following chapter place in the international system and look more closely at Japanese aspirations for hegemony. Included in this chapter will be an examination of how *gaiatsu* is used as a tool of the other Japanese agents of change. Data from the field research and further analysis of Japan's foreign policy restructuring will be woven into both chapters.

NOTES

[1] Charles F. Hermann, *Changing Course: When Governments Choose to Redirect Foreign Policy, International Studies Quarterly*, Vol. 34,(1990): 3.
[2] Some Japanese politicians, especially from the LDP, see the possibility of amending the *kenpou* as possible if it is done as a whole scale revision rather than just simply targeting Article Nine for revision. There seem to be some efforts to couch the need for a rewriting of the constitution also in nationalistic terms by emphasizing that the *kenpou* was written largely by Americans and is not Japanese in origin (See former Prime Minister Nakasone's comments in the PBS video series by Alex Gibney, *The Pacific Century: Reinventing Japan (#5)*, produced by the Pacific Basin Institute in association with KCTS/Seattle, 60 min., Jigsaw Productions, 1992, videocassette. The LDP has formed a constitutional committee to study the *possibility* of rewriting or amending the constitution as a whole. Some (mostly in the LDP) are hopeful, but many (mostly opposition members and members of the SDP are openly skeptical. Interview with Kei Hata, Member of the House of Councillors of the Japanese Diet, interview by the author, 18 May 1998, Tokyo, tape recording, in author's personal possession, Tempe, Arizona.
[3] For more on this concept see: Martin W. Sampson III and Steven G. Walker, *Cultural Norms and National Roles: A Comparison of Japan and France*, in Stephen G. Walker, ed., *Role Theory and Foreign Policy Analysis.* (Durham: Duke University Press, 1987), Chapter 7, P. 105–122.
[4] The author's interviews with several members of the opposition parties and even the Socialists (SDP) who were in a power sharing coalition with the LDP at the time, confirmed the need and desire for political consensus. Those interviewed expressed strong displeasure with the heavy handedness that was occurring in

Japanese politics. In other words, they felt that their views and concerns were being ignored by party leadership thus creating a loss of harmony.

⁵ The Social Democratic Party of Japan (SDPJ) was the predecessor of the current SDP.

⁶ A direct contrast to this concern about balance and consensus would be the US system which is probably the most open to outside influences, including foreign ones. The majority in Congress over the last 25 years has demonstrated an increasing willingness to push or block legislation regardless of the views of the opposition. This trend has been largely attributed to loose American campaign finance laws and the fallout of the Watergate scandal. Money buys influence in Washington but is limited to what constituents will *not* oppose at the polls. Based on Rinhard Drifte, *The US-Japan- China Security Triangle and the future of East Asian Security*, to be published in: *Security in a Globalized World: Risks and Opportunities*, Laurent Goetschel, ed., Nomos Verlag: Baden-Baden, 1999, P. 1 and a conversation with Former Republican Congressman and Minority Whip John Rhodes of Arizona, at the University Club, Arizona State University, Tempe, Arizona, Spring 1996, author's personal notes, in author's personal possession, Tempe, Arizona.

⁷ Sheryl WuDunn, and Nicholas D. Kristof, *Japan as No. 1? In Debt, Maybe, at the Rate Things Have Been Going*, New York Times, 1 September 1999, internet edition, <http://www.nytimes.com/yr/mo/day/news/financial/japan-debt.html>.

⁸ Some of these overseas jobs are designed to gain access to foreign markets and/or to escape high wages in Japan, but many are jobs that Japanese workers simply do not want to do anymore because they are menial or physically hard.

⁹ Data is the ratio of the total working age population to the retirement age population (the actual ratio is probably lower when non-worker from the working age group, such as housewives, are factored in.) and comes from the (Japanese)National Institute of Population and Social Security Research, *Selected Demographic indicators for Japan*, web page <http://www.ipss.go.jp/English/S_D_I/Indip.html>. For more on Japan's aging population please see Milton Ezrati, *Japan's Aging Economics*, Foreign Affairs, Vol.76 No. 3, May/June 1997, 96–104.

¹⁰ National Institute of Population and Social Security Research, *Selected Demographic indicators for Japan*, web page <http://www.ipss.go.jp/English/S_D_I/Indip.html>.

¹¹ Interview taken from John W. Kennedy, *Tokyo: Indifferent to the Risen Son*, Pentecostal Evangel, (5 December 1999): 10.

¹² Many couples cite the high cost of raising and educating children as the main reason for not having children or only having one child. Japanese municipal governments are so alarmed at this trend that they are offering financial incentives to couples to have more children. Such as paying for the medical costs and the first year's worth of diapers and formula. This is having little effect. Those that do have children are not willing to risk them in dangerous international conflicts. In several of the author's interviews with Japanese elites, the elite cited the need for Japan to concentrate its resources at home as Japan is facing tremendous issues at home that require all its resources. The clear implication is that while Japan is willing to do its part to protect its interests, it is unwilling to go the extra mile and place itself at risk for the interests of others (more on this later).

[13] Milton Ezrati, *Japan's Aging Economics*, Foreign Affairs, Vol.76 No. 3, May/June 1997, 101.

[14] This "family" style illustration is based on the US-Japan relationship since World War II, where the US wrote Japan's constitution and established many of its governmental institutions and norms. The "mother" in this scenario is the democratic values and economics that both nations share.

[15] A proverbial "loser" who has no real ambitions and never leaves the nest. Japan is clearly not in this category.

[16] During the occupation the U.S. broke up the *kiretsu*/cartels that worked hand in hand with the government and gave legal legitimacy and independence to trade unions etc. This permitted Japan to develop a much more truly capitalist economic system than it had before the war and it laid the foundation for Japan's post-war prosperity and economic boom.

[17] Nicholas D. Kristof, *Seeking to Be Tokyo's Governor, Politician Attacks U.S. Presence*, New York Times, 26 March 1999, A12.

[18] MOFA officials interviewed almost unanimously and in rote form said the "goals" of Japanese foreign policy were "The safety and prosperity of the nation." When probed for specifics these MOFA officials had difficulty in giving any and tended to repeat the same mantra, "The safety and prosperity of the nation." This "goal" of the nation seams to be drilled into bureaucrats working for MOFA from day one as their *raison de etre*. While this seems to be a good statement of purpose for MOFA, it does not specify tangible goals for the nation as a whole.

[19] Councillor Takemi has worked to create greater awareness of foreign policy issues by championing the creation of sub-committees in the Diet and having them hold hearings and issue policy statements rather than rely on MOFA as has been done traditionally. He was also instrumental in the formation and adaptation of LDP's foreign policy platform independent of MOFA.

[20] Ukeru Magosaki, *New Diplomatic Challenges in East Asia*, unpublished paper, Japanese Ministry of Foreign Affairs, 1998.

[21] Ichiro Ozawa, *Blueprint for a New Japan: The Rethinking of a Nation* (*Nihon Kaizo Keikaku*), trans. By Louisa Rubinfien and edited by Eric Grower, New York: Kodansha International, 1994.

[22] Shintaro Ishihara, *The Japan that Can say "No"* (*No to Ieru Nihon*), trans. and edited by Frank Baldwin, New York: Simon and Schuster, 1991.

[23] An example of this lack of foresight and desire for petty gratification is a Diet member who expressed a desire to see the American economic "bubble" collapse as the Japanese "bubble economy" did in 1989 just for the chance to *prove* to America that Japan was not as dumb as America thought and that such a collapse could happen to anyone. The member clearly had not thought through the impact that an American economic collapse would have on the already fragile Japanese economy, not to mention the disastrous impact on the rest of the world.

[24] Upon completion of the author's interview with Representative Eisuke Mori he asked to interview this author. He proceeded to ask a series of questions about Japan's international economic options. He was clearly looking for a solution to Japan's economic crisis that he could campaign on and possibly implement. Representative Mori clearly understood that if Japan was to have a larger role in the world it needed to solve its economic problems first. The question for him was

how to sell a workable solution to the electorate in a politically acceptable way that would not throw Japan into social turmoil at the same time. Eisuke Mori, Member of the House of Representatives of the Japanese Diet, interview by the author, 22 May 1998, Tokyo, tape recording. In author's personal possession, Tempe, Arizona.

25 Interview with a high ranking MOFA official who asked that his comments not be attributed or quoted directly with his name attached. Interview by author, during May-June 1998, Tokyo. Tape Recording. In author's personal possession Tempe, Arizona emphasis added.

26 Joseph M. Grieco, *Anarchy and the Limits of Cooperation: A Realist Critique of the Newest Liberal Institutionalism*, in *Neorealism and Neoliberalism: The Contemporary Debate*, ed. David A Baldwin, (New York: Columbia University Press, 1993), 118–119.

27 Hans J. Morganthau, *Politics Among Nations*, revised by Kenneth W. Thompson, New York: Knopf, 1985.

28 The terms institutionalism and neoliberalism are used interchangeably and are seen as synonymous for the purposes of this book.

29 The author is indebted to his friend and colleague Tong Ge for first introducing him to this concept of a realistic approach to institutionalism. Tong Ge argued in her Master's thesis/paper that China, in spite of a long standing (and continuing) opposition to institutionalist approaches to foreign policy, is now pursuing institutionalist foreign policy options out of a realistic need for international legitimacy. That is to say, China sees a realist need to use institutions for its foreign policy needs. Japan in the same way seems to have used institutionist approach for realist purposes. For more on this please see: Tong Ge, *Realism and Chinese Foreign Policy in East and Southeast Asia in the Post-Cold War Era*, (Master's thesis/paper Arizona State University: Department of Political Science, Spring 1999).

30 Grieco, 117.

31 The US-Japan Security Treaty is viewed by this author as a bilateral institution with multilateral implications rather than simply a bilateral security arrangement between Japan and the U.S. This is because of the three-fold role that the Treaty plays providing Japan its security guarantee, in promoting East Asian security, and the psychological benefit to other East Asian nations by "keeping the Japanese Genie in the bottle."

32 Sheldon W. Simon, *International Relations Theory and Southeast Asian Security*, *The Pacific Review*, Vol. 8, No. 1 (1995): 6.

33 Ibid. 7.

34 Grieco, 118, *emphasis added*. The idea of a partner exiting from a relationship is very significant for Japan in light of its fears of abandonment by the U.S. Japan can easily be seen as getting more from the relationship than the U.S. and thus according to Grieco is a possible candidate for abandonment by the U.S. Japan as a nation that is fundamentally practicing realism, realizes this and hence the fears of abandonment (More on this later in this chapter).

35 This concept of "localized rationality" partially comes from comments by Paul Bracken and Ralph Cossa at the National Bureau of Asian Research's *The Many Faces of Asian Security: Beyond 2000* conference at Arizona State University, Tempe Arizona on April 27, 2000, (the author's personal notes). This localized rationali-

ty reflects thinking from the perspective of the those locally making the decision. It may not appear to be rational from an outsider's perspective but it is very rational for those making the decision. Examples of this are Saddam Hussein's decision to invade Kuwait in spite of the strong interdependent relationship between the two states and Japan's decision to attack Pearl Harbor in spite of the fact that it knew that it would most likely lose a war with the United States. Both of these cases led to disaster, but this does not have to be the case. A "localized rationality" may be the best choice for a nation.

[36] Joseph M. Grieco, *Anarchy and the Limits of Cooperation: A Realist Critique of the Newest Liberal Institutionalism,* In *Neorealism and Neoliberalism: The Contemporary Debate,* ed. David A Baldwin, 116–140. New York: Columbia University Press, 1993; Robert Powell, *Absolute and Relative Gains in International Relations Theory, American Political Science Review,* Vol. 85, No. 4, December 1991: 1303– 1320; and *Anarchy in International Relations Theory: The Neorealist-Neoliberal Debate, International Organization,* 48, 2, Spring 1994: 313–344.

[37] I am grateful to my friends and colleagues Matt Stevenson and Seng Tan for their help and comments in talking through this analysis of relative and absolute gains.

[38] In addition to the benefits listed above, Japan is still exempted, because of the treaty, from having to provide its own security. In many ways part of the Yoshida Doctrine still works for Japan. Japan does not have to invest as much in its own defense as it would if the U.S. were not allied with it.

[39] Off the record interview with a government researcher in the employ of the Japan Defense Agency (JDA), Tokyo, May-June 1998, tape recording, in the personal possession of the author Tempe, Arizona.

[40] For more on Japan's role in regional fora please see Paul Midford's paper: *From Reactive State to Cautious Leader: The Nakayama Proposal and Japan's Role in Promoting the Creation of the ASEAN Regional Forum (ARF),* Columbia University: Department of Political Science, 1998.

[41] Gilles Paris, *Le Japonais Kochiro Matsuura da succeder a Federico Mayor a la tete de l'Unesco, Le Monde,* 22 October 1999 as cited by H-Japan <H-JAPAN@H-NET.MSU.EDU> #1999–91 5–7 November 1999.

[42] The inequalities in the Japanese electoral system resulted in the gap between rural votes and some city votes being 10 to 1 in favor of the rural voting districts. For more information see: Raymond V. Christensen and Paul E. Johnson, *Toward a Context-Rich Analysis of Electoral Systems: The Japanese Example, American Journal of Political Science,* August 1995, Vol. 39:3, 575–598.

[43] Major Takashi Motomatsu of the Japanese Ground Self Defense Forces and former commander of a SDF PKO mission to the Golan Heights, current station Planning Section of the Plans and Operations Department Japan Defense Agency. Interview by the author, 5 June 1998, Tokyo. Author's notes. In author's personal possession, Tempe, Arizona.

[44] Charles F. Hermann, *Changing Course: When Governments Choose to Redirect Foreign Policy, International Studies Quarterly,* Vol. 34,(1990): 3.

[45] Ibid.

[46] Ibid., 13.

[47] The idea here is that a leader or government that implements a foreign policy can be faced with three possible results from a policy: 1) They may be faced with positive feedback and may thus choose to accelerate or enhance the existing policy, 2) The policy maker may choose to continue the foreign policy (the status quo) with incremental changes in absence of either positive or negative feedback, or 3) In face of negative feedback from a foreign policy the policy maker may choose to change the foreign policy or implement a new one. This last choice obviously reflects restructuring and is the case for Japan. The same policy maker that implemented the policy is making the change. The second choice can be restructuring to a lesser extent. However, the first choice is foreign policy change but not restructuring. All foreign policy restructuring is foreign policy change but not all foreign policy change is restructuring. Foreign policy restructuring is the result of negative feedback causing the maker of the foreign policy to redirect (restructure) their foreign policy.

[48] Hermann, 4.

[49] Ibid., 5.

[50] Off the record interview with a government researcher in the employ of the Japan Defense Agency (JDA), Tokyo, May-June 1998, tape recording, in the personal possession of the author Tempe, Arizona.

[51] Grieco, 118, *emphasis added.*

[52] Japan's quest for allies while still maintaining its ties with the U.S. will be discussed in detail in Chapter six.

[53] Since the Korean War it is evident that the U.S. regrets allowing Article Nine to be part of the *kenpou*, no matter who the author was.

[54] Hermann, 10–11, emphasis added.

[55] The Cold War's end was the system change, but only the Persian Gulf War brought the realization that the Cold War was over and that the system had changed. In other words the Persian Gulf War constituted a wake up call for Japan.

[56] Hermann, 6.

[57] Ibid.

[58] Ibid., 7.

[59] *Oxford American Dictionary*, "cybernetics," New York: Avon Books, (1982): 212.

[60] Hermann, 9.

[61] Ibid., 8–9.

[62] Ibid., 10.

[63] Ibid., 10–11.

[64] Ibid., 11.

[65] Ibid.

[66] An interesting story was related to this author by an academic in Japan about the friction within the LDP during this time period. It would seem that Representative Hajime Funada (who was interviewed in the course of the field research, though he made no mention of this incident himself) was in a meeting where many of the older (Rep. Funada being one of the younger members of the Diet) members of the party opposed the PKO bill and were set to let the bill die as the Kaifu bill had done. Rep. Funada stood up in this meeting and physically blockaded the door; refusing to let any of the members out until they agreed to

back the PKO bill. In the end the older members relented and backed the bill in the full Diet.

[67] Hermann, 14.

[68] Ibid.

[69] This book is primarily interested in the decision making process as a whole rather than its stages. The detail needed to discuss the impact of each of these stages in detail on the Japanese decision to pass the PKO Law is beyond the scope of this chapter and book. Suffice it to say that the stages of Japanese decision making tend to closely follow the stages Hermann listed.

[70] George F. Kennan, Memoirs 1925–1950, (New York: Bantam Books, 1967): 54–55. The author is very grateful to his friend and colleague Seng Tan who introduced him to this quote.

[71] Yukihiko Ikeda, Former Foreign Minister and Member of the House of Representatives of the Japanese Diet, interview by the author, 16 June 1998, Tokyo, tape recording, in author's personal possession, Tempe, Arizona.

[72] In describing my research to others while in Tokyo, some responded that no changes had taken place. When reminded that Japanese troops were now being deployed overseas (under the PKO Law) for the first time since World War II many quickly retracted their assertion that no change had taken place. The PKO Law marked a significant change in Japanese post-war foreign and security policy. No one interviewed challenged the implicit assertion that change was taking place after hearing the PKO question.

[73] Several interviewees took the entire interview off the record (could quote but in no way attributable to them) right from the start. One of them actually put it all back on the record after the interview was over. Many took certain questions off the record as they might be politically sensitive if quoted in the open media. The offer to take it off the record seemed to be appreciated and was taken as a sign of respect in most cases and served the purpose of smoothing out the awkwardness of the initial few minutes of the interview.

[74] For a full text of the introduction used for the field interviews please see Appendix C.

[75] The Socialists were the most significant opponents of the PKO Law at the time of its passage, but Socialists interviewed were not as concerned with it six years later possibly reflecting their role as part of the governing coalition with the LDP.

[76] It was not felt that this subtle reminder would in any way bias the interviewee's answers as it is the norm for change to take place around us and few notice it until it is pointed out to them. This subtle prompt was designed only to awaken the respondent to the issues; not to direct or prompt answers.

[77] Eisuke Mori, Member of the House of Representatives of the Japanese Diet. Interview by the author, 22 May 1998, Tokyo, tape recording in author's personal possession, Tempe, Arizona.

[78] Off the record interview at interviewee's request at the Japanese Ministry of Foreign Affairs, Tokyo May-June 1998. Tape recording, in author's personal possession Tempe, Arizona.

[79] Kei Hata, Member of the House of Councillors of the Japanese Diet, interview by the author, 18 May 1998, Tokyo, tape recording, in author's personal possession, Tempe, Arizona.

⁸⁰ For the full text of the interviews in both Japanese and English please see Appendixes A and B at the end of this book.

⁸¹ This in and of itself is very fascinating in that it shows the low priority of foreign policy on the agenda of many of the elites that are responsible for making foreign policy decisions or are at least part of the process. Hideo Usui, Member of the House of Representatives of the Japanese Diet and former Defense Minister and Vice Defense Agency Minister (Career ministry appointment), interviews by the author, 26 and 29 May 1998, Tokyo, tape recording, in author's personal possession, Tempe, Arizona.

⁸² This low profile attitude may be changing based on conversations by the author with multiple people connected with the JDA. It seems that the success of the respective PKO missions has given the JDA confidence in taking up its own cause in the debate over its role in Japanese foreign policy.

⁸³ A "cold" phone call to former Prime Minister Koichi Miyazawa (with references of others whom we had interviewed) resulted in a positive answer to our request for an interview. Unfortunately scheduling conflicts kept this interview from ever taking place.

⁸⁴ The author is deeply indebted to Professor Tsuneo Akaha of the Monterey Institute of International Studies who introduced him to several of his academic friends in Japan and more importantly, introduced him to the Vice Minister of Foreign Affairs Shunji Yanai and opened the door for him at MOFA for further interviews.

⁸⁵ The author is extremely grateful to Yoko Takagi who worked as his research assistant for the first two weeks of the field research. Her initiative and hard work helped ensure the success of the field research. Yoko also proved to be a good sounding board for gaging the importance of non-verbal reactions to the questions. She was also very good at making cultural observations that would have escaped the notice of non-Japanese

⁸⁶ When the interviews were in Japanese the author relied on his own Japanese skill as much as possible, but he used a translator as a safety net which proved to be very wise. In most of the interviews in Japanese the author could understand over ninety percent of what was said, but in one interview with an older Diet member who did not like or understand the questions it was almost impossible to understand. He used very archaic Japanese and talked in circle to the point that the translator (who was a native speaker!) understood less than seventy percent of what was being said. The lesson was that it would always pay to have a translator on standby to assist and to avoid miscommunication even if the translator was not needed. It was also interesting to note the difference in behavior of the interviewee when the translator was a foreign male verses a Japanese female. When the foreign male translated, the attitude was a lot more respectful and professional.

⁸⁷ The author is also grateful to his former student Yuko Masaki who served as his receptionist and to her husband Rudy for all their help and their friendship.

⁸⁸ The author was continually impressed with the quality of the people working for MOFA, but at the same time it was disappointing to see such bright minds being locked into the organizational box, unable to freely explore and debate

ideas. Part of this is thought to be due to Japanese social and cultural norms which govern every aspect of Japanese life.

[89] Jiro Kodera, Director First International Economic Affairs Division of the Japanese Ministry of Foreign Affairs, interview by author, 20 May 1998, Tokyo, tape recording, in author's personal possession Tempe, Arizona.

[90] Karel van Wolferen, *The Enigma of Japanese Power*, Tokyo: Charles E. Tuttle Co., 1993.

[91] T. J. Pempel, *Structural 'Gaiatsu': international Finance and Political Change in Japan, Comparative Political Studies*, Vol. 32 No. 8, (December 1999): 907–932. For more on this also see the August 1999 online discussion of this subject between T. J. Pempel and Richard Katz, <ssj-forum@iss.u-tokyo.ac.jp>.

[92] *Daily Yomiuri, Defense Legislation Leaves Some Questions Unanswered*, 27 May 1999, internet edition, <http://www.yomiuri.co.jp/newse/0527po17.htm>.

[93] Noboru Yamaguchi, Colonel Ground Self Defense Forces, Deputy Chief of Defense Planning Division, Ground Staff Office, Japan Defense Agency, interview by author 2 June 1998, Tokyo, Japan, tape recording, in author's personal possession, Tempe, Arizona.

[94] Ryozo Kato, Director General, Foreign Policy Bureau of the Japanese Ministry of Foreign Affairs, interview by author, 21 May 1998, Tokyo, tape recording, in author's personal possession Tempe, Arizona.

[95] Ibid.

[96] Witness the Spring 1999 Tokyo governor's race and the accusations by candidate Shintaro Ishihara in the *New York Times* P. A12 March 26, 1999.

[97] Interview with Ryozo Kato.

[98] The research assistant, Yoko Takagi, noted this in her paper that an independent foreign policy vis-a-vis the US assumes conflict in areas that have no conflict. She was very surprised by Kato's attitude toward the US. Yoko Takagi, *Japan's Foreign Policy: Japan's decision making of the foreign policy and the PKO Law* (sic), Research Paper for Dr. Linda Rawles, Grand Canyon University, P.10–11.

[99] A notable exception to this was Professor Osomu Iishi of the Institute of Oriental Culture at Tokyo University. Professor Iishi expressed great dismay over this lack of discernment as to Japan's position and the benefits gained in the world as America's ally. Osamu Iishi, Professor Institute of Oriental Culture, Tokyo University, interview by author, 29 May 1998, Tokyo, tape recording, in author's personal possession Tempe, Arizona.

[100] Only one younger person interviewed seemed to want to stay in the older established ways of doing things. He was the son of a senior LDP member and had previously sought election to the Diet unsuccessfully. Part of the reason for his lack of success in spite of excellent connections and a family name to go with them might be his old fashioned style of politics that is not in tune with the country as a whole. Many of the younger Diet members campaign as young and hip (one even gave me a copy of a pop music CD he had cut). Many of their news clippings show them as "men" (or women) of the people. They are seen singing Karaoke, drinking beer, and laughing it up with constituents. Old style campaigning and paying ones dues to the party do not seem to matter so much any more.

101 *interflux*- being among a continuous succession of changes. From the prefix *inter*- meaning "between or among" and *flux* meaning a continuous succession of changes, *in the state of flux." Oxford American Dictionary*. New York: Avon Books, 1982.

102 See Ryozo Kato's observation earlier in this chapter that Japan only needs to wait until the World War II generation dies out and all will be forgotten as proof of this "head-in-the-ground" mentality.

103 The movie *Pride* is a revisionist attempt to rewrite Japan's wartime Prime Minister's life so that he is an Asian hero who stood up to America and the West and was martyred for his efforts. For more on this see Nicholas D. Kristof, *A Tojo Battles History, for Grandpa and for Japan, The New York Times*, internet edition <http://www.nytimes.com/library/world/asia/042299japan-tojo.html>, April 22, 1999, Setsuko Kamiya and Kanako Takahara, *Tojo film opens to applause, criticism, The Japan Times*, Sunday May 24, 1998, P. 2., and Ryuichiro Hosokawa, *Japanese need a good dose of 'Pride', The Japan Times*, Tuesday June 2, 1998, P. 18.

104 Ezra F. Vogel, *Japan as Number One: Lessons for America*, Cambridge, Mass.: Harvard University Press, 1979.

105 Yomiuri Shimbun, August 4, 1999. Internet: <http://www.yomiyuri.co.jp/newse/0805so07.htm>.

106 Howard W. French, *Two wary Neighbors Unite to Confront North Korean Arms, The New York Times*, August 4, 1999, P. A1 and A6.

CHAPTER 4
JAPAN'S SECURITY OPTIONS

". . . security is more than the objective physical state of being free from physical threat. It is also psychological: we are free from fear to the extent that we lack a feeling of fear." — Donald Snow[1]

Former Japanese Defense Minister Hideo Usui describes Japanese national security as the number one priority of Japan's foreign policy.[2] Yet as Masashi Nishihara of the Japanese National Defense Academy writes,

> Today political leaders rarely talk about comprehensive national security. Instead they talk about how to defend Japan and cope with emergency situations around Japan and in East Asia. Security debates are being dominated by subjects such as surveillance satellites, theater missile defense systems, in-flight refueling devices for jet fighters, anti-terrorist units in the SDF and the police organization, and the need for emergency laws. This is a clear indication that the Japanese have shifted their priority in national security.[3]

In light of this high priority that Japan seams to be placing on national security, this chapter will examine Japan's national security options. Fundamental to this will be the fact that Japan needs to be and is considering options beyond it current alliance with the United States. This is not to say that Japan wants to sever its relationship with the U.S., but rather that Japan needs to be considering alternatives, a "plan B" if you will, should Japan ever be abandoned by the U.S. or feel the need to demonstrate its independence from the U.S. by ending the U.S./Japan Security Treaty. Diet Member Shigeru Ishiba noted that, "Japan can not (afford) to be without allies and who can it really

103

trust except for the U.S.? Why? The U.S. bases here in Japan have (proven America's commitment to Japan)."[4]

As mentioned in chapter three, Japan has a very real fear of abandonment. During the Cold War the U.S. number one priority was security. When trade or economic conflicts between Japan and the U.S. occurred, U.S. security concerns took precedence over economic concerns. With the end of the Cold War Japan cannot count on the security concerns of the U.S. distracting it during trade conflicts. Japan's significance to America is much less important in the post-Cold War era than it was during the Cold War. The fear in Japan is not just that the U.S. might abandon it, but that its role it the world will be ignored or deemed insignificant by the nations of the world.

The origins of this fear go back to the world community's reaction to Japan's non-participation in the Gulf War. Japan was at the pinnacle of its economic power and yet its contribution to the war effort, while significant in economic terms, was deemed insignificant by Japan's allies because their was no human contribution. The Gulf War was fought with Japan sitting on the sidelines. There is even a term for it in Japanese which describes what Japan is feeling. It is called *"Japan's passing"* in Japanese.[5] The concept deals with Japan's fear that the world is passing it by and ignoring it as irrelevant. While these fears may be overstated because Japan has such tremendous economic influence; it does have a real fear of abandonment. In particular there is a fear, by many in Japan, that Japan will be abandoned by the U.S. in favor of China.

Part of the foundation for this fear is the Clinton Administration's alleged receipt of campaign contributions from sources in China which has given the appearance that the Clinton Administration is beholden to China. While in the U.S. it may seem to be outlandish or at best unproven in legal terms that the Clinton Administration traded influence for campaign contributions; outside of the U.S. it would seem foolish for other nations, particularly allies in the region like Japan, to assume that the Clinton Administration was not beholden to China. Common sense dictates that they must at least consider this possibility and factor it into their foreign policy calculations. Japan is no exception to this.

This fear of undue Chinese influence was reenforced by Clinton's refusal (at China's request) to stop off in Japan after visiting China in the summer of 1998 to brief the Prime Minister of America's most important ally in the Pacific on the summit with China's leaders as had been the custom of U.S. presidents returning from summits in China before Clinton.[6] The Clinton Administration's increasingly close ties with China have been noted outside of East Asia. As Ted Galen Carpenter writes in *Foreign Affairs*:

> The increasingly cozy U.S.-Chinese relationship— described by President Clinton and Secretary of State Madeleine K. Albright in

terms like "strategic cooperation" and "strategic partnership"—has alarmed Taiwan, unsettled longtime U.S. allies Japan and South Korea, and prodded India to unveil its nuclear weapons program. Such reactions will have long-term repercussions for Washington's political and military roles in Asia.[7]

While no Japanese leader would ever directly accuse an American administration of being unduly influenced by a foreign government, prudence would dictate that Japan's leaders consider the possibility and that Japan must be prepared to deal with such an eventuality as abandonment if it should ever happen.[8] It is in Japan's best interest to at least consider the possibility and lay the diplomatic groundwork for such an eventuality. Japan's national security depends on the abilities of its leaders to plan for multiple eventualities and possible setbacks.[9] As Ken Yamada wrote in the *Mainichi Shimbun* quoting "high-level" diplomatic sources in Japan, "Tokyo might be forced to review its strategy and become a political superpower that could contend with the United States and China."[10] Former Prime Minister Morihiro Hosokawa went so far as to argue that the U.S. military presence in Japan needs to be reduced and that "Japan play a far more vigorous role in the alliance."[11] The Japanese leadership is concerned and worried about Japan's national security and is exploring its options. This chapter will look at these options to see how they stack up against the dominant realism that is believed is guiding Japanese foreign policy as described in chapter three. In order to examine carefully Japan's foreign and national security options we must first look at the current status of Japanese national security.

JAPAN'S NATIONAL SECURITY

National security has traditionally been determined by a nation's political, military, and economic capacity.[12] In Japan's case it stacks up very well in each traditional area. Japan has capable domestic and foreign policy leadership, a very solid political system that espouses free and fair elections, and a strong respected constitution that has given Japan a stable government.[13] During the last part of the Cold War Japan's responsibility under the U.S./Japan Security Treaty was to secure the Sea Lanes of Communication (SLOCs) around Japan up to a thousand miles out. Thanks in large part to this responsibility, Japan has built a very modern and technologically advanced air and maritime defense force that is well able to protect the Japanese home islands. Japan's status as an island makes it considerably less vulnerable to conventional threats such as invasion. Furthermore, the Ground Self Defense Force (GSDF) is a modern well equipped fighting force generally capable of repulsing almost any attempt by a foreign invader to invade the Japanese home islands.

Beyond Japan's ability to defend itself there is the question of its ability to protect its interests abroad. Protecting one's interests abroad requires an ability to project power. Japan does not currently have military power projection capabilities beyond the defense of the home islands. Japan lacks the power to militarily enforce its interests beyond the areas surrounding Japan. Under the terms of the U.S./Japan Security Treaty Japan depends on the U.S. for this capability.[14]

At the same time Japan does have influence far beyond its military strength; largely due to its economic power and capabilities.[15] In economic terms Japan is second only to the United States in terms of Gross National Product (GNP). Its industrial and technological prowess are world renowned.

It is partially due to Japan's strength in these traditional areas that define national security that Japan has experienced no direct threat to its national security outside of the **possible** threat from North Korea if a Korean conflict spilled over into Japan and **possibly** the regional, hegemonic aspirations of China. A total breakdown of government in Russia might cause a refugee crisis for Japan, but this would probably not be a direct threat to its territory.

All of these concerns take into account the traditional definition of national security, but as Donald Snow writes:

> . . . security is more than the objective physical state of being free from physical threat. It is also psychological: we are free from fear to the extent that we lack a feeling of fear. Different people have contrasting notions about what makes them feel safe or secure; security will thus always, to some extent, be subjective. We may all agree on certain core conditions, primarily physical in nature, that define security, but there will also be areas where we disagree on what enhances or diminishes security. It is largely these disagreements that divide the traditionalists from the contemporary school.[16]

The contemporary school referred to by Snow takes into account areas of national security that have not been traditionally defined as national security. This larger definition of national security is often called *comprehensive security*. In the aftermath of the end of the Cold War there is a need for Japan to consider how it stacks up in terms of comprehensive security. Comprehensive security takes into account such divergent issues as narcotics, the environment, illegal immigration, and the strength of the national economy. These issues are increasingly considered as threats to national values as well as "the security and prosperity of the nation" to use the often repeated phrase given by MOFA to describe Japanese national goals.[17]

The concept of comprehensive security is actually of Japanese origin. In 1978, Prime Minister Masayoshi Ohira in the aftermath of America's defeat in Vietnam and the Middle East oil shocks commissioned a private study group in the Nomura Research Institute to study Japan's foreign policy options.

Japanese foreign policy up to this point had been very uni-directional. The shocks of the seventies showed Japan how dependent it was on foreign energy sources and raw materials and that America, its only formal ally, was not omnipotent and in decline. The Nomura Institute came up with the concept of comprehensive security. The idea was that Japan should, in light of its constitutional limitations, provide for its own security on a "holistic basis". In other words Japan was attempting to define itself in terms of its own internal stability, national development, and social harmony (*wa*)[18]. Japan would focus on more than just the military and aspects of national security. Japan would look at its national security from the perspective of its national needs in their entirety.[19] This led Japan to pursue a more active role in the U.N. It also began to take a more activist role in international organizations like the World Trade Organization (WTO) in order to lobby for issues like the continuation of the Japanese ban on imported rice.[20] Japan has also worked hard internationally to protect Japanese worldwide fishing rights and to preserve whaling as well as to preserve the environment in Japanese ocean fisheries.[21] These concerns reflect not only Japan's economic national security, but also cultural values and needs that go beyond the traditional concepts of national security.

In terms of comprehensive security Japan does not do as well as when only traditional terms are examined. Japan has an illegal immigration problem from China and Iran.[22] Though not on the scale of the American illegal immigration problem it is effecting the culture of Japan. Japan's population is declining, and most Japanese no longer wish to do the hard, dirty work that immigrants are willing to do. This has led to an influx of immigrants into Japan causing a slow dilution of Japanese ethnic homogeneity.[23] Homelessness, crime, and drugs are on the rise in Japan as traditional values break down and the economy remains stagnant. The domestic economy which is still stuck in a decade-long recession means that Japan is more heavily dependant on its international economy and thus the SLOCs which facilitate its international trade, than ever before to keep the country afloat economically.

In terms of comprehensive security the greatest potential threat to Japan is economic in the form of an interruption of commerce. It is for this reason that it is a very critical priority for Japan to maintain a strong allied relationship with the U.S. whose power has a global reach that can extend to areas that Japan cannot. Without the U.S. Japan would find itself exposed and its economic power stretched and potentially vulnerable.[24] This vulnerability is due to Japan's extensive investment abroad with no real means of protecting it except diplomacy. The alliance with the U.S. helps create a stability that protects Japanese economic investments and trade from foreign interference. Without the U.S. Japan would need to protect its own trade and its inability to do so makes it vulnerable. It is for this reason that Japan worries about abandonment.

When asked in interviews to name the top three security threats to Japan, Japanese foreign policy elites demonstrated a clear understanding of traditional threats and comprehensive threats to Japan's security. In terms of traditional threats 91% of the respondents named North Korea or in an attempt to be more politically correct the "Korean Peninsula".[25] China or a China/Taiwan conflict was second with 57%. This was followed by Russia and U.S. abandonment at 26% and 24% respectively. As expected, in terms of comprehensive security there were many different potential threats named. Some were surprising and some were not so surprising. For a full examination of the responses given please refer to figure 4:1. The opinions of the Japanese foreign policy elites are reflected but to a lesser extent in a 1997 *Yomiuri Shimbun* poll asking, "Which of the following countries or regions do you think could become a military threat to Japan?" Sixty-nine percent named the Korean Peninsula, 32% named China/Taiwan, 23% named Russia, and the Middle East and the United States were both named 15% of the time.[26] The next section will examine the possibility that Japan might be abandoned by the U.S. or that it might be forced through domestic political interests to sever its relationship with the U.S.

ABANDONMENT

Any astute student of American domestic politics realizes that there is some (though not probable) risk that the United States might abandon its security commitments to Northeast Asia. As Grieco writes, "For realists, a state will focus both on its *absolute and relative gains* from cooperation, and a state that is satisfied with a partner's compliance in a joint arrangement might nevertheless exit from it because the partner is achieving relatively greater gains."[27] Trade friction between the U.S. and Japan continues to present potential for a major U.S./Japan rift.[28] Some critics of Japan, such as Chalmers Johnson and E. B. Keehn, have long argued that America should use the alliance (and thus Japanese fears of abandonment) as a "tool" for American trade policy with Japan.[29] In an era where economics drives public opinion; popular opinion in the U.S. can easily drive American foreign policy. In the 1999 Chicago Council on Foreign Relations poll the defense of America's allies was listed as "very important" by only forty-four percent of the American public as opposed to sixty-one percent in 1990.[30] By way of contrast, in a *Yomiuri Shimbun* poll asking Japanese voters, "Do you think the United States would or would not help Japan militarily if Japan were attacked?", 68% felt that the U.S. would help. Only 22% felt that the U.S. would not help and 10% had no opinion.[31] As Kang argues:

Security Threats to Japan as Named by Foreign Policy Elites			
Threat	Countries	# of Times Mentioned	% of Respondents Listing in Top Three
1	North Korea Korean Peninsula *North Korea First Response Named* Total:	26 23 *33* 49	48% 43% *61%* 91%
2	China China/Taiwan Total:	25 6 31	57%
3	Russia	14	26%
4	U.S. Abandonment	13	24%
4	Nuclear Proliferation*	13	24%
6	Economy	10	19%
7	Oil/Middle East	8	15%
8	Natural Disaster	6	11%
9	Collapse of Multilateral Cooperation	4	7%
10	Constitutional Limitations	3	6%
10	None	3	6%
10	Falling Behind in Technology	3	6%
10	U.S. Bases in Okinawa	3	6%
11	Food Supply	2	4%

Question asked: What are Japan's top three security threats or concerns?

Total responses: 162 (N=54) Note: Some respondents listed four responses as they could not prioritize the third threat. Three respondents listed only one answer (None). Two respondents refused to answer the question.

There is a possible time bias here in that both India & Pakistan tested nuclear weapons during the period (May-June 1998) that the interviews were conducted. Under normal circumstances it might not have been this high. It is also very interesting to note that considering the time bias that only twenty percent of the respondents listed it as a top three foreign policy concern and only twenty-four percent listed it as a security threat.

Figure 4:1   Security Threats to Japan as Named by Foreign Policy Elites

There is a real danger that the United States might withdraw from or fundamentally rethink its security commitments in Northeast Asia. It must be kept in mind that not only "isolationists" but also prominent establishment figures such as Henry Kissinger think that the United States can, if necessary, play a "mediating" role between Japan and China. According to Kissinger, what the United States must do is to "help Japan and China coexist despite their suspicions of each other." Although he does not argue for an off-shore balancing strategy or disengagement for the United States in Northeast Asia, the logical implications of this view should be troubling to America's Asian allies and argues for a "community building" strategy that keeps democratic America actively engaged in a security community of Asian democracies.[32]

Japan needs the U.S. involved in Northeast Asian not just for its own security but also for regional stability. It is for this reason that the U.S./Japan Security Treaty serves not only as a bilateral alliance for Japan, but also multilateral needs by reassuring East Asia that Japan is peaceful and by keeping potential regional hegemons in check. The problem is that the importance of the U.S./Japan Security Treaty has never been as appreciated as much in the U.S. as it has in Japan.[33] According to polls taken in 1996 and again in 1997 by the *Nihon Keizai Shimbun* 56% of Japanese in each poll when asked, "What do you think of the Japan-US Security Treaty?" responded that it should be maintained. Thirty-three percent felt it should be abolished and 11% did not know.[34] Most Americans on the other hand do not even know or are hardly aware of the treaty's existence.

Another potential event that might spell the end of the U.S./Japan Security Treaty would be the collapse of North Korea and an ensuing reunification of the Korean peninsula. Without North Korea as the principal threat facing Japan, the need for the continuing existence of the U.S./Japan alliance could be questioned by the people in both countries. The obvious response that China still remains a threat may be politically impossible to verbalize. China would also likely feel threatened by the loss of the buffer zone of North Korea and would likely campaign loudly for the abolition of both the U.S./Japan Security Treaty and the U.S./Korea Security Treaty along with the withdrawal of U.S. forces from the region. This is one scenario in which the U.S./Japan Security Treaty could be abandoned, thus forcing Japan to go it alone.

Given the unspoken potential threat from China, Sino/Japanese relations are very critical for Japanese national security. There is a high level of awareness of this on the part of Japanese elites. It is very interesting to note that while the Japan/U.S. relationship is often called "the most important bilateral relationship in the world"[35] when asked in the interviews to name the top three priorities for Japanese foreign policy, Japanese elites named Japan's relationship with the China just as frequently as with the U.S.[36] It is also significant that when Japanese were asked in a *Jiji Press* survey, "Which of the following countries or regions do you think will become more important for Japan to form closer relationships with? (Choose up to three)" China polled 59% just behind the U.S. at 60%. Southeast Asia was a distant third at 39%.[37] However the prominence of the Japan/U.S. relationship was reenforced by a *Yomiuri Shimbun* poll which asked, "Regarding political relations, do you think the United States or China will be more important in Japan's future?" Fifty percent said the U.S., 25% named China, and 21% said both equally.[38]

Many have begun to talk about a trilateral relationship between the U.S., Japan, and China.[39] A noted Japanese foreign policy expert, Reinhard Drifte, writes, "Without a doubt, the US-Japan-China security triangle is becoming the determining security relationship on which will depend the maintenance of peace and security of a region ranging from Southeast Asia to Northeast Asia."[40] Several of those interviewed expressed the need for Japan to push for a triangular relationship among the U.S., Japan, and China in order for each side to play off the other's fears. They felt that if Japan did not do this it would become a victim of *Japan Passing* and be deemed irrelevant at worst. In light of Clinton's perceived slight of Japan in July 1998 Japan is feeling the need to aggressively cultivate its relations with both the U.S. and China in order to protect its status and power (security) in the region.[41]

A further area of concern for the Japan/U.S. relationship is the current budget debate over who should pay for the basing of U.S. troops in Japan. Japan wants the U.S. to pay and the U.S. is adamant that Japan continue to pay. This is principally due to the fact that if Japan were to stop paying for the stationing of U.S. troops in Japan, the U.S. Congress would likely balk at asking the American taxpayer to pay and call the troops home. If this were to happen, the result would likely be the end of the U.S./Japan Security Treaty in its present form. Japan would probably continue to have some kind of security guarantee from the U.S., but not a strong one on which it could depend in a crisis. Japan would be on its own to find new security guarantees. The next section will examine Japan's major security options one by one.

JAPAN'S OPTIONS[42]

The U.S./Japan relationship is seen as the number one bilateral relationship in the world, but Japan sees a need to work towards stronger relations with Asia in general.[43] According to former Foreign and Defense Minister Yukihiko Ikeda, "The end of the Cold War increased the number of players in Japanese foreign policy."[44] The problem for Japan is expanding its foreign policy to fit the post-Cold War realities that it faces.

When looking at Japan's foreign and security policy options there is a need to consider Japan's limitation and goals. As discussed earlier the greatest limiting factor for Japanese foreign policy is Article Nine. A major constitutional question of whether Japan can participate in bilateral or multilateral alliances would likely be revisited if Japan needs to consider formal alternatives to the U.S. in order to provide a security guarantee for itself.[45]

Furthermore, Japan is limited by the current weakness of its economy. Japan faces the hard fiscal reality of its domestic economic situation. The current weakness of the Japanese economy limits Japan's options internationally in that it can not afford to contribute as much as it did in the past. As Aurelia George Mulgan writes,

> "Japan's contributions to international organisations(sic), humanitarian activities, and socio-economic development have undoubtedly been squeezed by the country's long-standing strategy of securing its position in the international community through financial means.[46]

As mentioned previously the current economic crisis has also prompted the Japanese government to request that the U.S. pay for the basing of American troops in Japan.[47] This is something that the U.S. has been strongly resisting due to congressional opposition and the ongoing trade friction between the two countries over access to Japanese markets.[48]

The U.S. continues to view Japan as an economic giant and rightly so. Japan is the second largest economy in the world and has been a major beneficiary of the post-Cold War world *Pax Americana* and international free trade, etc., but it has largely failed to adapt its domestic economic policies and foreign economic policies to the opportunity presented by the end of the Cold War. Japan has stumbled each time that it was presented with an opportunity and it has spent the last ten years failing to capitalize on the possibilities of the post Cold War world due to domestic political concerns. The principal concern being the political need to protect its domestic economy from foreign trade and its markets from foreign goods.

Japan's domestic economy is the antithesis of what its international economy is. Domestically, Japan's economy is bloated and extremely inefficient; internationally Japan's economy is lean and extremely efficient.[49] Agriculture is a major area of Japanese economic weakness, but it is an unduly powerful sector of Japanese politics. Politically prudent protectionist acts by the Japanese government have created a lot of ill will between the U.S. and Japan. What might have been overlooked during the Cold War by the U.S. now is the focus of large scale trade disputes. Japan is stuck in a delicate balance between domestic politics and its international priorities.

These concerns have, so far, held Japan back from exercising new foreign policy options. The principal option being that the end of the Cold War permitted it the possibility of moving outside its alliance with the U.S.(or in conjunction with it). The problem for Japan is that options that did not make the U.S. the central feature were anathema for Japan under the Yoshida Doctrine. It has been very hard for Japanese elites, especially those in MOFA, to think beyond an alliance with the U.S. According to Masafumi Iishi, Director of the Foreign Policy Planning Division of MOFA, "(Japanese) bureaucrats must think about the unthinkable: the loss of the U.S. alliance!"[50]

The principal security reason that Japan needs the U.S. is its nuclear umbrella according to one senior Diet member. If Japan were abandoned, it would need to find an alternative way to deter nuclear attack upon itself.[51] The question is thus what options can Japan pursue if it loses or can no longer depend on the U.S. for its security guarantee? And how can it develop relationships to hedge against a loss of the U.S. security guarantee? What choices does Japan have beside the U.S.? What relationships should Japan be cultivating in order to hedge its bets for the future? The next several sub-sections will briefly examine the strengths and weaknesses of Japan's major alternative allies to the U.S., which are: China, North/South Korea, ASEAN, and/or Russia.[52]

OPTION #1: CHINA

In choosing alternative allies to the U.S. China is the first to come to mind in any discussion since it is the third part of the Northeast Asian security triangle. As mentioned previously, many scholars see a U.S.-Japan-China security triangle in which three powers balance against each other. Japan has large economic interests and investments in China. China desires these investments of capital and technology to continue and thus wants to have good relations with Japan. China is a major military power and a nuclear power complete with intercontinental ballistic missiles (ICBMs). It is also a permanent member of the U.N. Security Council. This combination of political power, size, and military strength makes China an attractive alternative to the U.S. for Japan at first glance. The problems are China's political ambitions and Japan's history in East Asia.

China in many ways is an aspiring regional hegemon others must face.[53] China wants to be **the** leader in Asia.[54] Some in Japan even believe that China wants to be a modern nineteenth century style expansive colonial power.[55] Japan would thus be the junior partner in any alliance with China. China would have it no other way. Japanese atrocities against China and the Chinese people during World War II would make it politically impossible for China to truly accept Japan on equal terms. Japan would be in a subservient role, more so than its present relationship with the U.S. This would be a political loss for Japan and would be seen as a desperate move by an abandoned Japan to ally formally with China. It would also require Japan to come to terms with its actions during World War II.

Coming to terms with Japanese actions in China during the Second World War is problematic and a proverbial political "hot potato" in Japan. Many of Japan's senior level officials are still in denial over Japan's role in the Pacific War. One senior MOFA official went so far as to describe China's anger at Japan as a ".. . . misunderstanding that frustrates the Japanese people (because of China's lack of understanding as to what Japan's real intentions were)."[56] When Former Japanese Prime Minister Hosokawa mentioned once at a press conference that he thought that Japan had made "mistakes" during World War II, there were calls on the floor of the Diet for him to be put to death by former ministers of cabinet rank. Japan is not ready to apologize to China for its actions in any meaningful way. This has bred suspicion in China over Japanese intentions in East Asia. It is also one of the reasons that China quietly accepts the U.S./Japan Security Treaty in that the treaty "keeps the Japanese genie in the bottle."

It is important to note the difference between Japan and Germany over the issue of atrocities by both nations during World War II. Because of its apology and remorse for its actions during World War II, Germany is seen as having repented. Thus neo-Nazi groups within Germany are seen as extremists atypical of the nation. In Japan on the other hand, right wing groups are often interpreted as representing the nation and the opinions of the nation because Japan has failed to adequately apologize and show remorse for its actions. Japan lacks the social capital with its neighbors that Germany enjoys with its neighbors. The primary historical reason for this is explained very well by Grieco,

> The Cold War, in a word, required Franco-German reconciliation and the development of trust between those two countries, and this set the stage and even served as the motor for a wider institutionalization of state relationships in Western Europe. In East Asia the Soviet and Chinese threat was met by an American network of bilateral defense treaties. By consequence, the countries in the region that received American protection did not have a need to reconcile with Japan. Moreover, when China joined the American-led coalition of Pacific Rim states against the USSR in the 1970s, its joining was based on an informal entente with the United States and not a formal regional arrangement involving other regional states. Thus, while the Cold War induced cooperation and reconciliation in Western Europe, and set the stage for the formation of institutions and social capital able to withstand the shocks of 1989–1990, it left Asia without either a habit of institutionalized cooperation or a reservoir of mutual trust able to contain or channel growing Chinese power.[57]

Japan does not enjoy reconciliation with its East Asian neighbors. It needs to forget about the propaganda of World War II that said it was liberating Asia from the West and face the fact that it was colonizing East Asia and behaving in a manner just as bad if not worse than any of the Western colonizers.[58]

Japan wants an interdependent relationship with China.[59] To have any hope of achieving this Japan must deal honestly and forthrightly with its past. It also needs to engage in confidence building measures with China.[60] Japan fears China's hegemonic aspirations almost as much as China fears a militarily independent Japan that once again is held in the sway of Japanese nationalism.

Japan also fears a close Sino-American relationship that leaves Japan on the outside looking in. China's actions in **over** protesting the accidental bombing of its embassy in Belgrade by the U.S. is playing into the hands of those who want to see some kind of stress or tension in the Sino-American relationship such as Japan (Russia and India too). Good relations between powerful rivals is not always welcomed by all when there are allies that fear abandonment (Japan).

Japan wants each side to depend on it to some extent. It prefers to keep its alliance with the U.S. but it knows that it must and should hedge its bets by bettering relations with China. While Japan may better its relations with China, China does not make a good ally for Japan. Japan would have to pay a huge political cost both at home and in pride to ally with China. Its best bet is to work with China to reduce tension in the China-U.S.-Japan triangle.

OPTION #2: RUSSIA

Russia is the "sick man" of Northeast Asia, but it is a strong "sick man". Russia is still the single biggest threat to Japan in terms of overall capabilities. A Japanese alliance with Russia would be a direct threat to China's (possible) regional hegemonic aspirations. For Japan an alliance with Russia is currently problematic since Japan and Russia have never signed a peace treaty formally ending World War II.[61] A dispute exists over the Japanese claim to four small islands called the Kuril Islands which are off the northeast coast of Hokkaido and have been occupied by Russia since August 1945. As one high level MOFA official put it, "These four islands shouldn't determine Japanese policy toward Russia, but the principle is (the) issue."[62] Japan needs to solve this island issue as soon as possible.[63]

An alliance with Russia has one great advantage which is Russia's nuclear capabilities.[64] A Russian nuclear umbrella over Japan could replace the U.S. nuclear umbrella. Whether Russia would be likely to offer this to Japan is questionable at best. A Russo-Japanese alliance would raise the tensions in Northeast Asia and be a cause of great concern to China. Improving relations with Russia and solving the territorial disputes would be advantageous to Japan, but given the shaky political and economic state of Russia today Russia would not likely make a good ally in the near future. Any alliance between Russia and Japan would likely end up with Japan being a "cash cow" for Russia and given the state of Japan's economy this would be difficult.[65]

OPTION #3: MULTILATERAL OPTIONS INCLUDING ASEAN/ARF

Japan has in general been very favorable towards most of the East Asian multilateral initiatives. However, Japan has approached most Northeast Asian initiatives from a purely bilateral perspective.[66] Given this, Japan has two major East Asian multilateral foreign/security policy options. One being the existing

ASEAN/ARF structure which now includes most of the nations of East, Southeast and Southern Asia. The second being any future Northeast Asian Security forum in which it chooses to participate. The great benefit of multilateral efforts for Japanese foreign policy is that not even the Communist Party (JCP) opposes multilateralism. Representative Mitsuo Higashinaka, the JCP's leading foreign policy expert, even went so far as to say that multilateral efforts should be a priority of Japanese foreign policy provided the fora are neutral like ASEAN and ARF.[67] Of the elites that were interviewed an overwhelming 83% favored Japanese multilateral efforts. Only 5% opposed Japan's having a role in multilateral fora. Five percent supported Japan having only a financial role and 7% had no opinion or did not know.[68]

In the absence of a security crisis or a threat (like an aggressor China or a China-Taiwan conflict that spills over into Southeast Asia or the SLOCs) which draws Japan and ASEAN together, an alliance is unlikely to occur. ASEAN is interested in Japan *economically* not militarily. ARF, on the other hand, offers Japan a chance to raise the level of it security dialog with the rest of the region and to work for regional stability though confidence building measures.

Northeast Asia lacks anything like Southeast Asia's ASEAN or ARF. The closest thing is KEDO (Korean Energy Development Organization). It is in Japan's interest to foster cooperation among Northeast Asian nations, but the dynamic is different in Northeast Asia than it is in Southeast Asia. Southeast Asia lacks a major power while Northeast Asia has several. The Northeast Asian nations are more confident in their own power, whereas Southeast Asian states seek to shore up their own security (insecurities) through multilateral efforts. Additionally, the U.S./Japan Security Treaty and the U.S./Korea Security Treaty make, in many ways, Japan, South Korea, and the U.S. a *de facto* alliance due to the U.S. bilateral security commitments to both nations.[69] The U.S./Japan Security Treaty also serves as a way to keep the U.S. closely tied to the region. As Professor Shin'ichi Ogawa of the National Institute for Defense Studies stated during an interview, "The U.S./Japan alliance has many merits for Japan and compliments any (potential) regional security alliances."[70] For a nation that worries that the U.S. will abandon it, the pursuit of a Northeast Asian regional security forum that includes the U.S. would seem to be an excellent way to keep the U.S. engaged and lessen the likelihood that the U.S. would totally abandon Japan.[71]

OPTION #4: SOUTH KOREA

South Korea is Japan's most natural ally in the region. Both nations have complimentary security needs. As Sheldon Simon, a noted expert on East Asian security, writes, "Both (Japan and South Korea) Asian states are dependent on the sea lanes of communications along the Pacific rim for energy and general international commerce."[72] The greatest evidence that Japan is hedging its bets against an unsought after abandonment by the U.S. is its efforts to repair relations with South Korea. Japan has apologized for it colonial occupation of Korea in a way that the South Korean government has chosen to accept.[73] In October 1998, Japanese Prime Minister Keizo Obuchi offered an unprecedented written apology that expressed regret for the suffering and harm that Japan inflicted as a colonial power on the Korean people.[74] Korea was ranked number three as the most mentioned foreign policy priority for Japan (behind the U.S. and China) in the field interviews.[75]

The stability of the Korean peninsula is critical to Japanese national security. The threat posed by North Korea gives the U.S./Japan Security Treaty its unspoken *raison d'etre* for Japan. North Korea represents the greatest single threat to Japanese national security. For this reason alone, Japan needs to advance its security relations with South Korea. Over ninety percent (n=54) of those interviewed during the course of the field research listed either North Korea or the Korean peninsula as one of the top three concerns for Japanese national security. Sixty-one percent listed it as the number one threat to Japan. This is in comparison to China which at fifty-seven percent, was the second most named threat to Japan; and less than ten percent listed China as the number one threat to Japan (for more detail see figure 4:1 above).[76] It is for this reason that Japan's relationship with South Korea is indispensable to its national security. In any renewed Korean conflict Japan and Korea would need to work closely together. While South Korea would probably never permit Japanese SDF troops on its soil, it would probably welcome Japanese naval and air power efforts against the North and Japan's assistance as a staging area for U.S. forces.

South Korea's potential as an ally has been often understated or overlooked. Korea has frequently been described as ". . . a shrimp swimming among whales."[77] The days during the Korean war when Korean troops were the first to flee in combat are in the past. Decades of staring at their Northern enemy across the DMZ (Demilitarized Zone) and training to face them have hardened South Korea forces into an potent military force. Even as far back as the War in Vietnam, South Korean forces earned the respect of their American allies for their professionalism and valor. A removal of the North Korean threat for whatever reason would free up the tremendous military reserve of the South Korean Army. Implicit in this is the threat this would pose to China even without the presence of U.S. forces in Korea. A Japan/unified Korea alliance would be a strong hedge against potential Chinese aggression in the region.

It is also in Korea's interest to reconcile its differences with Japan. One can better understand this when one looks at Korea's potential alternatives. Japan is South Korea's only potential regional ally. South Korea will try to build relationships with the other powers in the region, especially China, but it is Japan with its similar democratic values and capitalist economy that makes Japan the better potential ally.[78] It is for this reason that the South Korean government is willing to reconcile with Japan.[79] As Zbigniew Brzezinski argues, "...a true Japanese-Korean reconciliation would contribute significantly to a stable setting for Korea's eventual reunification, mitigating the international complications that could ensue from the end of the country's division....A comprehensive and regionally stabilizing Japanese-Korean partnership might in turn facilitate a continuing American presence in the Far East after Korea's unification."[80] South Korea needs peace and stability in Northeast Asia if it is ever going to successfully unify with the North. The economic costs alone would require the sum total of ROK resources and economic aid from the U.S. and Japan. A solid and amiable relationship with Japan would make this much easier.[81]

OPTION #5: NORTH KOREA

North Korea/Japan relations are strange at best. On one hand the Korean community living in Japan is P'yongyang's number one source of hard currency which flows from Japan to North Korea with Tokyo for the most part turning a blind eye to its transfer. On the other hand North Korea's nuclear and missile programs are Japan's number one traditional security threat. According to Professor Takasada of the Japanese National Institute for Defense Studies, an expert on Korea, Japan is the nation most threatened by North Korean nuclear weapons because it is unlikely that the North would use nuclear weapons on the Korean Peninsula itself unless forced to.[82] The same is not true for Japan. Japan's history in Korea makes it a politically low cost target for the North Koreans and it is unlikely that it would cause strong resentment in South Korea either.[83] Again Japan's history works against it.

North Korea is not really a true or practical option for Japan except if Japan were to be abandoned by the U.S. and the U.S. military presence were to be removed. Then Japan might choose to rid itself of its greatest threat by signing a nonaggression pact with North Korea and agree not to be a staging area for the U.S. in any renewed Korean conflict.[84] This would possibly permit Japan to sit out a Northeast Asian conflict, but would likely result in hard feelings all around by Japan's former allies and would be no real guarantee that the conflict would not spill over to Japan anyway.

OPTION #6: UNILATERAL OPTIONS OR GO IT ALONE

Japanese unilateral options may be an oxymoron. "There are so many obstacles to unilateral action by Japan," according to Kiichi Fujiwara of the Institute of Social Science at Tokyo University.[85] The number one obstacle being Article Nine. The most likely unilateral action by Japan would be to aquire nuclear weapons. Japan could pursue this course at tremendous political cost but it is not likely given the nearly universal condemnation it would face at home and abroad.[86]

There is an option for Japan to go it alone as an independent and neutral nation. This option has its benefits in that it is the most consistent with the current interpretation of the constitution. Japan would be allowed to defend itself from an external attack, and it is well able to repulse any attack on its home islands. Neutrality would reduce the risk of Japan being brought into a Korean conflict with the U.S. North Korea would be less likely to attack a neutral Japan with missiles than it would be if the U.S. was using Japan as a staging area for a Korean campaign.

The drawbacks of being a neutral nation would be the loss of prestige of being allied with the current hegemon, the U.S. Japanese neutrality would also likely cede regional hegemony to China. In order to make up for the loss of the U.S. nuclear umbrella and to secure Japan from nuclear blackmail, Japan would likely have to develop its own independent nuclear deterrent *if* faced with a threat like Chinese hegemony.[87] Japan's status as the only nation that has had atomic weapons used against it would make it very hard for Japanese leaders to convince the Japanese public to accept Japan as a nuclear power.

UNITED NATIONS

One final sub-option that Japan might pursue, if it goes it alone, is to step up it U.N. diplomacy and rely on the U.N. and the good will of its members for protection. This would be quite acceptable to the pacifist elements in Japan which have always favored a U.N. centered foreign and security policy. Since joining the U.N., Japan has pursued a U.N.-centric foreign policy as its only alternative to the U.S. as an ally. The peaceful goals of the U.N. and Japan's pacifist constitution work well together. The problem is can Japan depend on the U.N. when China, one of its major potential threats, sits on the Security Council as a permanent member with veto power. Russia, another potential threat, has the same advantage and potential to neutralize the U.N. as a protector of Japan.

CONCLUSION

Japan's options to the U.S. have many pluses and minuses. Figure 4:2 illustrates this. Clearly a continued relationship with the U.S. is Japan's best option. Better relations with South Korea help Japan in many ways, too, and permit Japan to solidify the triangular relationship with the region's most logical allies, Japan, South Korea, and the U.S., even if no alliance is ever formalized among the three. Japan should also continue to work on its relationship with China preserve peace and stability in East Asia.

Japan's Options: Pluses and Minuses		
Potential Ally	**Pluses**	**Minuses**
USA	- High return - Nuclear umbrella - Alliance with the reigning hegemon - Stability	- Lack of independence - Loss of some sovereignty - Potential to be dragged into conflict unwillingly
China	- Good return - No competitors in East Asia	- Junior Partner - Lack of independence - Must apologize for WW II
South Korea	- Equal match - Balance against China - North Korea -Shared democratic and capitalist values	- Must deal with WW II issues - North Korea
ASEAN/ARF	- Hedge against regional Chinese hegemony - ARF confidence building measures would add to regional stability	- Not militarily practical - ASEAN not formally an alliance; very little security benefit
Russia	- Nuclear umbrella - Strong hedge against China	- Loss of North Islands - Instability of Russia - Possibly an undependable alley -Financial drain
North Korea	-nonaggression pact might protect it from a Korean conflict spillover	-allied with a rogue state -No status -No potential to protect Japan from other threats -Financial drain
United Nations	-Constitutional -Acceptable to the Pacifist elements in Japan	-Both Russia and China can neutralize the U.N.'s ability to protect Japan.
Go It Alone	-True Independence and neutrality -Free to pursue U.N. centered diplomacy as a neutral nation -Constitutional (without power projection capabilities)	-No allies -Potential Loss of Influence -Need for Military Buildup -Loss of Nuclear Umbrella or the need to develop nuclear weapons itself -China gets regional hegemony

Figure 4:2   Japan's Options: Pluses and Minuses

Japan should also work towards the creation of a Northeast Asian security regime, although the creation of a Northeast Asian security regime will be an uphill battle at best for all those involved. As Henry Kissinger writes, "Wilsonianism has few disciples in Asia. There is no pretense of collective security or that cooperation should be based on shared domestic values, even on the part of the few existing democracies. The emphasis is all on equilibrium and national interest."[88] In the absence of a clear threat to regional security (for example: an aggressor China) the greatest argument for such a regime would be the necessity to keep the U.S. engaged in the region. This will not be easy. If Japan and Korea wish to have a strong security alliance with the U.S., similar to the American relationship with Europe, they must appeal to the sector in the American foreign policy community that believes that the U.S. must have close relations with the democratic capitalist nations of the world.[89] It is much easier to sell the American electorate "value-based diplomacy" than geopolitics.[90]

The logic of this idea would imply a trilateral relationship between the U.S., Japan, and South Korea. How far or how formal such a relationship would or should go depends on the threat or lack thereof posed by China. It is an essential element of both deterrence theory and strategic theory that one does not provoke one's adversary into aggressive behavior. Even hard-core realists would acknowledge that an alliance that precipitates aggression or hostilities on the part of an adversary is not helping one's national security (self help). As E.H. Carr points out, "the most serious wars are fought to make one's own country stronger, or, *more often*, to prevent another from becoming militarily stronger."[91] Fear of one's adversary(ies) is often a motive for aggression. As R. G. Hawtrey writes, "the principle cause of war is war itself."[92] *If* China were provoked into a more openly hostile or aggressive foreign and/or military policy in Northeast Asia by a formal trilateral alliance among the U.S., Japan, and South Korea then the national security of all three nations would not have been served. The flip side of this is if Chinese actions *cause* the formation of a three way alliance, then the national security of all three nations is served by the formation of an alliance.[93] Fortunately or unfortunately for Japan, the current interpretation of the constitution holds collective defense to be unconstitutional, and the Japanese public supports this view.[94]

A better scenario would be one that included China (*and* South Korea and Russia) in any security arrangement or fora in order to remove the potential "threat" posed by a formal alliance among the U.S., Japan, and South Korea that might be resented by a state left out.[95] Japanese/Korean cooperation will be needed for any security scenario to work in enhancing Japan's national security. While many see a triangular relationship in East Asia among the U.S., Japan, and China, considering the significance of South Korea and the potential of a unified Korea should the North collapse and the still formidable capabilities and power of Russia that it might be better to view North East Asian Security as a pentagon. This view of Northeast Asian security is closer to a multilateral forum in Northeast Asian that is similar to the ARF for Southeast Asia. Such a multilateral forum could lead to the confidence building measures that will be needed to ease regional tensions and provide for a strong and safe security environment for Japan. This concept is illustrated in figure 4:3.

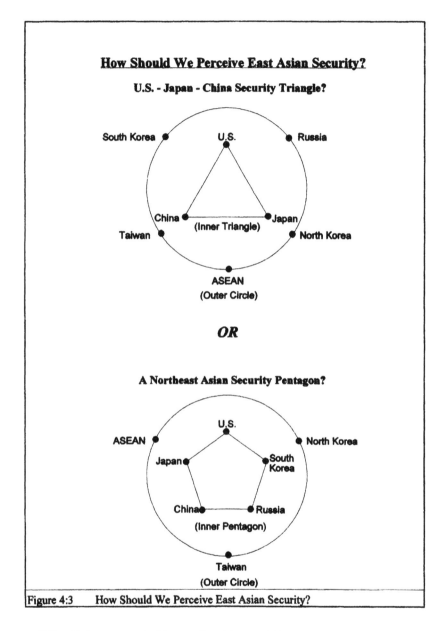

Figure 4:3   How Should We Perceive East Asian Security?

If the U.S.-centered alliance should ever fall apart, Korea is Japan's best alternative in the region. History aside Korea shares Japan's democratic values and capitalist system. Both countries are strong nations with modern militaries which complement each other well. It behooves Japan to continue to work to strengthen this relationship in the off chance Japan is abandoned. It

also is in Japan's interest even if the U.S. does not abandon its security commitments in the Pacific. With the exception of a possible China/Taiwan shooting match, Korea is the powder keg of East Asia. If conflict arises in Korea,
Japan **will** be dragged in one way or another. Japan needs to be prepared for
this eventuality should it ever occur.

Any security relationship for Japan will be difficult. Its relations with other
nations, for the most part, cannot be as equals. As Barry Buzan et al write,
"This relationship among subjects is not equal or symmetrical, and the possibility for successful securitization will vary dramatically with the position
held by the actor."[96]

Additionally in thinking about Japan's future options in East Asia, there is
always "the problem of memory". This is true whether one is talking about
Japanese relations with China or Korea. Nicholas D. Kristof, a Pulitzer Prize
winning journalist and former Beijing and current Tokyo Bureau Chief for the
New York Times, sheds a remarkable and disturbing light on the attitudes
toward Japan in East Asia. Kristof recounts this incredible and shocking story
from his days in Beijing shortly after the Tiananmen Square Massacre:

> The memory of a brief conversation nags me whenever I think
> about Asia's future. The conversation took place shortly after the
> Tiananmen Square crackdown, during a secret meeting with a leader
> of China's underground democracy movement. We met in a quiet
> corner of a Beijing restaurant, where he tapped the table suspicious-
> ly to see if it was bugged. This was a man whose vision I admired, so
> I listened intently when the waitress stepped away and he leaned for-
> ward to disclose his plans for promoting human rights.
> "We are going to kill Japanese," he said brightly.
> "What?"
> "We're going to kill Japanese businessmen. That'll scare them so
> they won't invest here. And the government will really be screwed!"
> "You're not serious?"
> "Of course we're serious. We can't demonstrate these days and we
> can't publish. The only thing we can do for democracy is kill Japanese
> businessmen."
> I protested that it seemed odd to promote human rights by mur-
> dering innocent businessmen. But he just smiled at my narrow-mind-
> edness, with a "you-will-never-understand-Asia" grin.
> "They're Japanese," my friend said dismissively. "Japanese devils."
> He never did kill anyone. But the vitriol in his voice underscored
> Asia's historical tensions, which are especially intractable because
> they exist between peoples, not governments.
> While Asia has seemed remarkably peaceful since the end of the
> Vietnam War the peace is a fragile one, concealing dormant antago-
> nisms and disputes that could still erupt.[97]

This story illustrates that even the most enlightened of people can be victims of culture and history. Japan is limiting its foreign policy options by its refusal to deal with the past effectively. Japan needs the trust of its neighbors in East Asia. This trust will not come without a sincere show of remorse and contrition for Japan's history in East Asia. The conservative right wing in Japan is in denial as to Japan's situation *vis-a-vis* the rest of the world and in particular Asia. Its steadfast opposition to apologies in general and China in specific for actions taken during World War II has led to an ongoing mistrust of Japan and its intentions.

A valuable lesson could be learned from the positive results of Japan's apology to South Korea. Japan has the potential to develop strong relations within East Asia, and it needs to do this sooner rather than later. If Japan can not do this, it will find itself very lonely in a region where allies are important. The next chapter will look at what Japan is doing and its perspective on the world. It will also look at the all important influence of *gaiatsu* on Japanese foreign policy making.

NOTES

[1] Donald Snow, *National Security: Defense Policy in a Changed International Order*, 4th ed. (New York: St. Martin's Press, 1998), 24.
[2] Hideo Usui, member of the House of Representatives of the Japanese Diet and former Defense Minister and Vice Defense Agency Minister (Career ministry appointment), interview by the author, 26 and 29 May 1998, Tokyo, tape recording, in author's personal possession, Tempe, Arizona.
[3] Masashi Nishihara, *Japanese Defense Policy: Issues and Options*, A paper presented at the International Symposium on Japan and Its Neighbors in the Global Village: Current and Emergent Issues. Nanzan University, Nagoya, Japan. 16–17 October 1999, 4, (*emphasis added*).
[4] Shigeru Ishiba, member of the House of Representatives of the Japanese Diet (LDP), interview by the author, 4 June 1998, Tokyo, tape recording, in author's personal possession, Tempe, Arizona.
[5] Pronounced in Japanese *katakana*: Ja-pa-nu pas-su-i-n-gu. This term was used in many interviews by the interviewees and even commented on by several academics as a major policy worry for Japan.
[6] The Clinton Administration told the Japanese government that Clinton wanted to be in the U.S. to spend the 4th of July with U.S. troops, some of which were stationed in Hawaii. A compromise was suggested that Clinton stop in Okinawa on the 4th of July and visit the troops there. The Japanese Prime Minister Ryutaro Hashimoto could then travel to Okinawa and be briefed by Clinton on his China visit. This compromise would have permitted all sides to save face as Clinton could say he was visiting U.S. troops, and thus in principle complying with China's request and Japan could feel that it was not "passed" over by the United States. The Clinton Administration rejected this compromise however and Japan was left with the feeling that it was "passed" over by its only ally the United States

even though Secretary of State Madeline Albright did brief the Prime Minister in the end.

[7] Ted Galen Carpenter, *Roiling Asia: U.S. Coziness with China Upsets the Neighbors, Foreign Affairs,* Volume 77 No. 6 (November/December 1998), 2. *Emphasis added.* The closeness of the Clinton Administration's relationship to China is especially ironic/interesting in that during the 1992 presidential campaign, the Clinton campaign continually hammered at George Bush's policy of engaging China as coddling China too much in the wake of the 1989 Tiananmen Square massacre. In a May 1, 1998 speech at Arizona State University, George Bush sarcastically noted Clinton's change of heart by saying that "he (Clinton) had finally got it (Clinton's China policy of engagement) right." Author's personal notes.

[8] Several of those interviewed, both inside and outside of government, stated off the record that they were worried about the Clinton Administration being influenced by China. The recent strains in Sino/American relations due to the bombing of the Chinese embassy in Belgrade, the Cox Report, and the difficulty over getting WTO through Congress are probably a relief to them. It is important to note that several other interviewees scoffed at the idea that the U.S. would abandon Japan in favor of China, but the reality is that many in Japan fear or at least wonder about the possibility of such a thing happening.

[9] Masafumi Iishi, Director Foreign Policy Planning Division of MOFA described this as a "worst case" scenario that Japanese bureaucrats need to plan for. Masafumi Iishi, Director Foreign Policy Planning Division of the Japanese Ministry of Foreign Affairs, interview by author, 1 June 1998, Tokyo, tape recording, in author's personal possession Tempe, Arizona.

[10] Ken Yamada, *Searching for Ways to Coexist: Clinton's First Trip to China,* Mainichi Shimbun, 25 June 1998 as cited by Carpenter, 4.

[11] Carpenter, 5.

[12] For more on the traditional definition of what constitutes national security please see: Donald Snow, *National Security: Defense Policy in a Changed International Order,* 4th ed. New York: St. Martin's Press, 1998 and Barry Buzan, Ole Wœver, and Jaap de Wilde. *Security: A New Frame Work for Analysis,* Boulder, Colorado: Lynne Rienner Publishers, 1998.

[13] In many ways the greatest legacy left by General Douglas MacArthur is Japan's constitution. In spite of its flaws, the *kenpou* is supported and respected by the Japanese people. The fact that it has never been amended is a testament to its durability as an institution in Japanese society.

[14] Since the test firing of the Taepodong-1 by North Korea in August 1998, the Japanese government has sought appropriations for the purchase of midair refueling aircraft in response to this threat to the Japanese homeland. If acquired, these planes would give Japan a limited power projection capability. The rationale behind this proposed purchase in light of the current interpretation of Article Nine is that it would be "self-defense" to destroy missiles that threaten the Japanese homeland in time of war. For more information on this please see: *Yomiuri Shimbun, Appropriation Sought for Refueling Aircraft,* 21 July 1999, internet edition, <http://www.yomiuri.co.jp/newse/ 0722po01.htm>.

15 It is very difficult to measure power outside of the terms of traditional military power. Japan obviously has power far beyond the reach of the SDF but it is difficult to quantify or to measure. As Donald Snow writes:

Measuring Power — Although the concept of power is so pervasive and attractive for describing the operation of the international system, its precise measurement remains elusive. The difficulty has two bases.

 The first is finding physical measures that adequately describe the abilities of states to influence one another. A common effort has been to try and find concrete, physical measures, such as the size or sophistication of the armed forces or the productivity of states' industrial bases that should indicate which is the more powerful country in any head-to-head confrontation. The problem is that such measures work only part of the time; there is, for instance, no physical measurement to compare national capacities that would have led to the conclusion that North Vietnam had any chance of defeating the United States in a war, but they certainly did.

 The second problem is that measures cannot get at the psychological dimension of will and commitment. How can an outside observer determine, for instance, when a clash of interests is clearly more important to one party to a dispute than it is to an adversary (at least before the fact)? Once again, the Vietnam War is illustrative; the outcome of that conflict (unification of the country) was clearly more important to the North Vietnamese and its southern allies than its avoidance was to the United States. That is clear in retrospect; it was not at all clear before and even during the conduct of hostilities. Being able to see clearly in retrospect is of very little comfort to the policymaker.*

*Donald Snow, *National Security: Defense Policy in a Changed International Order*, 4th ed. (New York: St. Martin's Press, 1998), 30.

16 Snow, 24.

17 When asked about Japanese foreign policy goals in question four, every interviewee from MOFA immediately said, "The security and prosperity of the nation." MOFA officials had to be pushed to give specific responses of how to achieve this "security and prosperity of the nation." None of the other interviewees ever gave this response to question four.

18 For more on this concept of the *wa* please see Martin W. Sampson III and Stephen G. Walker, *Cultural Norms and National Roles: A Comparison of Japan and France*, in Stephen G. Walker, ed., *Role Theory and Foreign Policy Analysis*. (Durham: Duke University Press, 1987), Chapter 7, P. 105–122.

19 Muthiah Alagappa, *Comprehensive Security: Interpretations in ASEAN Countries*, in *Asian Security Issues: Regional and Global*, edited by R.A. Scalapino, S. Sato, J. Wanandi, and S.-J. Han, (Berkeley, California: Institute of East Asian Studies, University of California-Berkeley Press, 1988) 50–78. Alan Dupont, *Concepts of Security*, in *Unresolved Futures: Comprehensive Security in the Asia Pacific*, edited by J. Rolfe, (Wellington: Center for Strategic Studies, 1995), 1–15. See Seng Tan, *Constituting Asia-Pacific (In)Security: A Radical Constructivist Study in "Track II" Security Dialogues*, (Ph.D. diss., Arizona State University, May 1999), 144–145. The author is very grateful to his friend Seng Tan for his help in talking through the concept of comprehensive security as it relates to Japan.

20 The Japanese government viewed Japanese self sufficiency in the production of rice, the primary food product consumed by Japanese, as a national security issue. The Japanese government had created a national myth around rice: that it was a centuries old staple food source for Japanese when in reality it only became a staple food for the Japanese early in this century with the introduction of modern farming methods. The ban on imported rice was never complete as it was never(in the post war era) possible for Japan to be totally self sufficient for its rice needs. The whole concept of self sufficiency collapsed in 1993 when the rice crop suffered a catastrophic failure and Japan was forced to import large quantities of rice from the U.S., Australia, and Thailand.

21 The Japanese environmental record outside of its immediate interests has been very spotty at best.

22 The illegal immigration problem from Iran stems from a loose visa laws for Iranian citizens (no visa is required in advance) and the Japanese government's unwillingness to offend the government of Iran by clamping down in a harsh way.

23 The influx of illegal immigrants into Japan has led to a backlash against foreigners in general which is upsetting Japan's normal welcoming but shy attitude. For more on this see Howard W. French, *Japan's Cultural Bias Against Foreigners Comes Under Attack, The New York Times*, internet edition <http://www.nytimes.com/library/world/asia/111599japan-discriminate.html>, November 15, 1999, Howard W. French, *Still Wary of Outsiders, Japan Expects Immigration Boom, The New York Times*, internet edition <http://www.nytimes.com/library/world/asia/031400japan- immigration.html>, March 14, 2000, and Calvin Sims, *Tokyo Chief Starts New Furror, on Immigrants, The New York Times*, internet edition <http://www.nytimes.com/library/world/asia/041100japan-immigrants.html>, April 11, 2000.

24 The level of Japan's vulnerability without the U.S. would depend on the stability of the world system supported by U.S. hegemony. If U.S. hegemony were to collapse Japan would be in serious need of powerful allies in other areas of the world. If U.S. hegemony were to continue Japan would probably be able to continue to benefit from the stability brought about by U.S. hegemony as a "free rider".

25 Note: The question was asked several months *before* the Korean Missile Crisis occurred and thus did not influence the high response rate for North Korea.

26 *Yomiuri Shimbun* survey of 1,952 national voters. Conducted 25–25 October 1997 by personal interview. Source: JPOLL, Roper Center for Public Opinion Research, University of Connecticut. (For required full disclaimer please see the Bibliography at the end of this book.) <http://roper1.ropercenter.uconn.edu>.

27 Grieco, 118, *emphasis added*. The prospect of a partner exiting from a relationship is very significant for Japan in light of its fears of abandonment by the U.S. Japan can easily be seen, on the surface, as getting more from the relationship than the U.S. and thus according to Grieco is a possible candidate for abandonment by the U.S. unless a strong case can be made that the U.S. can do without Japan. Japan as a nation that is fundamentally practicing realism, realizes this and hence the fears of abandonment.

28 The current strength of the U.S. economy and the weakness of the Japanese economy is making trade friction less of a concern, but the potential remains that

if the U.S. economy enters into a recession then trade conflicts might reemerge in the bilateral relationship.

[29] Chalmers Johnson and E. B. Keehn, *The Pentagon's Ossified Strategy, Foreign Affairs*, 74, 4 (July/August 1995): 103–114.

[30] John E. Rielly, ed., American Public Opinion and Foreign Policy 1999, (Chicago: Chicago Council on Foreign Relations, 1999), 16 & 38 as cited by C. S. Kang, *Korea and Japanese Security, International Journal of Korean Studies*, (vol. III, no. 1, Spring/Summer 1999): 107.

[31] *Yomiuri Shimbun* survey of 2,030 national voters. Conducted 18–19 January 1997 by personal interview. Source: JPOLL, Roper Center for Public Opinion Research, University of Connecticut. (For required full disclaimer please see the Bibliography at the end of this book.) <http://roper1.ropercenter.uconn.edu>.

[32] Kang, 108. Kissinger citation by Kang from: Henry Kissinger, *Diplomacy*, (New York: Simon and Schuster, 1994), 828.

[33] Marc Gallicchio, *Japan in American Security Policy: A Problem in Perspective*, (Working Paper #10) downloaded from: <http://www.seas.gwu.edu/ nsaarchive/japan/gallicciowp.htm> April 14, 1999.

[34] *Nihon Keizai Shimbun* survey of 1,774 national voters. Conducted 25–27 April 1997 by telephone. *Nihon Keizai Shimbun* survey of 1,776 national voters. Conducted 19–21 April 1996 by telephone. Source: JPOLL, Roper Center for Public Opinion Research, University of Connecticut. (For required full disclaimer please see the Bibliography at the end of this book.) <http://roper1.roper-center.uconn.edu>.

[35] Kang, 95.

[36] China and the U.S. were both mentioned twenty three times by elites when ask to name Japan's top three foreign policy priorities. Field Research interviews conducted May-June 1998 in Japan. Question number six or seven depending on the questionnaire. These views would undoubtably change if the U.S. abandoned Japan or seemed about to.

[37] *Jiji Press* survey of 1,430 national adults. Conducted 1 May 1996 by personal interview. Source: JPOLL, Roper Center for Public Opinion Research, University of Connecticut. (For required full disclaimer please see the Bibliography at the end of this book.) <http://roper1.ropercenter.uconn.edu>.

[38] *Yomiuri Shimbun* survey of 1,952 national voters. Conducted 25–25 October 1997 by personal interview. Source: JPOLL, Roper Center for Public Opinion Research, University of Connecticut. (For required full disclaimer please see the Bibliography at the end of this book.) <http://roper1.ropercenter.uconn.edu>.

[39] An examples of this perception of the U.S./Japan/China relationship as a triangular one are: Reinhard Drifte, *The US-Japan-China Security Triangle and the future of East Asian Security*, to be published in: *Security in a Globalized World: Risks and Opportunities*, Laurent Goetschel, ed., Nomos Verlag: Baden-Baden, 1999, David Arase, *Japan Needs Alliance-Plus in Northeast Asia*, editorial from the Nichibei Shimbun, internet edition, 20 March 1999, <http://www.nichibei.org/je/arase-march.html>, and Mark Berger, *Miracles of Modernization and Crisis of Capitalism: The United States-Japan-China Triangle and the Vicissitudes of the East Asian Model 1940s-1990s*, A paper presented at the International Symposium on Japan and Its

Neighbors in the Global Village: Current and Emergent Issues, Nanzan University, Nagoya, Japan, 16–17 October 1999.

[40] Reinhard Drifte, *The US-Japan-China Security Triangle and the future of East Asian Security*, to be published in: *Security in a Globalized World: Risks and Opportunities*, Laurent Goetschel, ed., Nomos Verlag: Baden-Baden, 1999, 1.

[41] Professor Takesada, National Institute for Defense Studies, interview by the author, 5 June 1998, Tokyo, tape recording, in author's personal possession, Tempe, Arizona. It is important to note that even *if* the U.S. abandoned Japan the U.S. as the reigning hegemon would still be an important factor in the East Asian and Japanese security equation.

[42] This section of the book is meant to be a *general* overview of Japan's options rather than a thorough treatment of them. A thorough and exhaustive treatment would be a book in and of itself.

[43] This view of closer relations within East Asia was mentioned by Naoko Saiki, Director International Peace Cooperation Division, Ministry of Foreign Affairs and others during the course of the field research. Naoko Saiki, Director International Peace Cooperation Division, Ministry of Foreign Affairs, interview by author, 4 June 1998, Tokyo, tape recording, in author's personal possession Tempe, Arizona.

[44] Yukihiko Ikeda, member of the House of Representatives of the Japanese Diet (LDP), former Foreign and Defense Minister, interview by the author, 16 June 1998, Tokyo, tape recording, in author's personal possession, Tempe, Arizona.

[45] There was great debate as to the legality of Japan's participation in the U.S./Japan Security Treaty, particularly when it came up for renewal in the late 1950s and early 1960s. The one sided nature of the current treaty (the U.S. is pledged to defend Japan and Japan is not expected to reciprocate) permitted the treaty to be interpreted as constitutional. Any future treaty with another nation is not likely to be as one sided thus raising the constitutionality question once again (if a country could be found who would want to ally with Japan).

[46] Aurelia George Mulgan, *Strategic Update - Japan*, School of Politics, University of New South Wales, Australian Defence Force Academy, conference paper, 1999, p.11.

[47] The Japanese government has traditionally paid for the costs incurred by U.S. forces in Japan such as labor, utilities, facilities (rent), maintenance and training. This cost Japan about 2.5 billion annually.

[48] For more on this see Calvin Sims, *U.S. Resists Cut in Funds by Japan for G.I.'s*, The New York Times, internet edition 17 February 2000, <http://www.nytimes.com/yr/mo/day/news/world/japan-us-troops.html>.

[49] As an example of how inefficient the Japanese domestic economy is, the average manufactured good travels through the hands of ten middlemen on its way from the manufacturer to the consumer. Much of this is due to Japan's arcane distribution system which relies heavily on the culturally imposed loyalty and obligation from one person to the next. Foreign companies have found this distribution system notoriously hard to open up to their merchandise.

[50] Masafumi Iishi, Director Foreign Policy Planning Division of the Japanese Ministry of Foreign Affairs, Interview by author, 1 June 1998, Tokyo, tape recording, in author's personal possession Tempe, Arizona.

⁵¹ Off the record comment by a senior Diet member. Interview by the author, May-June 1998, Tokyo, Japan, tape recording, in the personal possession of the author, Tempe, Arizona.

⁵² The following discussion in no way advocates that Japan seek other alliances. It merely examines at the possibilities that exist for Japan.

⁵³ Professor Takesada, National Institute for Defense Studies, interview by the author, 5 June 1998, Tokyo, tape recording, in author's personal possession, Tempe, Arizona.

⁵⁴ Hajime Funada, member of the House of Representatives of the Japanese Diet (LDP), Chairman of the Sub-Committee on Asia and the Pacific, interview by the author, 28 May 1998, Tokyo, tape recording, in author's personal possession, Tempe, Arizona.

⁵⁵ Shingo Nishimura, member of the House of Representatives of the Japanese Diet (Liberal Party), interview by the author, 17 June 1998, Tokyo, tape recording, in author's personal possession, Tempe, Arizona.

⁵⁶ Off the record comment by a senior member of MOFA interview by author, May-June 1998, Tokyo, tape recording, in author's personal possession Tempe, Arizona.

⁵⁷ Joseph M. Grieco, *China, Japan, and Germany in the New World Polity*, to appear in John Mueller, ed., 1999, chapter 8 page 163.(Faxed copy of publisher's proof in possession of the author).

⁵⁸ For more on the problem of Japan's history in East Asia and the problems it is causing for its foreign policy please see: Steven T. Benfell, *Profound Regrets: The Memory of World War II in Japan and International Relations in East Asia*, a paper presented at the 40th Annual Conference of the International Studies Association, Washington, D.C. February 17, 1999.

⁵⁹ Many of those interviewed at MOFA said that Japan needed to work towards interdependence with China to hedge against China size *vis-a-vis* Japan.

⁶⁰ Professor Takesada, National Institute for Defense Studies, interview by the author, 5 June 1998, Tokyo, tape recording, in author's personal possession, Tempe, Arizona.

⁶¹ During the last Russian/Japanese summit in Tokyo both sides agreed to set a deadline for signing a formal peace treaty by the end of the year 2000. Whether this deadline will be met is currently unclear. The sticking point is the Kuril islands which are a political "hot potato" for the ruling LDP and a nationalist issue for Russian leaders. Boris Yelstin tried to return the islands to Japan in 1994, but nationalist interests in the Russian parliament forced him to abandon the idea.

⁶² Off the record comment by a high level MOFA official. Interview by author, May-June 1998, Tokyo, tape recording, in author's personal possession Tempe, Arizona.

⁶³ For more on the Kuril island dispute with Russia please see: Yakov Zinberg, *In Search for Alternative National Interests: Russio-Japanese Territorial Disputes After the Cold War*, a paper presented at the 40th Annual Conference of the International Studies Association, Washington, D.C. February 17, 1999.

⁶⁴ China also has nuclear capabilities, but these are currently limited in quantity and in sophistication. It is unlikely that China would be willing to extend its limited nuclear deterrent to ensure Japan's safety.

[65] For more on Japan's relations with Russia please see: Tsuneo Akaha, *Japanese-Russian Relations: An Overview or Japanese Views of Russia: Through the Eyes of Others*, a paper presented at the International Symposium on Japan and Its Neighbors in the Global Village: Current and Emergent Issues, Nanzan University, Nagoya, Japan. 16–17 October 1999.

[66] Akihiko Tanaka, *Japan and Regional Integration in Asia-Pacific*, a paper presented at the 40th Annual Conference of the International Studies Association, Washington, D.C. February 17, 1999, 11.

[67] Mitsuo Higashinaka, member of the House of Representatives of the Japanese Diet (JCP), interview by the author, 19 May 1998, Tokyo, tape recording, in author's personal possession, Tempe, Arizona.

[68] Field research interviews conducted in Japan May-June 1998. (N=41)

[69] B. C. Koh, *U.S.-Japan Security Cooperation and the Two Koreas*, a paper presented at the International Studies Association 41st Annual Convention, Los Angeles, California, 17 March 2000, 1.

[70] Shin'ichi Ogawa, Professor, National Institute for Defense Studies, interview by author, 11 June 1998, Tokyo, tape recording, in author's personal possession Tempe, Arizona.

[71] For more on Japanese multilateral efforts and options please see the following three papers: Akihiko Tanaka, *Japan and Regional Integration in Asia-Pacific*, a paper presented at the 40th Annual Conference of the International Studies Association, Washington, D.C. February 17, 1999, Takashi Terada, *The origins of Japan's APEC policy: Foreign Minister Takeo Miki's Asia-Pacific policy and current implications*, The Pacific Review, Vol. 11 No. 3, 1999: 337–363, and Paul Midford, *From Reactive State to Cautious Leader: The Nakayama Proposal and Japan's Role in Promoting the Creation of the ASEAN Regional Forum (ARF)*, unpublished paper, Columbia University: Department of Political Science, 1998.

[72] Sheldon W. Simon, *Multilateralism and Japan's Security Policy*, The Korean Journal of Defense Analysis, Vol. XI, No. 2, (Winter 1999): 91.

[73] It is important to note that while the South Korean government of Kim Dae Jung might have accepted Japan's apology, many Koreans did not. They feel that Japan has not been especially remorseful or frank in its apologies. There is also the lingering issue of compensation for Korean "Comfort Women". For more on Japan's troubled "history" of apologizing for its actions during the Second World War please see: Nicholas D. Kristof, *A Big Exception for a Nation of Apologizers*, The New York Times, 12 June 1995, A1 and A4.

[74] The very fact that Prime Minister Obuchi was able politically to make this apology to South Korea considering right wing opposition within the LDP (Obuchi's party) to apologies on the part of Japan for **any** actions taken during World War II may be testimony to the shock that Japan suffered when North Korea sent a ballistic missile over Japan on August 31, 1998. This test firing of the Taepodong-1 ballistic missile by the North Koreans awakened many in Japan to the fact that their safety and security was closely tied to South Korea's and the stability of the Korean Peninsula. Several Diet member whom I interviewed personally contacted me by email to express their concern over the test firing. The political pressure of the moment may have permitted Prime Minister Obuchi to issue an apology to South Korea when in other circumstances he never would have been able to

do so. This may also be further evidence of the reactionary nature of Japanese foreign policy making that was discussed in chapter three.

75 Field Research interviews conducted May-June 1998 in Japan. Question number six or seven depending on the questionnaire.

76 Field Research interviews conducted May-June 1998 in Japan. Question number six or seven depending on the questionnaire.

77 Kang, 97.

78 South Korea's relationship with Japan has progressed to the point in which the two are now conducting joint naval exercises together. For more on this please see: Associated Press, *Japan, S. Korea Hold Naval Exercise*, New York Times, internet edition, <http://www.nytimes.com/apoline/i/AP-Koreas-Japan-Military.html>, 4 August 1999.

79 Ibid., 101.

80 Zbigniew Brzezinski, *A Geostrategy for Eurasia*, Foreign Affairs, 76, 5 (September/October 1997), 62–63 as cited by Kang, 109.

81 For more on the relationship between Japan and Korea please see: Eunbong Choi, *Balancing the past and the future: A Korean View of the Korea-Japan Relationship*, a paper presented at the International Symposium on Japan and Its Neighbors in the Global Village: Current and Emergent Issues, Nanzan University, Nagoya, Japan, 16–17 October 1999.

82 Professor Takesada, National Institute for Defense Studies, interview by the author, 5 June 1998, Tokyo, tape recording, in author's personal possession, Tempe, Arizona.

83 By low cost it is meant that North Korea would pay a lower cost (in relative terms) by attacking Japan with nuclear weapons than South Korea and if North Korea has developed the capability of reaching the U.S. then there is the question if the U.S. would use nuclear weapons if it can be targeted with nuclear weapons. Even if the U.S. is safe from North Korean nuclear weapons there is the question of whether they would be used on the Korean Peninsula over the likely objections of the ROK.

84 This potential loss of Japan as a staging area for the U.S. in a renewed Korean conflict is probably the greatest reason that the U.S. would choose not to abandon Japan. However if the threat of a renewed Korean conflict were to be removed then the U.S. might feel confident to withdraw from Japan. This scenario assumes that the U.S. and Japan are no longer allies for whatever reason.

85 Kiichi Fujiwara, Professor, Institute of Social Science, Tokyo University, interview by author, 11 June 1998, Tokyo, tape recording, in author's personal possession Tempe, Arizona.

86 The only scenario in which Japan might choose the nuclear option is one in which Japan faced a direct threat in which only a Japanese nuclear deterrent would potentially alleviate.

87 In the author's interview with Director Masafumi Iishi of MOFA's Foreign Policy Planning Division, Mr. Iishi in talking about Japan's options, stated that nuclear weapons represented a cheap and feasible deterrent for Japan but only in a "worst case" scenario in which Japan has been abandoned by the U.S. Masafumi Iishi, Director Foreign Policy Planning Division of the Japanese Ministry of Foreign

Affairs, Interview by author, 1 June 1998, Tokyo, tape recording, in author's personal possession Tempe, Arizona.

[88] Henry Kissinger, *Diplomacy*, (New York: Simon and Schuster, 1994), 826.

[89] The values of this sector of the American foreign policy community are based on the Democratic Peace Theory in Political Science which purports that democracies do not fight each other. The Clinton Administration has made democratization an American foreign policy goal based on the assumed validity of this theory.

[90] Kang, 108.

[91] Edward Hallett Carr, *Twenty Years' Crisis, 1919–1939: An Introduction to the Study of International Relations*, (New York: Harper & Row, 1939), 111.

[92] R. G. Hawtrey, *Economic Aspects of Sovereignty*, 105 as cited by Carr, 111.

[93] How China views the U.S./Japan/South Korea relationship is of critical importance. As Kang writes, "This view (the U.S./Japan/South Korea relationship) was expressed to the author (Kang) by senior Chinese diplomats in Tokyo, December 1997. The author would like to note that in his ongoing informal survey of Chinese officials and scholars, he has observed that there appears to be a generational divide regarding the Chinese view of the Japan-United States and South Korea-United States alliances. The older Chinese appear more comfortable with the alliances, to the extent that they ensure limited Japanese armament, but the younger ones are prone to see them as tools for containing rising Chinese power." Kang in footnote number 14, 114.

[94] Kang, 111. The constitutional limitations imposed by Article Nine work in Japan's favor here by reassuring China (and Korea) of Japan's benign intentions. A constitutional reinterpretation or the amendment of Article Nine would remove this reassurance. Note: The U.S./Japan Security Treaty is the U.S. guarantee of Japan's security/defense. It is not an alliance by Japan with the U.S. where both sides have pledged to support the other in a conflict. It is because of this that the Japanese government can interpret the *kenpou* to permit the Treaty on the grounds that it is *not* collective security because the U.S. is providing a one way guarantee and Japan has only to provide for its own self defense in cooperation with the U.S.

[95] North Korea might be better left out of any future Northeast Asian security fora as it might prove too disruptive for the fora to be successful. However the flip side of this is that the inclusion of North Korea **might** bring North Korea into a more cooperative relationship with the U.S. and the other states in the region thus diminishing the threat posed by the North Korean regime. The success of North Korea in the ARF, which it has been invited to join, might be a good indication of its potential in a Northeast Asian forum.

[96] Barry Buzan, Ole Wœver, and Jaap de Wilde. *Security: A New Frame Work for Analysis*, (Boulder, Colorado: Lynne Rienner Publishers, 1998), 31.

[97] Nicholas D. Kristof, *The Problem of Memory*, *Foreign Affairs*, Volume 77 No. 6 (November/December 1998): 37–38.

HOW JAPAN VIEWS ITS PLACE IN THE WORLD AND THE "MYTH" OF GAIATSU

"There is no sadder sight in the world than to see a beautiful theory killed by a brutal fact."—Thomas H. Huxley[1]

I t is difficult to argue that the U.S. military presence in East Asia has not been the major factor in the stabilization of the region in the post World War II era. Japan's geo-strategic position in East Asia has been the foundation of the American presence in Asia. The U.S./Japan Security Treaty and the U.S./South Korean Security Treaty have been the cornerstones of the U.S. military presence in the region especially since the closing of the Philippine bases. In the post-Cold War era, the U.S. presence has been both a blessing and a curse for Japan. Japan has benefitted greatly from the U.S. presence in the region. The region's peace and stability have permitted Japan to grow and flourish under the Yoshida Doctrine. At the same time Japan's potential for regional leadership remains weak in the light of the U.S. larger presence. To many both inside and outside Japan the presence of U.S. forces based in Japan is an infringement on Japanese sovereignty.[2] They see Japan as still occupied by the U.S. and feel that Japan must find a way to assert itself in world affairs independent of the U.S.

The problem for Japan is that, head to head conflicts with the U.S. aside, most of Japan's international needs and interests coincide with America's needs and interests. Japan as the world's second largest economic power profits just as much as the U.S., if not more so, from the *Pax Americana* that the world currently enjoys. Peace and stability are good for Japan and Japanese business interests. National sovereignty issues aside, Japan has a stake in supporting continued U.S. hegemony.[3] The question for Japan is how to support U.S. hegemony while at the same time independently asserting itself. This chapter will examine Japan's foreign policy. It will also look at the concept of *gaiatsu* which is often given as the reason that Japan does many of the things it does.

ADJUSTING TO THE POST-COLD WAR WORLD

The end of the Cold War brought about an unexpected independence from the U.S. for which Japan was not prepared. The sudden demise of the Soviet Empire made Japan's role as ally much less necessary for the U.S. It was no longer as geo-strategically important to the U.S. as it was during the Cold War. Japan was not prepared for this when the Persian Gulf War broke out. Tokyo struggled in the face of vocal condemnation on the part of its allies for not sending its men and women into combat when it had no real choice to do so under Article Nine. From the world's point of view Japan had the third largest defense budget (in dollar terms) in the world. A nation spending so much on defense should be able to contribute to the protection of commerce and freedom (and oil). The concept of a nation with a constitutional ban on armed force having such a large defense budget just did not compute.

From Japan's point of view, Article Nine of the constitution and internal politics were hard enough to explain or comprehend domestically much less by the world at large. The leadership in Japan realized that a new interpretation of the *kenpou* was the best way for Japan to deal with this issue in a way that was constitutionally acceptable.[4] From this the PKO Law was born as described in Chapter 2.

Looking to the U.N. for an answer to its problem was a natural thing for Japan to do. Since the end of the U.S. occupation, Japan has made the U.N. a central focus of its foreign policy. The U.N. charter with its commitment to the peaceful resolution of conflict reflects Japan's constitution's pacifist nature. The Japanese people are some of the most pro-U.N. people on Earth. U.N. clubs and UNESCO chapters exist all over the country. That Japan should look to the U.N. to get itself out of its post-Cold War predicament is no surprise. Nevertheless, there are limits to its U.N. based foreign policy. These limits are forcing Japan into new areas of foreign policy which it has traditionally avoided due to constitutional limitations under Article Nine.

The problem for Japan is that except for its U.N. based pacifist foreign policy it has no other principle as a guide except for MOFA's "creed", "the safety and prosperity of the nation." As one Diet member who asked to remain anonymous said, "Japan has no firm principle guiding its foreign policy."[5] Another senior government official felt that foreign policy is not and should not be goal oriented; it is rather a day to day business of avoiding conflicts.[6] Japanese foreign policy has therefore become a crisis to crisis foreign policy. It prepares very well to deal with the *last* crisis not the next one.

One important aspect of foreign policy is how to set the nation's priorities. During the field research the foreign policy elites were asked to name what they thought were the top three foreign policy concerns for Japan.

Many of the responses were predictable, but the number and variety were a testimony to the lack of focus in Japanese foreign policy. China and the U.S. alliance were predictable top vote getters with 43% of the respondents naming them as a foreign policy priority. Some showed remarkable foresight by recognizing the need to keep up with high technology and the information revolution,[7] the need to search for alternative allies should the U.S. abandon Japan, or the need to support other democracies. What was surprising was that only 4% named Japan's acknowledged and high profile quest for a permanent seat on the U.N. Security Council as a foreign policy priority. Other surprises included the fact that Russia was the third most often listed threat to Japan (see Chapter Four), but only 11% of the interviewees listed Russia as a foreign policy priority![8] The responses fanned out all over the spectrum. For a complete list of responses please see figure 5:1.

Another example of the lack of foreign policy focus and awareness came from an interview with the former Defense Minister and Upper House Councilor Hideo Usui. Councilor Usui after hearing my first few questions ran out of time and had to go to an important meeting. On his way out he instructed his secretary to schedule a second interview and to make sure we had at least 90 minutes. At the conclusion of this second interview, before I could ask for references to other Diet members, he asked me if he could schedule appointments with other colleagues in the Diet and the defense/security community because he wanted them to be thinking about the questions that I was asking. He stated that he had been trying to get his colleagues to think about these things and my interviewing them would demonstrate the need to be thinking about the direction of Japanese foreign policy. The idea being that if foreigners were asking these questions about Japan should not the Japanese be asking them of themselves? He proceeded to personally call and schedule appointments for me with five senior Japanese Diet members and ministry officials.[9]

The significance of this is that it demonstrates that there is very little serious thinking (by the foreign policy community as a whole) on the major foreign policy questions that face Japan today by the very people who are responsible for making these decisions. The national debate on foreign policy seemed to be very muted. My interviews in a small way were influencing the direction and thought of the foreign policy debate in Japan by in a small way creating it and helping it open up. A further example of this lack of solid debate was my interview with Councilor Ichiro Yamamoto. Councilor Yamamoto saw me only as a favor (obligation in Japanese) to a colleague. Our interview was rescheduled at least six times before he finally granted me a short 20 minute interview. Having been educated in the U.S. he was very American (as opposed to Japanese) in his criticism of me before I even could ask any questions. He figured that I was a waste of his time. Upon hearing the questions he became much more interested and when I offered to end

Concern	Countries	# of Times Mentioned	% of Respondents Listing in Top Three
	Top Foreign Policy Concerns as Named by Foreign Policy Elites		
1	China	22	
	MFN for China	1	
	Total:	23	43%
1	U.S./Japan Alliance	23	43%
3	Korea	14	26%
4	Nuclear Proliferation*	11	20%
5	Economic Integration/Trade	10	19%
5	Multilateral Institutions (support of)	10	19%
6	Russia	6	11%
7	Environment	5	9%
8	Southeast Asia	4	7%
8	U.S./Japan/China Trilateral Relationship	4	7%
8	Defense/Security Policy	4	7%
11	Middle East	3	6%
12	Apology for WW II	2	4%
12	Pursuit of High Technology	2	4%
12	U.N. Security Council Seat	2	4%

Also listed: Improving U.S./China Relations, Food Sources, Japan/Europe Relations, PKO, Taiwan, Search for new allies, Democratization (support of). Total responses: 130. (N=54)

*There is a possible time bias here in that both India & Pakistan tested nuclear weapons during the period (May-June 1998) that the interviews were conducted. Under normal circumstances it might not have been this high. It is also very interesting to note that considering the time bias only twenty percent of the respondents listed it as a top three foreign policy concern and only twenty-four percent listed it as a security threat.

Note: Totals do not add up to 162 (54x3) as some respondents refused to answer or could/would not name more than one or two. Two respondents refused to answer the question. Most respondents took their answers off the record.

Figure 5:1   Top Foreign Policy Concerns as Named by Foreign Policy Elites

the interview after 20 minutes he extended the meeting another 25 minutes into his next appointment. At the end of the interview he got on the phone (without being asked by me) to schedule another appointment for me with another Diet member because he thought that what I was asking was important.[10]

Internal substantive debate would seem to be lacking in the higher circles of both the elected and career foreign policy establishment. Very little thought, it would seem, is given to long range goals. Part of this can be ascribed to the fact that the Japanese public has even less interest in foreign policy than do Diet members.[11] What matters is what interests one's constituents. If one's constituents believe it is important, then it is important. Image is everything. One of the reasons that foreign policy takes such a back seat is the influence of *gaiatsu* and its impact on Japanese political life. The next section will look at the concept of *gaiatsu* and how it influences the formulation of Japanese foreign policy.

GAIATSU

It is important to note the role of the United States in the process of the formation of the SDF and Japanese foreign policy. U.S. pressure is an issue that runs throughout the formation of Japanese defense and security policy. Japanese politicians have been able to explain many of their bolder actions regarding the SDF by referring to pressure from the United States.[12] This "American Pressure" is called **gaiatsu**. *Gaiatsu* can literally be translated as, "pressure from the outside" and is a common term in any newspaper reporting on foreign policy or security related matters. The official Japanese explanation for many of their defense and security policy decisions is essentially that, "the Americans made us do it."[13]

This makes the concept of *gaiatsu* akin to the argument that "the devil made me do it." It denies personal responsibility and choice for one's actions when in reality one is making a choice in a given set of circumstances or situation. Furthermore it denies Japan's sovereignty as a nation by giving the impression, both at home and abroad, that it is incapable of making its own decisions and worse is a possible puppet of the U.S. *Gaiatsu* is part of the situation and part of the decision. All nations, including hegemons like the U.S., face foreign pressure. Japan is not unique in this regard. The ability to deal with foreign pressure depends on one's position *vis-à-vis* the pressure. In the scheme of Hermann's model, the role of external or foreign pressure should be represented as part of the decision making process. Figure 5:2 illustrates this.)

Reinhard Drifte supports this argument in his book: *Japan's Foreign Policy for the 21ˢᵗ Century: From Economic Superpower to What Power?* In it he argues that Japan's continual trade conflicts with America are the true sign that it is a world power.[14] A "poor little Japan" argument is not valid when one considers the scope and breadth of Japanese power. As Drifte argues,

> The question of Japanese power has implications for the policies of other countries which for example expect Japan to contribute to the international system in a way commensurate with its economic power. They exert strong influence (commonly referred to in Japan as '*gaiatsu*') on Japan to this effect. As a result it is most opportune to

appreciate in a more systematic way what sort of power Japan has, how and if at all this power is exerted, whether the demand for 'commensurate contribution' is compatible with the internal and external conditions that Japan is facing, and whether those making these requests are conscious of the implications. It is obvious, but often not fully realized, that such contributions imply the exertion of power, and this has important implications for the world system, including for the relative power of the other countries. There are even Japanese who have to ask themselves whether the outside world really wants to face these consequences.[15]

In fact, Japan makes its own decisions because of its own needs and desires, NOT just in response to *Gaiatsu.*

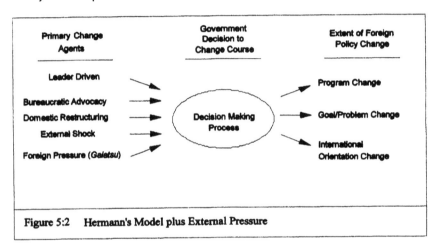

Figure 5:2   Hermann's Model plus External Pressure

THE "MYTH" OF *GAIATSU*

As the strain of the Cold War grew, the Americans were "making Japan do" more and more in terms of its own defense. Even with the one percent GDP limitation, the size of the Japanese economy raised the Japanese defense budget to the third largest in the world behind the United States and the former Soviet Union's by 1990.[16]

As mentioned previously, image is everything in the eyes of the electorate. America's image has taken a beating in recent years in Japan. America comes across as a bully to many in Japan. Professor Osamu Iishi of the University of Tokyo gives this illustration of how every year he asks his incoming students to name who Japan's top three allies and top three enemies are. Up till 1990 the U.S. was always listed as one of Japan's top three allies. Then in 1991 America started showing up as one of Japan's top three opponents. When asked why the students would say that America is a "bully" and cite the Persian Gulf War and America's trade disputes with Japan as examples of America telling and forcing weaker nations to do what it wants.

This was reinforced by a conversation I had with a woman at a sushi bar in Tokyo. She had asked why I was in Japan and after explaining what I was doing she started to talk about her opinions on foreign policy. She felt that America as the most powerful nation on Earth could not be trusted to protect Japan because it was not in America's interest. America only used Japan to do its bidding (she used the term *gaiatsu*) and saw Japan only as a tool of its foreign policy.

These illustrations of the changing perception of America can in many ways be traced back to the increased use of *gaiatsu* by Japanese leaders to convince the public that Japan needs to do something that America wants it to do. It is also important to note that in spite of the hostile feelings most Japanese still want to remain allied with the U.S. in the future. In a 1997 *Yomiuri Shimbun* poll national voters were asked, "Do you want the United States to be an ally in the 21st century, or not?" Sixty-eight percent of the respondents said "Yes I do". Only 23% said "No I don't". Nine percent had no response.[17] Most Japanese also feel that U.S./Japan Security Treaty in conjunction with the SDF is the best way to "maintain the peace and safety of Japan." In the Prime Minister's Office poll 68% wanted to maintain the current treaty and SDF.[18]

During two months of field interviews with Japanese foreign policy elites in Japan only two interviewees out of fifty-six mentioned *gaiatsu* as a reason that a Japanese foreign policy choice was made. One was a member of the JCP and the other was an academic.[19] Japanese foreign policy choices were always discussed in the context of Japanese sovereignty and what was best for Japan. This was very surprising in that *gaiatsu* is a very common term in the literature on Japanese foreign policy.[20] Robert Putnam in his paper, *Diplomacy and domestic politics: the logic of two-level games*, describes an occurrence of gaiatsu in Japan,

> . . . in Japan a coalition of business interests, the ministry of Trade and Industry (MITI), the Economic Planning Agency, and some expansion-minded politicians within the Liberal Democratic Party pushed for additional domestic stimulus, using U.S. pressure as one of their prime arguments against the stubborn resistance of the Ministry of Finance (MOF). Without internal divisions in Tokyo, it is unlikely that the foreign demands would have been met, but with external pressure, it is even more unlikely that the expansionists could have overridden the powerful MOF. "Seventy percent foreign pressure, 30 percent internal politics," was the disgruntled judgment of one MOF insider. "Fifty-fifty," guessed an official from MITI.[21]

The nearly total lack of allusion to *gaiatsu* by Japanese foreign policy elites caused this author to question whether *gaiatsu* was truly the factor in Japanese foreign policy that it is alleged to be. However, when one reads cases like the one cited above by Putnam it is easy to see that it is a factor in some form or another. Putnam notes that without the divisions within the Japanese government *gaiatsu* would not have been a factor.[22] Foreign pressure is clearly an agent of change that belongs in Hermann's model.

The more that the concept of *gaiatsu* was examined the more clear it became that *gaiatsu* was related to the **implementation** of Japanese foreign policy choices rather than only a *cause* of Japanese foreign policy choices. Putnam describes the "two-level games" that nations and leaders play to get what they want.[23] He cites the example of Helmut Schmidt playing this "game" at a summit in Bonn,

> Publicly, Helmut Schmidt posed as reluctant to the end. Only his closest advisors suspected the truth: that the chancellor "let himself be pushed" into a policy that he privately favored, but would have found costly and perhaps impossible to enact without the summit's package deal.[24]

In the case of Japan it seams that there is a two-level game at work. For example, the U.S. wants Japan to do something that is in Japan's overall or long term interest, such as sending forces to contribute to international peace and stability. Japanese leaders want the same outcome as they are trying to make Japan a "normal nation" but without violating the constitution which inhibits Japan's normalization. Because the public and even political interests within the ruling party(s) are not likely to support it, Japanese leaders then use foreign pressure as a way of convincing internal interests both in government and in the public at large that Japan is being forced to pass the PKO Law and that Japan can not afford to say "no" to the foreign interests (the U.S.). This sells the idea to an unwilling public because "America is big and powerful and 'little' Japan cannot say 'no' to America."[25]

In this way *gaiatsu* becomes the "lightning rod" for unpopular decisions that Japanese leaders want to make. America or other foreign countries take the heat. Often foreign pressure does exist, but it is pressure to do something that internal leadership already has decided to do. The first draft of the PKO Law was written in the early 1980s. Japanese leaders were just looking for a chance to implement it.[26]

The "myth" of gaiatsu is that it is the sole explanation for why Japan does so many things in foreign policy that are unpopular. The reality is that, as Putnam describes, without some internal support or division foreign pressure has no chance.[27] All nations make their own choices. National sovereignty can be defined as a nation's ability to make its own choices or decisions in

the absence of controlling foreign interests.[28] This is to say that a nation incapable of making its own choices is not sovereign. An example of this would
be a nation that is militarily occupied by another nation as Japan was after
World War II. Japan has been a sovereign nation since the allied occupation
ended in 1952. The U.S. is a powerful ally and because of this is a great influence on Japan, but there are plenty of examples of Japan defying U.S. wishes in a public way. The problem for Japan is that with the end of the Cold
War the U.S. is more vocal about its disagreements with Japanese policy. This
combined with the overuse of *gaiatsu* is contributing to the image of America
as a bully.

All nations no matter what their size or power face external pressure.
Foreign pressure is a norm in foreign policy making. Thus, Japan is not unique
in that it faces foreign pressure. Internal needs dictate what foreign pressures
will make a nation acquiesce to external stimuli. An example of this is the U.S.
during the Cold War. The U.S. often sacrificed its economic priorities for
National Security concerns. It often chose to ignore unfair economic advantages taken by allies such as Japan or simply gave into them. When this
author interviewed Ryozo Kato, the Director General of the Foreign Policy
Bureau for MOFA, he expressed the view, that seemed to speak for MOFA as
well, that Japan has always given in 100% of the time to the U.S. and would
like to have the U.S. give in sometimes in order to be fair.[29] This begs the
question: Does Japan give in to the U.S. 100% of the time? No way. During
the Cold War the U.S. permitted/let Japan build up its economy (under the
Yoshida Doctrine) at what was often American expense because the
American priority was security. With the waning and end of the Cold War the
U.S. became more permissive with Japan on security issues and more
demanding economically.

Many in Japan feel that Japan has given in to the U.S. too many times.
They look for ways to "show" Japan's independence by disagreeing with the
U.S.[30] What they ignore is that for most of the Cold War it was America that
looked the other way. Director General Kato described Japan as suffering
from "interdependent fatigue syndrome" and related it to the
Anglo/American relationship where the U.S. and Britain often have identical
foreign policies on most issues.[31] Britain however does not seem to suffer
from this "interdependent fatigue syndrom" as Japan does. Britain is confident; Japan is not. The trouble for Japan in this case is that what is good for
America is often good for Japan too.

This may be one reason why Japan is so heavily influenced by American
pressure. Another possible reason that Japan is susceptible to American pressure is that American foreign policy is largely based on *power politics* whereas Japan's foreign policy is based on *goodwill*, particularly American goodwill.
Japan needs American goodwill because of its constitutional limitations under
Article Nine. There is a need for Japan to realize that it cannot always depend

on goodwill.[32] It needs to chart its own course. However, the course that it is currently following (America's course) is a course of its own choosing.

According to Councillor Keizo Takemi the real pressure for change in Japanese foreign policy is coming from business and the younger generation.[33] The pressure is from the inside rather than the outside. The outside (America) is encouraging change, but it is the needs of business and the generational shift in power that is causing Japan to move forward with change. With this in mind we also have to remember that the main reason for almost any political action by a politician is to gain support for the next general election. If the public does not feel that it is in Japan's best interest, no amount of *gaiatsu* will ever be effective at persuading elected political leaders to take action that is against their own political interests. The concept of *gaiatsu*, at its core and the way it is used in Japan in the public arena, implies that Japan is not an independent nation. It postulates that foreign powers control its policy making apparatus or at least have a veto power. This is the "myth" of *gaiatsu*.

In arguing that *gaiatsu* is a myth, this author is not arguing that it does not exist. Rather, it is argued that external pressure exists as it does for every other nation and that Japan is no exception. Reality is that Japanese leaders make a cost benefit analysis and implement decisions on that basis. What is interesting is how *gaiatsu* is used domestically in Japan. *Gaiatsu* is an excuse or cover for a national need. A senior member of MOFA described *gaiatsu* as a politically easy out for Japanese leaders.[34] The frequent use of *gaiatsu* reflects a need by Japanese foreign policy leadership to often sell publicly unpopular choices that are in Japan's long term interests by scapegoating the U.S. for actions that could cause adverse political consequences.

Japanese elites want Japan to be a normal nation. Article Nine prevents this. *Gaiatsu* is a way of normalizing Japan without risking public displeasure over the rejection of Japan's pacifist constitution. Japanese elites are using foreign pressure to their own ends. *Gaiatsu* has permitted Japan to develop the second largest defense budget in the world. It has given Japan a modern fighting force. While many in Japan still do not accept the legitimacy of the SDF and the Defense Agency, they are a source of pride for others.

Military might is a source of pride for the peoples of many nations and Japan is no exception. When this author was living in Japan on the north island of Hokkaido a Japanese Maritime SDF vessel (Aegis class) made a port call at the city of Otaru. The ship was opened for visitors and their families to come aboard. While the tours emphasized the role of the vessel in search and rescue operations and maritime safety, the highlight of the tour for most was the weapons systems. Many questions were asked about how the systems worked and there was a clear pride in the fact that this was a Japanese warship. At an air show in Chitose a similar scenario played out in that there was noticeably greater interest in the military aircraft over the civilian aircraft.

The images and attitudes of the people were remarkably similar to similar events that the author had attended in Europe and America. There was a noticeable awe and sense of pride that Japan can protect itself. This demonstrates that the Japanese people's attitudes toward the tools/symbols of modern warfare are changing. In spite of the pacifist leanings of the majority in Japan they see the SDF as a source of pride and an example of what Japan can do. This helps Japan down the path to normalization. The clear desire, on the part of Japanese elites, to see Japan behave as a normal nation is reflected in their willingness to give in to *gaiatsu*.

WHAT IS JAPAN DOING?

Japanese security depends on the U.S./Japan Security Treaty, but given Japanese fears of abandonment Japan needs to be considering its options. As Sheldon Simon, an expert on East Asian security writes, "For Japan, security still depends primarily on the U.S.-Japan Defense Treaty, but in the post-Cold War era, Japanese leaders realize that reliance exclusively on the United States is insufficient.[35] Japan's constitutional limitations under Article Nine bridle what it can do. Its history in East Asia further constrains it. As Hendrik Spruyt writes:

> Ever since the Second World War, Japan has emphatically distinguished itself from its previous expansionist policies. Institutional and ideological constraints on the level of military spending and the prohibition on the deployment of troops abroad have made Japan a distinctly atypical great power. Such restraints have been augmented with substantial foreign aid and foreign policy declarations that aim to allay any fears of renewed Japanese might.[36]

Due to Japanese limitations Japanese foreign policy is for all intents and purposes very narrow in its primary focus: the U.N., China, the Koreas, the U.S., and more recently multilateral efforts. Japanese nationalists desire Japan to have an independent foreign policy towards all of these nations.[37] The next several sections will be an overview of what Japan is doing to foster better relations with these nations.

CHINA

China represents the most powerful threat to any possible Japanese aspirations of regional hegemony. Shin'ichi Ogawa of the National Institute for Defense Studies stated that, "(There is a need to) manage the relationship with China carefully or conflict will be inevitable."[38] China and Korea are the unnamed foci of the "areas surrounding Japan" statement in the 1997 revisions to the Japan/U.S. Security Treaty Guidelines. Neither Japan nor the U.S. wishes to see China upset the regional status quo. The key to China's containment, as seen by many in MOFA, is the U.S. being able to establish a good working relationship with China (without abandoning Japan).[39] Japan is also working itself to establish better military ties with China. Both China and Japan are attempting to upgrade a bilateral security forum between the two to the deputy ministerial level.[40]

The political problem with deterring China is that as one senior MOFA official stated, "The Socialist fear that deterrence will make peace disappear."[41] There is an attitude that peace will stay if everything is left alone. Japan prefers an interdependent relationship with China. The problem with this is there is no word in Chinese for interdependence.[42] Japan wants something from China that China has no concept of in its own language.

MULTILATERAL EFFORTS

Multilateralism in the Asia-Pacific region is still in its infancy. The problem for East Asian multilateralism is that the distances are so vast that what may be a security threat to one country may not be a concern to others in the region.[43] However as Simon writes,

> Great distances among regional actors have been reduced as factors, favoring protection by increases in navel and air power projection as well as the proliferation of missile technology. The resultant higher levels of security interdependence provide incentives for greater security cooperation.[44]

When one considers the issue of Japan and multilateralism, the question that invariably comes up is "why?" Hendrik Spruyt put it succinctly,

> > Given Japan's ability to build a reasonably strong, and modern, self-defense force, and given the US security guarantee, it is perhaps not obvious why Tokyo would choose to upgrade its multilateral commitments rather than rely on more conventional means of managing its security environment specifically through internal balancing and alliances.[45]

Given Japan's fear of abandonment that was discussed in chapter four it becomes obvious that Japan is seeking to hedge its bets because with or without the U.S. alliance it is still constrained by its limitations. Some (particularly those on the left) would say that Japan's multilateral efforts are an alternative to the bilateral relationship with the U.S., but as Professor Osamu Iishi argues, Japan needs to be developing both bilateral and multilateral relationships. He stated that the bilateral relationship with the U.S. was more important to Japan than multilateral relationships, but that multilateral relationships could not and should not be ignored by Japan.[46] Japan's economic power gives it tremendous potential for regional leadership in the creation of multilateral fora.[47]

Japan needs to cooperate with other nations if it is to achieve its primary foreign policy goal of national security.[48] There is the legitimate worry that if nations do not cooperate the result will be a loss of stability and order. Fear could lead to arms races throughout the region. As C. S. Kang argues:

> Realists worry that contemporary economic and political develop-ments in East Asia are leading to uneven rates of growth among nations, impacting differential growth power. Even liberals worry that, compared to post-cold war Europe, East Asia suffers from a "thinness" of multilateral organizations as well as democracy, institu-tions they believe mitigate the instability of multipolarity.[49]

Of the elites that were interviewed in Japan an overwhelming 83% strongly favored Japanese multilateral efforts. Only 5% opposed Japan's having a role in multilateral fora. Five percent supported Japan having only a financial role and 7% had no opinion or did not know.[50]

There seems to be almost universal support for Japanese multilateral efforts. This support crosses party lines from the right to the left. As Simon states, "Broad support for multilateralism in Japan stems from diverse expec-tations about its potential benefits."[51] For those on the conservative right in Japanese politics, they see a way for Japan to be active in collective security—something the *kenpou* has forbidden up till now. For those on the left wing of Japanese politics multilateralism provides an opportunity to free Japan from it U.S.-centered security policy. Those on the left see multilateralism as cooperative security rather than collective security.[52]

Japanese elites see multilateral participation on the part of Japan as the direction for the future. Limited by its inability to engage in collective defense, Japan is throwing itself into the next best option: multilateralism. Again Spruyt writes, "the reason why Japan will gravitate to Multilateral fora such as the UN (*and ARF*), in addition to its other policy options, resides in its (still) artificially constrained repertoire of choice."[53] Simon notes two major reasons why Japan is pursuing multilateralism in East Asia. They are:

> The first concerns the country's evolution toward a normal state with security interests independent of—though not incompatible with—its American ally.
> The second reason coincides with the concerns of most other Asian actors: how best to cope with a rising China.[54]

The problem is that Japan does not seem to be able to develop a long term multilateral policy. As Professor Akihiko Tanaka argues, ". . . Japan has yet to produce a coherent policy or strategy on regional cooperation. Part of the reasons seem to be that Japan is not sure about its long-term regional orientation especially in relation to its very close relations with the United States."[55] The problem seems to be in how Japan should adapt itself to Asian multilateralism while at the same time balancing its relations with the U.S. Again Professor Tanaka writes,

> "Since the first diplomatic bluebook published in 1957 posited three elements of Japan's foreign policy—the importance of the ties with the free world, the affinity with Asia, and the importance of the United Nations, the Japanese have been struggling to find out the appropriate priority between the ties with the U.S. and the relations with Asia."[56]

This effort is increasingly financial with over $42 billion spent by Japan to help Asia.[57] Economics continues Japan's best tool for its foreign policy. As it develops its multilateral foreign policy, Japanese investment and ODA are opening new doors for Japan. Japan is increasingly trying to create goodwill for itself through checkbook diplomacy. In spite of the setback caused by the Gulf War Japan is increasingly proud of its record of giving. In many interviews the interviewee notes that Japan's aid was greater than the U.S. and that Japan is paid up in full on its U.N. dues while the U.S. is not. Money buys a lot friends, but the real question for Japan should be does it buy security?

THE UNITED NATIONS

\As noted earlier the U.N. has long been the center of Japanese foreign policy. One foreign policy goal for Japan that was clearly expressed by Ryozo Kato, Director General of Foreign Policy Planning at MOFA, was to strengthen the U.N. and its various functions as an international governing body. Japan would like to see Security Council reform but it recognizes that whatever reform takes place it should and will be gradual.[58] While security council reform is a governmental priority it draws a surprisingly lukewarm response from the public with only 50% supporting it in a mixed way (only 14% supporting Japan's bid for a seat), while a solid 30% oppose Japan's reform agenda.[59]

Japan's efforts to make a personnel contribution through the UNPKO are growing. The PKO mission served the political purpose of selling the Japanese people on greater SDF deployment outside of Japan. As Ogawa noted, "PKO is not a military mission, it is a political mission."[60] Each successful mission strengthens future use of the SDF in more and more dangerous missions. Many in Japan would like to see Japan's contribution be enlarged to include PKF missions. While this is not likely in the near future, due to domestic politics, it is likely that Japan will expand its current contributions under the existing PKO Law. Of the elites that were interviewed, 80% supported the expansion of Japan's responsibilities under the current PKO Law.[61] The Japanese public also tends to support Japan's PKO role. In a poll sponsored by the Prime Minister's Office Japanese adults were asked, "Do you think Japan should continue participating in PKO activities, or not?" Of the respondents, 24% felt that Japan should be a more active participant while 46% felt that Japan should maintain the current level of participation. Only 19% felt that Japan should reduce participation and 4% felt that Japan should not participate. Seven percent did not know.[62] A Yomiuri Shimbun poll the following year asked, "Do you approve or disapprove of the Self-Defense Forces participating in United Nations Peace-Keeping Operations throughout the world?" A whopping 74% approved while only 17% disapproved.[63] All of this public support should be encouraging to Japan's U.N. diplomacy but as any astute politician would tell you, public opinion can be fickle and moreover can change overnight. If Japan overreaches too quickly with the SDF and if a PKO (or future PKF) mission goes badly, public support could dry up. However, public opinion may not be as fickle as it might seem at first glance. People support Japan taking on a greater role in the world; the question is what kind of role, and this question must be answered in the political arena. Most of the major political parties recognize Japan's need to do something. Japan and the SDF should be able to work *under U.N. command* on PKO and PKF missions without violating the constitution, but this is a minority view.[64]

THE UNITED STATES

It is called the most important bilateral relationship in the world. The U.S. is and will remain the true center of Japanese diplomacy. Indicative of the priority given the U.S. in Japanese politics is the fact that two of the highest posts in MOFA are the ambassadorships to the U.S. and the U.N. Japan is doing what it needs to do to keep it relationship with the U.S. strong. The September 1997 revision to the Guidelines marked a watershed event in U.S./Japan relations.

For the first time Japan is trying to legitimize and legalize what it would have probably done anyway in a crisis. As Kiichi Fujiwara of the Institute of Social Science at Tokyo University said in an interview, "The Guidelines just give legitimacy to what Japan would have done anyway. They have no effect on foreign policy."[65] But they do have an effect on the perception of Japanese foreign and security policy. Japan appears more normal. It is a nation that is sending its men and women in uniform overseas for the good of international order. The limitations placed on the SDF by the Japanese government do little to destroy the perception that Japan is doing something. The "Catch-22" of this is that if a shooting conflict erupts on a PKO mission, the withdrawal of SDF would be devastating to Japan's image especially with the nations whose troops stayed behind to fight.

The revised Guidelines are seen by some as being only in favor of the U.S. but not being a real change for Japan.[66] Reality, however is that while the U.S. gains from a more able ally because Japan has a clearer definition of its role within the alliance. The revised Guidelines have moderately strengthened Japan's role in the alliance.[67] Japan's primary motivation for revising the Guidelines was to preserve the U.S. commitment to Japan. Japan primarily wants and needs the U.S. to be engaged in the region. *Gaiatsu* played a part in selling the revisions, but Japan's leadership wanted these revisions and used American pressure to get the Guidelines past their detractors. U.S. and Japanese detractors aside, Japan can and will do all it can to keep America allied with it. As it had often done before, it disguised its desires in order to sell the changes to its public under the auspices of *gaiatsu*. Furthermore, the changes made in the Guidelines, for Japan, were made "on its own terms."[68] The problem for Japan here is that while the Guidelines give Japan more direction in its security policy, it also restricts its foreign policy options. As Muligan writes,

> Moreover, even though Japan desires more freedom of diplomatic action in the US-Japan security relationship, the guidelines may mean it ends up with considerably less. Keeping an appropriate diplomatic distance from the United States on regional issues will become more problematic in the same way that insulating Japan's strategic options will.[69]

Japan will face increasingly tougher choices than it did before the Guidelines. In a China/Taiwan crisis in which the U.S. chooses to involve itself, Japan could be faced with choosing between its ally and its pacifism.[70]

When one looks at public opinion in general, there is strong support for a continued American role in Japanese security. In a national survey by the *Nihon Keizai Shimbun* 70% of the Japanese electorate think that the current level of U.S. support for Japan's national defense is fine. Twenty-seven percent thought that it should be increased.[71] In the same poll a surprisingly large plurality felt that Japan's laws should be changed to back the U.S. in a conflict in the Far East.[72] Sixty-three percent of Japanese felt that the U.S./Japan Security Treaty is useful in providing the Asia-Pacific Region with security.[73]

THE KOREAS

"The areas surrounding Japan" that are mentioned in the Guidelines probably include, but do not specifically name the Korean Peninsula. Before and particularly since the North Koreans sent a missile over Japan, the Japanese government has increasingly been focusing on improving relations with

South Korea and studying how it should deal with North Korea.[74] The North Korean threat has served as a unifying factor for Japan, South Korea and the U.S. The three countries warned and worked jointly to persuade North Korea to halt future missile tests.[75]

Japan's apology to South Korea has gone a long way to healing government to government relations. The two nations are cooperating more closely with each other. They are conducting joint naval exercises together and are working to solve their territorial disputes peaceably.

The North Korean situation is causing Japan to rethink it definition of self-defense. Japan is now considering the idea that it can be considered self-defense to destroy missile sites in foreign countries if they threaten Japan. To this end the Japanese government has submitted bills to the Diet requesting funding for refueling aircraft in order to permit Japanese strike aircraft to destroy targets in Korea and elsewhere if needed. Furthermore, Japan is already sending air crews to the U.S. for training on mid air refueling. This marks a dramatic change in Japanese defense policy. For the first time the SDF will have power projection capability. This is a long way from the SDF that once believed that possessing jet fighters was unconstitutional.[76]

CONCLUSION

In conclusion it is important to note what Japan is not prepared to do in its foreign policy. Japan, like many nations, is not prepared to take on primary responsibility for the maintenance of world order.[77] The principal reason is constitutional limitations, but secondly there is a strong feeling among Japanese elites that Japan can not or will not take on the costs of maintaining world order by itself. Seventy-eight percent of those interviewed felt that Japan could not pay the price to be a true leader or would be willing but that it could not pay the price of world leadership. No one felt that Japan was able to be a true world leader and 22% felt that they did not know whether Japan was able or not. Most however expressed the idea that Japan would be willing if it was able.[78] Polls of the Japanese public indicate the same thing. When asked during an *Asahi Shimbun* survey, "If Japan was asked to cooperate in solving international conflicts, do you think it would be able to play its role adequately under the current constitution?" Only 24% felt Japan would do an adequate job. Sixty percent felt that Japan would do an inadequate job.[79] Part of this is the fact that economics can not be separated from defense and foreign policy.[80] Japan's economic recession of the last 10 years leaves it in a weak position to take up world leadership. It much prefers to follow U.S. leadership. Another reason that might be causing Japan to feel inadequate is that 67% of Japanese voters feel that Japan is not respected by other countries.[81] Fifty-three percent feel that raising the level of its foreign diplomacy is the best way to increase respect for Japan.[82]

It appears that in spite of right wing rhetoric to the contrary, Japan is not pursuing global leadership. It has too much to lose if it does. There also seems to be a realization that Japan is limited in what it can do by itself. In concert with other great powers Japan can do much but alone it sees its own weaknesses and is not willing to risk its position in the world in pursuit of greater power.

One thing that is clear for Japan is that its people do not want war again. The peoples of most nations would express the same sentiments but in Japan it can be said that the aversion to war is stronger than most national interests that force could be used to protect.[83] Professor Fujiwara stated that, "Japan is addicted to pacifism like an alcoholic is to alcohol."[84]

On the other hand Japan wants the respect of its fellow nations. As Professor Akihiko Tanaka of Tokyo University's Institute of Oriental Culture stated, "Japan felt it was a loser in the Gulf War and it wants to avoid the same situation in the future."[85] The problem is that Japan is better at reacting than acting. Toshiya Hoshino of the Osaka School of International Policy, Osaka University noted that, "It is harder to be active than reactive."[86] As Professor Ogawa asserted, "Japan has been a reactive state since the 19th century."[87] What Japan seems to be lacking is firm goals and policies for the actions it takes. Professor Hoshino feels that, "Japan is not good at the 'vision thing'."[88] Professor Tanaka confirmed this when he contended that,"Japan has no real long term goals. It is a status-quo power in realist terms."[89]

Japan still needs to further mature politically. Japan still operates under too many constraints to be a "normal state". If Japan wants normalization in the eyes of its own people, the concept of *Gaiatsu* must be abandoned. Japan must stand independent and take credit for its own actions for better or worse. If Japan is sovereign, then *gaiatsu* is irrelevant. Is Japan a sovereign nation? Of course. Japan then needs to stop complaining and start playing the game. This must even be done when siding with the U.S. Professor Tanaka stated that, "Japan prefers to be bashed rather than passed."[90] Japan needs to have strong priorities if it wants to avoid being passed over. It must formulate its own direction and priorities for its foreign policy. Professor Kubata, formally of the *Asahi Shimbun*, already has one, "It should be a foreign policy priority to find more friends in Asia."[91] Whether this priority or another Japan must make its own choices.

NOTES

[1] As cited by Robert Markman, *A Whole Lot of Bull $*#%!, Worth*, February 2000, 118.
[2] Chalmers Johnson would be an example of a person who feels this way outside Japan and the Communists (JCP) and the conservative far right of Japanese politics would be examples of those who oppose the U.S. presence on grounds that it violates/undermines Japanese sovereignty.

[3] One of the strengths of U.S. hegemony is that so many other nations have a interest in seeing it continue. Japan is not alone in preferring U.S. hegemony to an unknown alternative.

[4] This realization that a new interpretation of the constitution was indeed needed was confirmed by Vice Foreign Minister Shunji Yanai and Former Foreign Minister Yukihiko Ikeda during this author's interviews with them. For more on the origins of the PKO Law and the political origins of the law please see Shunji Yanai, *Law Concerning Cooperation for United Nations Peace-Keeping Operations and Other Operations: the Japanese PKO Experience*, The Japanese Journal of International Law, 36 (Tokyo: The International Law Association of Japan, 1993): 33–75. Shunji Yanai, Vice Minister Japanese Ministry of Foreign Affairs, interview by author, 20 May 1998, Tokyo, tape recording, in author's personal possession Tempe, Arizona. Yukihiko Ikeda, Member of the House of Representatives of the Japanese Diet and former Foreign Minister. Interview by the author, 16 June 1998, Tokyo, tape recording, in author's personal possession, Tempe, Arizona.

[5] Interview with a lower house Diet member who asked that his comments not be attributed or quoted directly with his name attached. Interview by author, during May-June 1998, Tokyo, tape recording, in author's personal possession Tempe, Arizona.

[6] Interview with a senior government official who requested that the entire interview be off the record. Interview by author, during May-June 1998, Tokyo, tape recording, in author's personal possession Tempe, Arizona.

[7] Councillor Kei Hata is an example of this in her spearheading the Diet drive to bring Japan into the information revolution. Her paper, *Urgent Recommendation Regarding Information Infrastructure Strategy*, sets out what the goals of Japan should be in technology. Kei Hata, Member of the House of Councillors of the Japanese Diet (LDP), interview by the author, 18 May 1998, Tokyo, tape recording, in author's personal possession, Tempe, Arizona and Kei Hata, *Urgent Recommendation Regarding Information Infrastructure Strategy*. Paper presented to Prime Minister Hashimoto, 8 December 1997 (English version, April 1998). Downloaded from: <http://www.k-hata.or.jp/itproe>.

[8] Field Research interviews conducted May-June 1998 in Japan. Question number six or seven depending on the questionnaire.

[9] Hideo Usui, member of the House of Representatives of the Japanese Diet and former Defense Minister and Vice Defense Agency Minister (Career ministry appointment), interview by the author, 26 and 29 May 1998, Tokyo, tape recording, in author's personal possession, Tempe, Arizona.

[10] Ichiro Yamamoto, member of the House of Councillors of the Japanese Diet, interview by the author, 18 June 1998, Tokyo, tape recording, in author's personal possession, Tempe, Arizona.

[11] This is not to say that the public is not aware of foreign policy issues. They are just not motivated to vote by them. In a 1994 *Asahi Shimbun* poll asking, "How closely would you say you follow news about world affairs and foreign policy issues?", 75% of the respondents said "very closely" or "somewhat closely". *Asahi Shimbun* survey of 1,192 national adults. Conducted 5–6 March 1994 by personal interview. Source: JPOLL, Roper Center for Public Opinion Research, University

of Connecticut. (For required full disclaimer please see the Bibliography at the end of this book.) <http://roper1.ropercenter.uconn.edu>.

[12] Michael W. Chinworth, ed. *Inside Japan's Defense: Technology, Economics Strategy*, (Washington: Brassey's (US), Inc., 1992), 9.

[13] Ibid.

[14] Reinhard Drifte, *Japan's Foreign Policy for the 21st Century: From Economic Superpower to What Power?*, (Oxford: St. Antony's Press, 1998), 1–14.

[15] Ibid., 3.

[16] For a complete analysis of this see Auer's complete article. James E. Auer, *Article Nine of Japan's Constitution: from Renunciation of Armed Force "Forever" to the Third Largest Defense Budget in the World, Law and Contemporary Problems*, Spring 1990: 171–187

[17] *Yomiuri Shimbun* survey of 1,952 national voters. Conducted 25–26 October 1997 by personal interview. Source: JPOLL, Roper Center for Public Opinion Research, University of Connecticut. (For required full disclaimer please see the Bibliography at the end of this book.) <http://roper1.ropercenter.uconn.edu>.

[18] Prime Minister's Office survey of 2,114 national voters. Conducted 6–16 February 1997 by personal interview. Source: JPOLL, Roper Center for Public Opinion Research, University of Connecticut. (For required full disclaimer please see the Bibliography at the end of this book.) <http://roper1.ropercenter.uconn.edu>.

[19] One reason that so many Japanese did not mention *gaiatsu* in the interviews is that they may have been embarrassed to do so. *Gaiatsu* implies a lack of sovereignty and many Japanese could be embarrassed to tell a foreigner that foreign pressure is a major part of foreign policy formation in Japan. Mitsuo Higashinaka, member of the House of Representatives of the Japanese Diet (JCP), interview by the author, 19 May 1998, Tokyo, tape recording, in author's personal possession, Tempe, Arizona and an academic researcher who asked that all his comments be off the record.

[20] For example Leonard J. Schoppa, *Two level games and bargaining outcomes: why 'gaiatsu' succeeds in Japan in some cases but not in others, International Organization*, 47, 3, Summer 1993, 353–386.

[21] Robert Putnam, *Diplomacy and domestic politics: the logic of two-level games, International Organization*, 42, 3, Summer 1988, 429.

[22] Ibid.

[23] Ibid., 427–460.

[24] Ibid., 429.

[25] The PKO Law is just an illustration of how this form of gaiatsu might be applied, but evidence (from field interview questions) indicates that this seems to be the way it happened.

[26] Yanai interview.

[27] Putnam, 429.

[28] This is the author's own definition of sovereignty based on his study of the literature over the years.

[29] Ryozo Kato, Director General, Foreign Policy Bureau of the Japanese Ministry of Foreign Affairs, interview by author, 21 May 1998, Tokyo, tape recording, in author's personal possession Tempe, Arizona.

[30] Witness the Spring 1999 Tokyo governor's race and the accusations by candidate Shintaro Ishihara. *New York Times*, 26 March 1999, A12.

[31] Kato interview.

[32] Colonel Yoshihisa Nakamura, Professor at the National Institute for Defense Studies, Japan Defense Agency, interview by the author, 28 May 1998, Tokyo, tape recording, in author's personal possession, Tempe, Arizona.

[33] Keizo Takemi, Member of the House of Councillors of the Japanese Diet, current Cabinet Vice Foreign Minister and past House of Councillors Chair of Foreign Relations Committee and founding chair of the subcommittee on Pacific Affairs. Interview by the author, 25 May 1998, Tokyo, tape recording, in author's personal possession, Tempe, Arizona.

[34] Jiro Kodera, Director First International Economic Affairs Division of the Japanese Ministry of Foreign Affairs, interview by author, 20 May 1998, Tokyo, tape recording, in author's personal possession Tempe, Arizona.

[35] Sheldon W. Simon, *Multilateralism and Japan's Security Policy*, The Korean Journal of Defense Analysis, Vol. XI, No. 2, (Winter 1999): 79.

[36] Hendrik Spruyt, *A New Architecture for Peace?: Reconfiguring Japan Among the Great Powers*, The Pacific Review, Vol. 11 No. 3 1998: 367.

[37] Jiro Kodera, Director First International Economic Affairs Division of the Japanese Ministry of Foreign Affairs, interview by author, 20 May 1998, Tokyo, tape recording, in author's personal possession Tempe, Arizona.

[38] Shin'ichi Ogawa, Professor, National Institute for Defense Studies, interview by author, 11 June 1998, Tokyo, tape recording, in author's personal possession Tempe, Arizona.

[39] Kodera interview.

[40] Hisane Masaki, *Japan, China consider upgrading security forum*, The Japan Times, internet edition, 14 September 1999. <http://www.japantimes.co.jp/news/news 9– 99/news.html>.

[41] Off the record comment by a senior official in MOFA.

[42] Kato interview.

[43] Simon, (Winter 1999): 80.

[44] Ibid.

[45] Spruyt, 370.

[46] Osamu Iishi, professor Institute of Oriental Culture, Tokyo University, interview by author, 29 May 1998, Tokyo, tape recording, in author's personal possession Tempe, Arizona.

[47] Simon, (Winter 1999): 80.

[48] Hideo Usui, member of the House of Representatives of the Japanese Diet and former Defense Minister and Vice Defense Agency Minister (Career ministry appointment), interview by the author, 26 and 29 May 1998, Tokyo, tape recording, in author's personal possession, Tempe, Arizona.

[49] C. S. Kang, *Korea and Japanese Security*, International Journal of Korean Studies, (vol. III, no. 1, Spring/Summer 1999): 101.

[50] Field research interviews conducted in Japan May-June 1998. (N=41)

[51] Simon, (Winter 1999): 82.

[52] Ibid.

[53] Spruyt, 371. (*and ARF*) added.

54 Simon, (Winter 1999): 94.
55 Akihiko Tanaka, *Japan and Regional Integration in Asia-Pacific*, a paper presented at the 40th Annual Conference of the International Studies Association, Washington, D.C. February 17, 1999, 11.
56 Ibid., 11–12.
57 Yanai interview.
58 Kato interview.
59 *Yomiuri Shimbun* survey of 2,030 national voters. Conducted 18–19 January 1997 by personal interview. Source: JPOLL, Roper Center for Public Opinion Research, University of Connecticut. (For required full disclaimer please see the Bibliography at the end of this book.) <http://roper1.ropercenter.uconn.edu>.
60 Ogawa interview.
61 Field research interviews. When asked about whether or not they would like to see the current PKO Law expanded 80% said "yes", 20% said "no". (N=35)
62 Prime Minister's Office survey of 2,015 national adults. Conducted 3–13 October 1996 by personal interview. Source: JPOLL, Roper Center for Public Opinion Research, University of Connecticut. (For required full disclaimer please see the Bibliography at the end of this book.) <http://roper1.ropercenter.uconn.edu>.
63 Yomiuri Shimbun survey of 2,031 national voters. Conducted 30–31 August 1997 by personal interview. Source: JPOLL, Roper Center for Public Opinion Research, University of Connecticut. (For required full disclaimer please see the Bibliography at the end of this book.) <http://roper1.ropercenter.uconn.edu>.
64 Kenjiro Monji, Cabinet Councillor, Cabinet Councillor's Office on External Affairs, Cabinet Secretariate, Prime Minister's Office, interview by author, 11 June 1998, Tokyo, tape recording, in author's personal possession Tempe, Arizona.
65 Kiichi Fujiwara, Professor, Institute of Social Science, Tokyo University, interview by author, 11 June 1998, Tokyo, tape recording, in author's personal possession Tempe, Arizona.
66 Jiro Kodera, Director First International Economic Affairs Division of the Japanese Ministry of Foreign Affairs, interview by author, 20 May 1998, Tokyo, tape recording, in author's personal possession Tempe, Arizona.
67 Aurelia George Mulgan, *Strategic Update - Japan*, School of Politics, University of New South Wales, Australian Defence Force Academy, conference paper, 1999, p.10.
68 Ibid., 9.
69 Ibid., 15.
70 This may be the very position that some Japanese leaders would like Japan to be in order to force the Japanese public to give up its pacifism.
71 *Nihon Keizai Shimbun* survey of 1,776 national voters. Conducted 19–21 April 1996 by telephone. Source: JPOLL, Roper Center for Public Opinion Research, University of Connecticut. (For required full disclaimer please see the Bibliography at the end of this book.) <http://roper1.ropercenter.uconn.edu>.
72 Ibid.
73 *Asahi Shimbun* survey of 2,307 national voters. Conducted 16–17 September 1996 by personal interview. Source: JPOLL, Roper Center for Public Opinion Research, University of Connecticut. (For required full disclaimer please see the Bibliography at the end of this book.) <http://roper1.ropercenter.uconn.edu>.

[74] *Asahi News, North Korea focus of defense white paper*, internet edition, 27 July 1999. <http://www.asahi.com/english/enews.enews.html>.

[75] Miyuki Hokugo, *Japan, S. Korea, U.S. warn N. Korea against missile test, Asahi News*, internet edition, 27 July 1999. <Http://www.asahi.com/english/enews.enews.html>.

[76] Please see chapter two for more on the evolution of the SDF.

[77] Former Defense Minister Hideo Usui made this abundantly clear. Japan is willing to help. But its role should be one of support rather than leadership. Hideo Usui, member of the House of Representatives of the Japanese Diet and former Defense Minister and Vice Defense Agency Minister (Career ministry appointment), interview by the author, 26 and 29 May 1998, Tokyo, tape recording, in author's personal possession, Tempe, Arizona.

[78] During field research in May-June 1998 Japanese 56 elites were asked, "Countries that are seen as world leaders are seen as willing to bear the costs of world order. (For example the U.S. keeping forces in East Asia and Europe.) Is Japan prepared to undertake a world leadership role and what cost would it be willing to pay in order to take on that role? (Or to put it another way is Japan willing to sacrifice for the good of the world?) The answers were coded by the author into three categories: Can, Can not/only under U.S. leadership, and Don't Know.

[79] *Asahi Shimbun* survey of 2,251 national voters. Conducted 20–21 April 1997 by personal interview. Source: JPOLL, Roper Center for Public Opinion Research, University of Connecticut. (For required full disclaimer please see the Bibliography at the end of this book.) <http://roper1.ropercenter.uconn.edu>.

[80] Interview with Hideo Usui.

[81] *Nihon Keizai Shimbun* survey of 1,725 national voters. Conducted 15–17 December 1995 by telephone interview. Source: JPOLL, Roper Center for Public Opinion Research, University of Connecticut. (For required full disclaimer please see the Bibliography at the end of this book.) <http://roper1.ropercenter.uconn.edu>.

[82] Ibid.

[83] Repeatedly during the field research interviews, the interviewees expressed concern over the foreign policy "problem" of the Japanese people's aversion to war and military conflict. Japanese pacifism is strong and represents a problem for policy makers when considering the entire scope of foreign policy options.

[84] Fujiwara interview.

[85] Akihiko Tanaka, Professor, Institute of Oriental Culture, Tokyo University, interview by author, 16 June 1998, Tokyo, tape recording, in author's personal possession Tempe, Arizona.

[86] Toshiya Hoshino, Professor, Osaka School of International Policy, Osaka University, interview by author, 10 June 1998, Tokyo, tape recording, in author's personal possession Tempe, Arizona.

[87] Ogawa interview.

[88] Hoshino interview.

[89] Tanaka Interview.

[90] The terms *Japan Passing* and *Japan Bashing* sound almost the same in Japanese and are sometimes used together as a pun.

[91] Seiichi Kubota, Professor, Faculty of Modern Culture, Tokyo Junshin Women's College (former Journalist with the Asahi Shimbun) interview by the author, 1

June 1998, Tokyo, tape recording, in author's personal possession Tempe, Arizona.

WHERE IS JAPAN GOING?

Japan is an example of a nation working very hard not to be a great power. —Kenneth Waltz[1]

The post Cold War world of *Pax Americana* has experienced wars and uprisings on all fronts. For Japan, the simple world it knew during the Cold War became complex. Choices for Japan are no longer clear. Decisions are difficult. This final chapter of the book will look at the sources of Japanese foreign policy including the growing role of the Diet in future foreign policy making. It will also examine the prospect of Japanese hegemony and possible world leadership. The role of the SDF in Japanese foreign policy will also be examined and recommendations will be made for the continued normalization of Japanese foreign policy. Finally the book will conclude by revisiting Hermann's model and the theoretical foundations of this book. The Chapter will conclude with an assessment of future research needs.

FUTURE SOURCES OF FOREIGN POLICY

Most previous studies of Japan have looked at the Prime Minister's office or MOFA as the primary sources of Japanese foreign policy. This book, while not denying the great and continuing influence of these two entities, sees change in the wind. In Japan there seems to be a growing influence of the Diet on foreign policy at the expense of MOFA' s power. In the future the Prime Minister's office will more likely be providing leadership and the Diet providing direction with MOFA reduced to more of a moderating role as well as implementation of foreign policy more than the making of it. The reason for this change comes from the changes within the Diet which give it greater voice.

At the same time MOFA is losing its influence because of stagnation within MOFA. The decline of MOFA's power can be seen in the effort to raise the JDA to ministry status. With the JDA as a full and legitimate ministry MOFA will no long hold a monopoly on the bureaucratic side of foreign and security policy. Another reason for the decline of MOFA's power is its bureaucratic rigidity. While serious thinking occurs in the ministry, it seems to suffer from a group mind set. Very little dissenting opinion from the official ministry line was found in the interviews. Open policy debate is frowned upon within the organization. Original thinking and genuine policy debate seem to be suppressed from the top down. Mid level bureaucrats within the ministry are not used to their full potential. MOFA does not normally tolerate dissent from ministry policy. Senior level bureaucrats seem to be the only ones who have the freedom to speak out and debate issues.[2]

THE DIET

Overall there seems to be an effort to decentralize political systems within Japan to bring more power into the Diet and away from the bureaucracies. The bureaucracies in Japan will no doubt resist this but given that the *kenpou* legally places policy making power in the Diet there is little the bureaucrats can do if the Diet choses to exercise its prerogative. Foreign policy will be no exception to this decentralization of the policy making apparatus. MOFA will still wield tremendous influence but the direction of foreign policy will be governed more generally by politics rather than foreign policy elites. Japan's foreign policy under Diet control will be less stable and predictable, but it will be more democratic and reflective of the nation as a whole.

Traditionally the Diet has not intervened in foreign policy making. The reason for this is that foreign policy does not get Diet members elected. This is changing according to Upper House member Ichiro Yamamoto, "People are becoming more aware of foreign policy."[3] Japanese politicians have traditionally been fearful of public reaction and constitutional limits, but public opinion is changing. As Japanese foreign policy becomes more high profile people are paying more attention to it. There is a growing awareness of how the world is interlinked and that national interests can not be secured only from domestic sources.

There is also a growing popular pride in Japanese contributions to the international community. As one Diet member proudly commented, "(Japanese) ODA (Official Development Assistance) is the pillar of Japanese foreign policy and Japan is number one in the world."[4] The support of the Japanese public for ongoing SDF participation in PKO missions is further evidence of what Councilor Yamamoto is arguing. Yamamoto disclosed further that the upper house of the Diet is taking particular interest in ODA and has formed a sub-committee on ODA because ODA is Japan's "most important (foreign policy) card."[5] Kuniko Nakajima, former MOFA official and now a researcher with the Okazaki Institute, concurs with Yamamoto's opinion that there is a shift in public opinion toward foreign policy. She feels that the Gulf War marked a turning point for Japanese foreign policy and that the PKO Law and the support of the Japanese people for PKO missions was a sign that attitudes are changing with respect to Japan's responsibility for sending its own personnel on international peace missions.[6] Nakajima and Yamamoto's opinions are supported by polling data. It seems that attitudes toward the SDF being sent overseas seem to be changing. The Japanese public now supports what would have been unthinkable before 1990: sending the SDF overseas to handle natural disasters (**Note:** This would be independent of U.N. missions[7]).

In a poll commissioned by the Prime Minister's Office, 78% of Japanese "agreed" or "somewhat agreed" with the "idea of sending the Self-Defense Forces overseas to handle natural disasters in foreign countries." Only 12% "disagreed" or "somewhat disagreed" with the idea.[8] The Japanese public has also warmed to the idea of SDF participation in exchange programs that are part of multilateral confidence building measures. In the same survey by the Prime Minister's Office, 67% "approved" or "somewhat approved" of the SDF participation in exchange programs. Only 7% disapproved in any way.[9] Earlier in this book it was said that some nations live by the sword and perish by the sword. In Japan's case, since World War II it has lived by the dove and now it seems to be choosing not to let its role in the world be limited by a self-imposed pacifism. Rather, it is taking up a military role for the SDF in the name of international peace and stability and risking the consequences of such a role.

Japan in the future is less likely to behave in a highly risk-averse way if the Diet exerts some control over the reins of foreign policy. Ideologues who do not let their ideology stop at the water's edge may be a new element in Japan's foreign policy. Japanese foreign policy will likely contain a broader array of interests than it currently does.

Some would say that the Japanese people have no power over Japanese foreign policy.[10] But in many ways they have the ultimate power over Japanese foreign policy in the sense that they must approve any changes to the *kenpou* and Article Nine. Article Nine controls Japanese foreign policy through its ability to limit Japanese military efforts. The constitution gives the people the ultimate right to amend the constitution. Article Ninety-six of the constitution describes how the constitutional amendment process works. It reads as follows:

> Amendments to this Constitution shall be initiated by the Diet, through a concurring vote of two-thirds or more of all the members of each House and shall thereupon be submitted to the people for ratification, which shall require the affirmative vote of the majority of

all votes cast thereon, at a special referendum or at such election as the Diet shall specify.[11]

The final power over foreign policy is in the hands of the people. There will be no changes to the constitution without the people's consent.

THE SDF IN JAPANESE FOREIGN POLICY

With the passage of the PKO Law the SDF for the first time became an official part of Japanese foreign policy. Japan now has the ability to make a human contribution to international order and stability. Japanese foreign policy can be more than just "checkbook" diplomacy. As mentioned earlier the SDF is becoming a source of pride for the Japanese people, but it is also a worry for Japan's neighbors because of Japan's history in the region. Initial Japanese PKO missions met with harsh criticism within the region. Nonetheless, the peaceful nature of the PKO missions which Japan has participated in have muted most of the most vocal opponents such as China.

Another aspect of the growing influence of the SDF is its expanding capabilities which are mostly directed at North Korea. If Japan continues to modernize and upgrade the SDF's capabilities, it might provoke or give North Korea an excuse to continue/resume missile testing. This can be a proverbial "Catch-22" for Japan. If it fails to develop adequate defenses to prepare for a missile attack or deter a possible attack it may find itself in an unthinkable position. It could find its cities and population vulnerable to attack and its foreign policy subject to blackmail. On the other hand, if it does develop a missile defense system, it may invite the very kind of threat that it seeks to avoid.

Under the revised Guidelines the SDF has a much clearer mission than before while at the same time strengthening the U.S./Japan Security Treaty which had been under attack as having lost its significance in the post-Cold War world. The greatest current threat to the continuation of the U.S./ Japan Security Treaty is if the North Korean threat would disappear. Without the threat of North Korea the only true remaining threat to Japan is China and currently it is a political impossibility for either nation to name China as the reason for the treaty's existence.

There is one major problem if the U.S./Japan Security Treaty is ever abandoned. Japan loses its nuclear umbrella. As Professor Masashi Nishihara of the National Defense Academy said, "If there is no alliance (with the U.S.) then Japan must consider the nuclear option if there is a threat that justifies it."[12] The loss of the U.S. alliance would push Japan down a dangerous road that may give strength and credibility to nationalist/militaristic elements in Japanese society which would likely cause further alarm to Japan's neighbors.

The role of the SDF in Japanese foreign policy is likely to grow. There is a role for the SDF to balance Chinese power and possibly Russia and India in the future. There is also a need to initiate confidence building measures in

East Asia to ensure the peace and stability of the region.[13] But first a new legal foundation for the SDF to take on this increased role must be laid.[14] Geoffrey Smith reported in the *Washington Times* that:

> ". . . US experts said that Japan appears ready to assume a greater defense role to promote stability in East Asia. Joseph Nye, dean of the Kennedy School of Government at Harvard University, said that trends over the past 10 years that show Japan to be increasing its security role in the world are expected to continue and probably even accelerate in the years ahead. Nye said at a conference on US-Japan relations at the Center for Strategic and International Studies (CSIS) last week that "Japan is doing drastically more in the world than it was 10 years ago." Defense Attache Major General Noboru Yamaguchi said in a speech last week at Johns Hopkins University's School for Advanced International Studies that "new types" of threats have appeared in the region. Yamaguchi specifically cited the August 1998 DPRK launch of a Taepodong missile and increased tensions over Taiwan. Yamaguchi said, "Japanese sea lines go through and around Taiwan, so Japan also is going to lose [if there is a war]. My personal feeling is that if something happens over the Taiwan Strait, everyone is going to lose." William Breer, who holds the Japan chair for CSIS, said that the US seems mixed in its reaction to Japan's efforts to build a stronger military. Breer said, "I think most thinking Americans would say that if [a stronger Japanese military] happens through Japan's revisional process, then it's OK." Breer said that efforts were under way to amend the constitution in Japan "to bring the constitution in line with the current reality" but not to "remilitarization a la the 1930s."[15]

The U.S. clearly has no problem with Japan's rearming and trusts it to do so. The problem is that Japan must deal with this issue domestically as well as internationally in order to find a larger role for the SDF.

Japan must also modernize its laws for dealing with the SDF. The lack of laws governing crisis/emergency situations is a critical problem for the SDF. Japanese tanks are currently required to stop at traffic lights in a battle situation. This represents a silly but consistent oversight in the development of law concerning the actions that may or may not be taken by the SDF within Japan.

CONSTITUTIONAL REFORM

As mentioned earlier Article Ninety-six gives the power to amend the *kenpou* to the people. Most of those interviewed from the LDP supported the first paragraph of Article Nine which states: *Aspiring sincerely to an international peace based on justice and order, the Japanese people forever renounce war as a sovereign right of the nation and the threat or use of force as a means of settling international disputes.*[16] It is the second paragraph that many conservatives in Japan find inconsistent with Japan's status as a leader in the world. It states: *In order to accomplish the aim of the preceding paragraph, land, sea, and air forces, as well as other war potential, will never be maintained. The right of belligerency of the state will not be recognized.*[17] This paragraph is in reality inconsistent with the existence of the SDF. Many in the Japanese Diet feel (68% of those interviewed) that the rewording or revision of this second paragraph would go a long way to establishing Japan as a normal nation. The problem is that it may only be politically possible to change this part of the *kenpou* if the constitution undergoes a total rewrite in the context of a constitutional convention. Of those in government interviewed during the field research phase of this book, 62% favored revising/deleting all or part of Article Nine. Thirty-six percent felt that Article Nine should be left alone, and 2% had no opinion.[18] By way of contrast those outside of government favored keeping Article Nine as is, 56%-44%.[19] Overall, Japanese elites favored revising Article Nine in some way 58%-40% with 2% having no opinion.[20]

It is very important to keep in mind that the enduring legacy of the efforts of MacArthur's staff in writing the *kenpou* is that Japan is a democracy with power resting in the hands of the people. Any constitutional changes will have to be the *will* of the Japanese people. Changes in the *kenpou* will be governed by the people's will not the desires of the politicians according to one senior MOFA official.[21] Public attitudes will govern how far Japan can go in its interpretation of the constitution and whether any changes can or will ever be made. Fifty percent of those who favored revising the *kenpou* were very pessimistic that it would happen in the near future.[22]

Those who support Article Nine believe that Japan's leadership can come from its peaceful relations with the world through the example of its "Peace Constitution". Mitsuo Higashinaka of the JCP argued that Japan should be encouraging other nations to renounce war.[23] The public in general seems to reflect this same opinion. In a poll conducted by the *Asahi Shimbun* in April 1997, Japanese voters were asked, "Do you think the renunciation of war (article) in the Constitution will help attain world peace in the future, or not?" Seventy-three percent of those responding felt that it "will help".[24]

Despite the efforts by the LDP and other conservatives in Japan to jump start a constitutional revision process, these attempts are not likely to be successful. The same pacifist attitudes that MacArthur and his staff tapped into during the occupation are still strong today. Some would say that Japan needs Article Nine. Japan has the second largest defense budget in the world. Article Nine keeps Japan in check by placing moral pressure on it.[25] The current interpretation of Article Nine may make it look like a worthless scrap of paper, but it does make Japan think about its actions and it gives those actions principles to guide them. However as Professor Jun Morikawa said in an interview, "When Japanese say they have principles, there are always exceptions."[26]

WORLD LEADERSHIP

Japan is not ready to become a global leader. According to Kenjiro Monji of the Cabinet office of the Prime Minister, "(Japan) couldn't send people when most needed (the Persian Gulf War). Economic strength is not enough to be respected. Some power is needed to have some 'teeth'."[27] According to one senior Japanese official, "Japan needs to be prepared to spill (its own) blood."[28] These are the lessons that Japan learned from the Gulf War and hence the push for passage of the PKO Law and the search for new ways to use the SDF. There is also the fear (unjustified) that if Japan takes on a more active role in the world this will result in militarism on the part of Japan.[29] Until Japan deals with its history, this issue will continue to haunt Japan.

One of the major problems with Japan being a world leader is that the country has become more inward looking as its economy struggles to recover from a decade-long recession. Japan has lost its confidence. Its people do not see Japan as a world power and furthermore they do not see Japan in a world crisis which would require Tokyo's leadership.[30] As one senior MOFA official, put it, "There is a general feeling that Japan should be like (the) U.S., but I disagree. Japan should play (the) foreign policy (game) based on its abilities (not on its aspirations)."[31] The idea being that capable nations work from their strengths. This official went on to say that, "Japan's military contribution could never be more than a minor one."[32] Japan's people will need a very good reason to make a major contribution to a multinational military effort. The Japanese people do not seem to be eager to play a major military role. The legacy of the disaster of World War II lives on in this sense. According to this MOFA official the majority of Japanese do not believe in the PKO solution because they see it as non-essential for Japan. However, they do see it as a significant and acceptable contribution for Japan to make even if they feel that it is unnecessary for Japan.[33] In this sense the Japanese public is becoming more acceptant of Japan's responsibilities in the world, but with reservations or limits on these responsibilities.

According to Ryozo Kato the director General of Foreign Policy Planning at MOFA, Japan's unwillingness to take risks is a risk in and of itself.[34] Japan risks world condemnation for its inaction and the possibility of being ignored and passed by by the rest of the world if it fails to take leadership where genuine risk is involved.

Japan must cooperate with nations other than the United States if it is to achieve its primary foreign policy goal of national security.[35] The problem is Japanese pacifism. The Japanese people hold Japan's pacifism as an example for other nations. They do not want to give up Article Nine.[36] This faith in pacifism represents a great stumbling block for Japan in its quest to make itself a normal nation. Hideo Usui stated that Japan needs to "...remove the barriers..." to making "...Japan an ordinary nation as soon as possible."[37] Article Nine represents a fundamental barrier that may be insurmountable in the near term. The revision or removal of Article Nine from the constitution is not likely to happen without a crisis to motivate the Japanese people to change attitudes. The Japanese people do not want to talk about the possibility of Japan being attacked. They see Japan as a nation with no enemy and ask, "So why would any nation attack Japan?"[38] The Japanese leadership tends to take a very realist view of the world while the Japanese people take an idealist view of the world. This is the frustration of Japanese policy makers.

JAPAN'S LIMITATIONS

As stated before the primary obsticle to the normalization of Japan's foreign policy is Article Nine. As noted earlier the quest to revise the *kenpou* is in the hands of the people. As one senior MOFA official said, ". . . the behavior of the Japanese people is not limited by the constitution, but by the people's feelings (towards the constitution).[39] Japan needs to play the foreign policy game based on its limitations and it abilities rather than its potential.[40] According to Diet member Shigeru Ishiba, "Unless Article Nine is changed Japan can not be a leader in the world."[41]

According to Professor Ogawa Akira of the Okazaki Research Institute in Tokyo, the greatest failure of the present generation of leadership in the Diet is the fact that they have not trained the next generation to lead Japan.[42] The political leadership of Japan is heavy with old men who will not step aside and let a new generation take control. Neither is this older generation grooming the next generation to succeed them. This will hurt Japanese world leadership potential in the future as the current younger generation, which is biding its time till it can seize the reins of power, will not be prepared for leadership in the international arena.

JAPANESE HEGEMONY?

There is a general feeling among the foreign policy elite in Japan that Japan needs the U.S. Japan will not be a hegemon if it is dependent on the U.S. Thus it can be safely said that Japan has no hegemonic aspirations for the next 5–10 years.[43] It does however, want to be like Britain and France, playing a major support role. Given this desire to have a significant support role and the limitations placed on Japan by Article Nine, the U.N. is likely to be the focus of Japan's non-U.S. foreign policy in the future. Japanese leaders want to feel the pride again of being a major international player, while at the same time clinging to pacifism. This schizophrenia is reflected in public attitudes toward Japanese foreign policy initiatives abroad. Japan may dispatch forces abroad as long as there are no significant casualties to the SDF.[44]

The fact that the Japanese public, in general, shows little interest in foreign affairs and that Japan's elected leadership in the Diet has similarly shown little interest is a strong indication, in and of itself, that Japan is not seeking hegemonic status. The reality of Japan's decade old economic crisis is that Tokyo is more concerned with things at home than things abroad. Professor Toshiya Hoshino of the Osaka School of International Policy, Osaka University says that, "Without a healthy economy it is hard to pursue an international role."[45] Witness Japan's desire to cut funding for U.S. bases in Japan. Japan does not feel that it has the financial capability to support its international commitments.

America's slow withdrawal from a forward deployment in the Philippines and elsewhere in Asia is often cited as evidence that America is a declining hegemon. In the 1980s Japan was touted as a rising hegemon that would supplant America's hegemonic status.[46] This raises the question, are Japan's economic troubles and inability to make a significant international commitment a sign that it is a potential/rising hegemon in decline or merely a sign that Japan was never a candidate for hegemony? According to Professor Akihiko Tanaka of the Institute of Oriental Culture at Tokyo University, "Japan has no tradition of missionary zeal (to help the world). It has only the memory of bad mistakes (World War II). Japan needs ulterior motives."[47] Furthermore, "economic conditions limit future (options).[48]

It is a combination of Japan's war role (World War II) and Article Nine that prevent Japan's foreign policy normalization. While Japan's foreign policy is slowly maturing, its normalization is held back by its history and its inability to seem sincere. Sincerity is at the heart of the issue. Many feel that China is just using Japan's history in East Asia as a tool of its foreign policy.[49] Yet if Korea and China use Japan's history for political purposes, it is Japan's lack of sincerity that gives resonance to the issue with the peoples of East Asia. Germany is seen as sincere. Its actions in monetary terms and in education testify to this. Japan's efforts to sweep these issues "under the rug" or to bury them as already dealt with hurt Japan. Japan must show that it understands the suffering it caused by waging war in East Asia in the first place. The government of Japan may not have approved all the actions (crimes by the Imperial Army), but the government created the conditions for the atrocities to be committed. Japan must deal with this legacy before becoming a normal nation.

Japan is not ready to take on a leadership role comparable to the U.S. One of the most surprising findings during the field interviews was that when asked the following question,

> Countries that are seen as world leaders are seen as willing to bear the costs of world order. (For example the U.S. keeping forces in East Asia and Europe.) Is Japan prepared to undertake a world leadership

role and what cost would it be willing to pay in order to take on that role? (Or to put it another way is Japan willing to sacrifice for the good of the world?),

not a single respondent said that Japan **could** undertake a "world leadership role"! Seventy- eight percent said that Japan could not and 22% said that they "did not know." However, 48% said that Japan would be willing to assume a leadership role *if* it could.[50]

It is for this reason Japan is continuing its pursuit of a U.N. centered foreign policy. The U.N. is critical to Japanese foreign policy in that its peaceful ideals reflected in the U.N. Charter conform with the pacifist sentiments in Japan and its constitution. It is for these reasons that the U.N. will likely remain the focus of Japanese foreign policy efforts. This is a constitutionally valid aspiration on the part of Japan in that it is in line with both the preamble and the current interpretation of Article Nine that permits action by the SDF under U.N. auspices.

Japan's foreign policy elite are searching for a more prominent global role for Japan. But at the same time Japan is a pacifist nation that cannot independently flex its military strength abroad. Its twentieth century history argues against a more prominent role, but its history is not a defining factor when one studies the attitudes of the Japanese today. Pacifism is more important in the understanding of Japanese attitudes toward foreign policy today than past aggression. Japan has no intention of repeating its World War II mistakes. Rather, it seeks to be a positive influence and part of the world community by making a contribution to international and regional peace and stability as a pacifist nation.

To do this Japan must walk a fine line internationally and domestically. Japan has the desire to be a normal nation, but is it willing to bear the costs? Can Japan take casualties in support of international and regional peace and stability? Perhaps, but only after facing a few more Gulf War-like criticisms for inaction or if Japan finds itself truly threatened.

JAPAN'S FUTURE

During the Cold War Japan was part of the West which made its foreign policy formulation straight forward and easy. Since the end of the Cold War the task has been much more difficult. Japan needs a new role fore itself in international affairs.[51] Japan definitely wants to be seen as the leader in Asia. It already represents Asia by being the only Asian nation in the G-7(8), but it wants it global standing to mature so that it can be Asia's bridge to the West.[52] Japan has often found itself caught between Asia and the West. It is now seeking to use this position to its advantage by being both East and West. The problem is China's opposition to Japanese leadership. China believes that it should represent Asia and that Japan should subordinate its ambitions to China's. China uses Japan's history in China to undermine Japan's ambitions.

Japan has it in its own power to rid itself of this problem of history, if it is willing. The greatest hindrance to Japan's future is its unwillingness to deal with its past. If Japan fails to deal with its past, it is likely to remain isolated (as a security player) in East Asia with continued dependence on the U.S. As Sheldon Simon argues, Japan needs "to accept responsibility and sincerely apologize for past misdeeds. It may still take years before Japan can earn the confidence of potential security partners."[53] In a world that is integrating faster every day, Japan may also lose its potential for regional leadership because no one in East Asia will be willing to fully trust it. Japan should fully apologize for its actions during the Pacific War. Given Japan's muddled history of insincere and half/semi expressions of remorse by various Prime Ministers, the Emperor, "as the symbol of the nation" should be the one to make the apology. The government's official position on this is that this is an unconstitutional exercise of power by the Emperor.[54] However, many of those interviewed outside of government felt this to be untrue and that only the Emperor could truly apologize for the nation.[55]

In dealing with Japan's past there also seems to be a generation gap among Japanese elites. Ninety-six percent of young Japanese elites interviewed favored an honest look at Japanese history and the issuance of a sincere formal apology to those whom it harmed. On the other hand older interviewees opposed an honest look at Japanese history during World War II, and they rejected any apology 72% to 28%. Overall the elites of all ages favored an honest look at the past by a margin of 61% in favor and 39% opposed.[56]

Japanese participation in Peace Keeping Forces (PKF)[57] is the next step for Japan. Japanese participation in PKF under U.N. auspices would move the SDF towards a more normal military force which has heretofore been absent. It will also raise the prestige and visibility of Japan in international crises.[58] The Ground SDF is the most resistant to expanding its PKO role; "but Japan has to sweat," according to Col. Noburo Yamaguchi of the SDF.[59] The key here being that Japanese forces would serve under U.N. command rather than under the Japanese chain of command. The SDF would be "borrowed" by the U.N. This would remove the possible constitutional obstacle to the SDF being in combat. However, the public would have to be "sold" on the idea that it was necessary for Japan to send the SDF in harms way (under U.N. command) for the good of international order.

The younger generation in Japan desperately wants Japan to be normal. According to Nobuto Hosaka, "Young Diet members want Japan to be a ordinary/normal nation. There is a need to get rid of the image of a Japan that just sells and (replace it with) one that gives."[60] Naoko Saiki of MOFA noted that, "Internationalization or Mass Culture is taking away Japanese identity.

Youth want to be identified with the world not as Japanese. Japan embarrasses them."[61] Japan needs normalization in order to have its own youth respect it.

SUGGESTIONS FOR FOREIGN POLICY NORMALIZATION

Here are some important points to consider for Japan to normalize its foreign policy:

1. The generation gap in Japanese politics must be overcome if Japan is to move forward.[62] The younger generation is realist and pragmatic and very internationalized. They want a Japan that they can respect.

2. If Japan is ever to achieve normal status as a nation, Article Nine must be revised. Article Nine takes away a basic and useful tool of foreign policy; the threat of force. Japan's quest for normalcy will hinge on the future of Article Nine. However, the desires of the LDP and others on the right in Japanese politics to see a constitutional revision will likely remain wishful thinking for the time being. It would take a crisis that threatens Japan or something Japan holds dear for Japan to abandon Article Nine.

3. Japan needs new thinking if it is to flourish in the post-Cold War world. However, many feel that the current Japanese leadership (MOFA and the Prime Minister's Office) are too cautious to innovate.[63] Nevertheless, one of Japan's greatest problems is the lack of vision and leadership by the governing elites concerning the future direction of Japanese foreign policy. Tokyo governor Shintaro Ishihara is a vocal critic of Japan's governing elite. He believes that, "Japan has no worthy political leadership, no real intellectual or political debate and, worst of all, *no direction*."[64] This will make aggressive new thinking unlikely in the near term.

4. Japan should offer a sincere apology and show of remorse in the next few years before the last of the World War II generation dies off. Issues such as the legalization of a national Anthem and flag are good for restoring national pride, but they hurt efforts to show that attitudes have changed toward Japan's East Asian neighbors.

5. Change is not likely to occur unless there is a crisis which forces Japan to change. Japan needs to plan for the next crisis not the last one.

6. Japan has to prove its value to the U.S. while at the same time becoming more independent from the U.S. It needs a strong U.S./Japan Security Treaty as well as a strong constructive relationship with China.[65]

Japan is likely to be much more activist in its foreign policy in the future.[66] Given the uncertainties of the post-Cold War world Japan must have a greater voice in its own security. The problem for Japan will be one of vision and direction. It needs to chart its course rather than sail blindly from crisis to crisis. Japan may also be forced to take sides in a conflict, like a Taiwan/China clash or a renewed Korean conflict, in order to keep the U.S.

as an ally. As Mulgan writes, "Japan runs the risk of becoming a mere pawn in American strategy because it is now more locked into this strategy than ever before....Japan may be forced to take sides even when reluctant to do so."[67]

Japan must alter the free rider attitude that developed under the Yoshida Doctrine. The free rider attitude of many Japanese toward foreign affairs has resulted in Japan's general inability to act as a major world player. Japan did as little as possible for the world community until the end of the Cold War. "The problem is that Japan is having to do something more and Japan needs principles to guide its foreign policy, currently it has none in foreign policy," according to Representative Shozo Azuma.[68]

The largest obstacle to the development of principles and reform in Japanese foreign policy will be the bureaucracy. The legislature may attempt reform but MOFA may fight it. Just as Pempel argued in the arena of economic reform this author argues in foreign policy. Institutional change is difficult without a crisis.[69] A crisis like the Gulf War and the end of the Cold War gave Japan the push to make changes. PKO enlargement primarily depends on conflict or crisis in order to justify Japan increasing the role of the SDF.[70] Shin'ichi Ogawa of the National Institute for Defense Studies in Tokyo argues that, "(The Japanese) people need a big event, crisis, or shock to be woken up."[71] However, Japan must wake up before the crisis hits and look toward the future and its role beyond its borders. The next sections will examine what we have gained theoretically from our study of Japanese foreign policy in the post-Cold War and outline the need for future research.

IMPLICATIONS FOR HERMANN'S MODEL: WHAT HAVE WE LEARNED?

Hermann's model helps clarify much of what we see in Japanese foreign policy in the post-Cold War era. It teaches us that the formation and restructuring of Japanese foreign policy are no different than any other nation. Hermann's model describes what happens when a government sees a need to change or restructure a foreign policy that it has implemented for a new one that better reflects its current needs. In Japan's case this is exactly what has happened; however there is one dynamic that Hermann's model fails to account for. This oversight is the generational shift in attitudes toward foreign policy within the Diet.

Hermann's model assumes to some extent a relatively constant influence by the Primary Change Agents (see figure 6:1). It does not take into account the possibility for major shifts in the change agents. In the case of Japan this was initially true (that there were no major shifts in the change agents) but as observed during the field research there seems to be a shift in power from MOFA (Bureaucratic Advocacy) to the Diet (Leader Driven). This internal shift requires no political reorientation; rather it requires only a change in sources

of influence on the part of foreign policy elites. In Japan's case the generational shift in Diet representation seems to be giving more power to the Diet
in foreign policy decisions at the expense of MOFA. MOFA will continue to
be a strong influence on Japanese foreign policy but on a more equal footing
with the Diet and with the Diet taking greater leadership. This change is illustrated in figures 6:2 and 6:3.

One of the primary omissions of Herman's model is that it did not
include foreign pressure as a change agent. All nations face foreign pressure
or *gaiatsu* in Japan's case. The addition of foreign pressure to the list of
"change agents" helps us to understand why nations choose to redirect their
foreign policies. Foreign pressure can be a key reason for nations to change
the direction of their foreign policy especially if that pressure comes from a
particularly important ally. This is an external source of foreign policy change,
and it can be part of an equation in which nations choose to redirect their
foreign policy. Nations normally choose foreign policies that represent their
best interests despite foreign pressure. However, in the case of Japan, foreign
pressure will often move Japan in a direction that it may not have chosen
without *gaiatsu*. At the same time, this pressure may conform to the Japanese
leadership's own preferences. Foreign pressure becomes a device to justify an
apparently unpopular policy.

Additionally we have learned that *gaiatsu* is often used as a two-level
game in selling unpopular foreign policy choices. Japanese leaders like all
political leaders struggle to direct policy in the direction that they desire it to
go. In the face of public opposition many leaders will drop these policies. In
Japan, political leaders frequently blame a powerful foreign power, ie., the
U.S., and thus justify an unpopular policy with little political cost to themselves. This is the "myth" of *gaiatsu* in that political leaders purport that it is
foreign pressure that is solely responsible for an unpopular policy when in
fact it is often the case that many in leadership desire the same policy as the
foreign entity.

The addition of constants/intervening variables to Hermann's model
helps us to understand how the situational dynamics may play out when
decisions are made. These constants, such as Article Nine in the case of Japan,
have the potential to change over time but usually are relatively stable over
time in the decision making "matrix" (process). Understanding the influence
of constants or intervening variables helps us to better predict the outcome
of the decision making process.

PRAGMATIC REALISM

As I argued in chapter three, Japan is fundamentally practicing a form of realism, but Japan's limitations under Article Nine prevent it from practicing
power politics *a la* Morgenthau. Recognizing these limitations, Japan has
adapted its approach to foreign policy by pragmatically pursuing an institu-

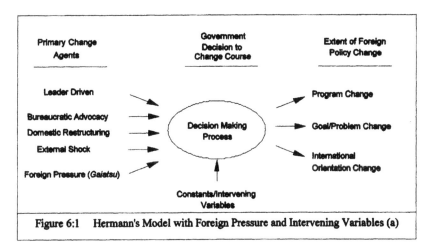

Figure 6:1 Hermann's Model with Foreign Pressure and Intervening Variables (a)

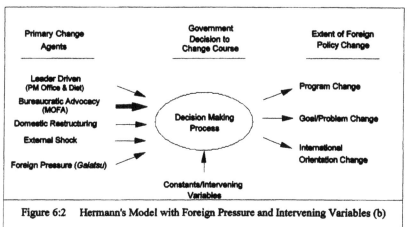

Figure 6:2 Hermann's Model with Foreign Pressure and Intervening Variables (b)

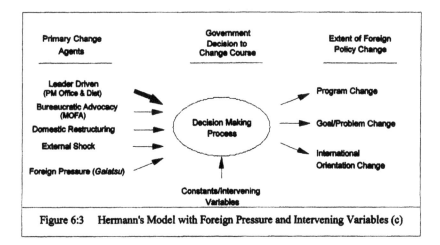

Figure 6:3 Hermann's Model with Foreign Pressure and Intervening Variables (c)

tionalist foreign policy. Grieco[72] argued and this author concurs that states may cooperate internationally (institutionalism) in an anarchical world while the motives for such cooperation are realist in nature. The premise guiding this perspective is that realism dominates or influences all calculations going into relations between nations. States want relative gains, but with the survival of the state as the primary goal of a nation's foreign policy, a state will choose *absolute gains* over a net loss in *relative gains*. It is for this reason that we can see both realism and neoliberalism occurring in East Asia as noted by Sheldon Simon.[73] The book adds to the debate between Grieco and Powell over the nature of relative and absolute gains in international relations theory. It notes the simultaneous nature of relative and absolute gains by Japan. Japan may desire pure relative gains in security and economics in an ideal world but given its limitations Japan will continue to pursue absolute gains in hope of making relative gains in terms of intangibles such as goodwill and influence, particularly vis-à-vis its relations with the United States.

This pursuit of absolute gains/relative gains is demonstrated by the fact that Japan has maintained a U.N.-centric foreign policy while relying on the U.S. for its security guarantee because of Japan's constitutional limitations. As demonstrated in chapters three and four, the end of the Cold War has weakened the security guarantee of the U.S., (The U.S. does not need Japan as much now as during the Cold War.). Japan is now faced with seeking other options while dealing with the same existing limitations. Japan needs to be more independent, *vis-a-vis* the U.S., in its foreign policy and more active in both regional and international affairs. Multilateralism offers the best hope for absolute gains while at the same time making relative gains in terms of goodwill and influence, but Japan's steadfast refusal to deal with its history in East Asia limits its ability to gain the trust that is needed for multilateralism to work in Northeast Asia.

The questions that were asked in chapter one are: "What is Japan's new role in the world?", "What accounts for the gradual change in the role of the SDF?", "What are the driving forces domestically behind these changes?", and "What is Japan's long term foreign policy agenda?" This book has endeavored to answer these questions. Japan's role in the world is increasing through U.N. PKO missions and its growing participation in multilateral fora. The gradual increase in the role of the SDF comes from a desire on the part of Japan to make a contribution towards international peace and stability. Additionally there is a desire, on the part of some Japanese elites, to continue the process of Japan's normalization through the reinterpretation of Article Nine. This process is being implemented by giving the SDF greater responsibilities and duties overseas in order to normalize it as a military force.

The driving forces behind the changes in Japanese foreign policy are primarily two fold. One force is the change agent of foreign pressure (*gaiatsu*); pressuring Japan to contribute to the international community at a level commensurate with its economic strength. The second is the generational shift in Japan which is redirecting the source of foreign policy from MOFA to the Diet. While the World War II generation is content with the status quo under Article Nine, the younger generation wants Japan to be a normal nation. Finally Japan's long term foreign policy agenda is still in the making. Japan, as all nations, wants to guarantee its peace and safety. However, there seems to be no agenda for discussion or real debate over the question of where Japan should direct its foreign policy in the next five to ten years.

FURTHER RESEARCH

Further research is needed into foreign pressure as a change agent in Hermann's Model as well as whether foreign pressures are constants/intervening variables in the foreign policy decision making process. In the case of Japan scholars must consider the limitations imposed by Article Nine and the cultural pacifism that is held by the majority of the public in Japan as constants.[74] Also to be considered are the foreign policy norms that have been created over time, which direct responses to a given situation. The question of the influence of foreign pressure should also be related to the question of national sovereignty.

Japan, as the rest of the world, was taken by surprise by the sudden end of the Cold War. Japan has been endeavoring to adapt to the New World Order over which it has had little control and as most other nations has been struggling with this task. Japanese foreign policy faces many challenges; and its experience offers others both positive and negative examples.

CONCLUDING REMARKS

The stated goal of this book is to explore the inner workings of Japanese foreign policy making. The central thesis is a challenge to the conventional wisdom in the existing literature which believes that Japan is not really changing. This author observed change in the Japanese foreign policy making community to an extent greater than was thought possible at the beginning of this project. The drafting and the passage of the PKO Law in reaction to the Gulf War, as described in chapter two, marked the beginning of this change process which is adapting Japanese foreign policy to the realities of the post-Cold War world.

Chapter three challenged the belief that Japan is merely pursuing an institutionalist foreign policy by noting that under Article Nine Japan does not have the choice of pursuing relative gains but is pursuing absolute gains for realist reasons in hopes of making intangible relative gains. Furthermore, the chapter described the application of Hermann's model to Japanese foreign policy and noted the omission of foreign pressure as an agent of change. Also noted was the need to include constants, such as Article Nine and cultural norms like Japanese Pacifism, as intervening variables in the foreign policy decision making process. The decision making matrix is influenced both internally by cultural norms and externally by foreign pressure. These variables are part of the process from which foreign policy changes occur and should be considered in any study of foreign policy change.

The field research exceeded the author's original aspirations in both quality and quantity and offers great potential for future ongoing study of the foreign policy decision making process. These interviews provided insight into the making of Japanese foreign policy and yielded two important findings: The first was a surprise that much of Japanese foreign policy is made on an emergency basis. There seemed to be few planned response scenarios for the government to fall back on when a major foreign or security policy event took place.

Considering what an important event the nuclear tests conducted by India and Pakistan were for Asian security, I was surprised to observe first hand that the Japanese foreign policy community was very unprepared to react to these events. The lack of contingency planning on the part of the government of Japan that was evidenced by the slow government response to the Kobe earthquake or the lack of emergency laws (tanks having to stop at traffic-lights) governing the SDF and U.S. forces in Japan seems to pervade the foreign policy community as well. While no nation can plan for every eventuality, Japan does not seem to plan at all for very many. With the exception of the new policies put in place by the September 1997 Revised Guidelines (which are intentionally vague in many areas), Japanese foreign and security policy is ill-prepared for future crises. Excluding its general capitalist, democratic, and pacifist tendencies, Japan does not seem to have a particular ideology or philosophy to guide its strategic planning. This means that Japan has been very slow to react to an international security event in a timely and appropriate manner.

The second major finding was the power shift that is moving major foreign policy issues from the more cautious MOFA to the more volatile Diet largely due to the generational shifts taking place in Japan. The Diet as the source of foreign policy offers many new and interesting considerations for the Japanese foreign policy community and the scholars studying it. What was left unexplored for future research is MOFA's response to the Diet's more assertive role in the foreign policy decision making process and how MOFA will adjust to a reduced role in the decision making process.

Chapter four delved into the concept of security and Japan's security options in a changing environment. Japan's original innovative comprehensive security concept may have to be modified and revert to more traditional security concerns. The more normal Japanese foreign policy becomes the more Japan must think in traditional terms. Thus, absolute and relative gains both become important for Japanese foreign policy.

Many in Japan believe in Japanese exceptionalism or uniqueness. The research found that Japan is not unique in that it experiences the same situations and events that the rest of the world faces. What makes Japan different is Article Nine. It is because of the limitations imposed by Article Nine that Japan needs to plan its responses to world events better so it can respond in a timely and appropriate manner. Japan needs to build the internal structures to deal with crises. These structures are best to be built in conjunction with the U.S. so that Japan's responses, particularly in East Asia, are coordinated with its only ally.

Chapter five looked at how Japanese view themselves in the world through the use of existing survey data and the author's field research. Japan's desire to be an active member of the world community commensurate with its economic status was noted. It was further seen that both the Japanese people and the foreign policy elite recognize Japan's limitations and that Japan has no interest in East Asian hegemony despite its economic strength. It is also important to note that it has just as strong an interest in seeing that no other nation in the region becomes a regional hegemon. Japan's efforts to raise its world standing through the U.N. and other multilateral organizations represent its alternative to hegemony. Continued pursuit of multilateral options offers Japan a way of ensuring its security along with continued efforts to improve relations with South Korea. The book found that multilateral efforts have broad support across the political spectrum.

One of the most important contributions of this book to the understanding of the making of Japanese foreign policy was the description offered in chapter five of *gaiatsu* being a two- level game. Japanese foreign policy elites will use *gaiatsu* to force an issue, that they desire to see approved, through for the purpose of shifting the blame to the U.S. for "making" Japan do something. This use of *gaiatsu* runs counter to the existing literature which fails to note the use of *gaiatsu* as a two-level game or acknowledge the questions that it raises about Japanese sovereignty if a two-level game does not exist.

The problem of Japan's unwillingness to deal with its history in East Asia was noted throughout the book, particularly in chapters two, four, and five. Contrary to the conventional wisdom among the ruling elite, Japan will never gain its full stature as a nation until it deals with its historical responsibilities in a forthright and honest way. The documentation of an obvious generation gap regarding the issue of an apology for World War II was another major finding of the research. Japan's quest for normalcy in its foreign relations in East Asia will be obstructed until it adequately addresses this issue.

In conclusion, further research is needed on the sources of change in Japanese foreign policy. The differences between the older and younger generation of elites in Japan over an apology by the emperor for World War II will be *a* defining event in Japanese history and of great interest to scholars of the decision making process and Japanese politics in general. The slowness of Japan to react in a crisis is symptomatic of a larger problem within Japan as a whole, but the power shifts that are now underway offer the best hope for a more responsive foreign policy that will serve and protect Japan throughout the twenty-first century.

NOTES

1 Kenneth Waltz, conference comment January 1999, Scottsdale, Arizona, author's personal notes, in the author's personal possession, Tempe, Arizona, January 1999.

2 During the interviews with various mid-level members of MOFA a paranoia seemed to be evident on the part of interviewees. While they seemed to be grateful to be able to express their own views, they seemed to behave as if the walls had ears. They were very careful to take anything that diverged from the official line "off the record." Senior level directors seemed the opposite and much more relaxed and willing to offer differing opinions.

3 Ichiro Yamamoto, Member of the House of Councillors of the Japanese Diet, interview by the author, 18 June 1998, Tokyo, tape recording, in author's personal possession, Tempe, Arizona.

4 Ibid.

5 Ibid.

6 Kuniko Nakajima, former career diplomat with the Japanese Ministry of Foreign Affairs and currently a researcher with the Okazaki Institute, interview by the author, 18 June 1998, Tokyo, tape recording, in author's personal possession, Tempe, Arizona.

7 This is a marked change in policy in that chain of command in the field would be exclusively Japanese. One of the strongest arguments for the constitutionality of the PKO Law is that the SDF troops are on loan to the U.N. and are commanded by U.N. commanders. The SDF troops are thus not being commanded by Tokyo except for being ordered to and from the field with conditions on what they can and can not do. The authorization for the potential future use of SDF troops in natural disasters quietly steps over the line by permitting Tokyo to command troops on overseas missions.

8 Prime Minister's Office survey of 2,114 national adults. Conducted 6–16 February 1997 by personal interview. Source: JPOLL, Roper Center for Public Opinion Research, University of Connecticut. (For required full disclaimer please see the Bibliography at the end of this book.) <http://roper1.ropercenter.uconn.edu>.

9 Ibid.

10 Several Diet members stated off the record that the people have no real voice in foreign policy. What they were alluding to is the control of foreign policy by MOFA and not by the people's representatives in the Diet. Other Diet members, particularly younger Diet members, stated that the Diet was taking a greater hands on approach to foreign policy and that MOFA was not the ultimate source of foreign policy.

[11] Article Ninety-six of the Japanese Constitution as cited by *Yomiuri Shimbun*, Law on Constitutional Poll Needed, 9 August 1999, internet edition, <http://www.yomiuri.co.jp/newse/0809ed16.htm>.

[12] Masashi Nishhara, Professor at the National Defense Academy, Japan Defense Agency, interview by the author, 31 May 1998, Tokyo, tape recording, in author's personal possession, Tempe, Arizona.

[13] Ibid.

[14] Aurelia George Mulgan, *Strategic Update - Japan*, School of Politics, University of New South Wales, Australian Defence Force Academy, conference paper, 1999, p.3.

[15] Geoffrey Smith, *Japan Expanding Defense Role, The Washington Times*, 7 March 2000, 11, as cited by Northeast Asia Peace and Security Network Daily Report For Tuesday, March 7, 2000, from Berkeley, California, USA, <NAPSNet@nautilus.org (NAPSNet)>.

[16] *The Constitution of Japan. Law and Contemporary Problems*, Spring, 1990: 200–214

[17] Ibid.

[18] Field research interviews conducted with both elected and career government foreign policy elites in Japan May-June 1998. (N=39).

[19] Field research interviews conducted with academics in Japan May-June 1998. (N=9).

[20] Field research interviews conducted in Japan May-June 1998. (N=48)

[21] An off the record comment by a senior MOFA official. Interview by the author, May-June 1998, Tokyo, tape recording, in author's personal possession, Tempe, Arizona.

[22] Field research interviews conducted in Japan May-June 1998. Of the twenty-four government elites answering in favor of revising Article Nine twelve felt that it would not happen. (N=48)

[23] Mitsuo Higashinaka, member of the House of Representatives of the Japanese Diet (JCP), interview by the author, 19 May 1998, Tokyo, tape recording, in author's personal possession, Tempe, Arizona.

[24] *Asahi Shimbun* survey of 2,251 national voters. Conducted 20–21 April 1997 by personal interview. Source: JPOLL, Roper Center for Public Opinion Research, University of Connecticut. (For required full disclaimer please see the Bibliography at the end of this book.)

[25] Kenichi Nakamura, Dean of Law, Hokkaido University (Top Japanese Researcher on the PKO Law), interview by author, 20 June 1998, Tokyo, tape recording, in author's personal possession Tempe, Arizona.

[26] Jun Morikawa, Professor Rakuno Gakuen University, interview by author, 22 June 1998, Tokyo, tape recording, in author's personal possession Tempe, Arizona.

[27] Kenjiro Monji, Cabinet Office of the Prime Minister, Office on External Affairs, Office of the Prime Minister of Japan, interview by the author, 11 June 1998, Tokyo, tape recording, in author's personal possession, Tempe, Arizona.

[28] Off the record interview by the author, May-June 1998, Tokyo, tape recording, in author's personal possession, Tempe, Arizona.

[29] Yamamoto interview.

[30] Jiro Kodera, Director First International Economic Affairs Division of the Japanese Ministry of Foreign Affairs, interview by author, 20 May 1998, Tokyo, tape recording, in author's personal possession Tempe, Arizona.

[31] An off the record comment by a senior MOFA official. Interview by the author, May-June 1998, Tokyo, tape recording, in author's personal possession, Tempe, Arizona.

[32] Ibid.

[33] Ibid. This might seem contradictory on the surface, but given that public opinion often contains such contradictions the Japanese public is not being totally hypocritical. For example, most Americans supported the President's recent actions in Kosovo while at the same time they expressed the feelings that America did not belong there. Japan is much the same. Most support the SDF and see the need for the PKO missions while preferring at the same time that the SDF not be deployed overseas.

[34] Ryozo Kato, Director General, Foreign Policy Bureau of the Japanese Ministry of Foreign Affairs, interview by author, 21 May 1998, Tokyo, tape recording, in author's personal possession Tempe, Arizona.

[35] Hideo Usui, member of the House of Representatives of the Japanese Diet and former Defense Minister and Vice Defense Agency Minister (Career ministry appointment), interview by the author, 26 and 29 May 1998, Tokyo, tape recording, in author's personal possession, Tempe, Arizona.

[36] Repeatedly during the field research interviews, the interviewees would express concern over the foreign policy "problem" of the Japanese people's aversion to war and military conflict. Japanese pacifism is strong and represents a problem for policy makers when considering the entire scope of foreign policy options.

[37] Interview with Hideo Usui.

[38] Interview with Hideo Usui.

[39] Off the record statement by a senior member of MOFA. Interview by the author, May-June 1998, Tokyo, Japan, tape recording, in the personal possession of the author, Tempe, Arizona.

[40] Ibid.

[41] Shigeru Ishiba, member of the House of Representatives of the Japanese Diet (LDP), interview by the author, 4 June 1998, Tokyo, tape recording, in author's personal possession, Tempe, Arizona.

[42] Akira Ogawa, Professor Okazaki Research Institute, Tokyo, Japan, interview by author, 18 June 1998, Tokyo, tape recording, in author's personal possession Tempe, Arizona.

[43] Nishihara interview.

[44] What would qualify as significant is anybody's guess. It could be one or as high as a hundred. It would depend on the situation or the mission.

[45] Toshiya Hoshino, Professor, Osaka School of International Policy, Osaka University, interview by author, 10 June 1998, Tokyo, tape recording, in author's personal possession Tempe, Arizona.

[46] An example of this is Paul Kennedy, *The Rise and Fall of the Great Powers: Economic Change and Military conflict from 1500–2000*, New York: Random House, 1987.

⁴⁷ Akihiko Tanaka, Professor, Institute of Oriental Culture, Tokyo University, interview by author, 16 June 1998, Tokyo, tape recording, in author's personal possession Tempe, Arizona.

⁴⁸ Ibid,

⁴⁹ One interviewee felt that Japan was hiding behind the issue of World War II in order to not have to contribute to world order. Hajime Oshitani, Professor at Rakuno Gakuen University, interview by author, 25 June 1998, Tokyo, tape recording, in author's personal possession Tempe, Arizona.

⁵⁰ Field research interviews conducted in Japan May-June 1998. (N=50)

⁵¹ Ryozo Kato, Director General, Foreign Policy Bureau of the Japanese Ministry of Foreign Affairs, interview by author, 21 May 1998, Tokyo, tape recording, in author's personal possession Tempe, Arizona.

⁵² Kei Hata, member of the House of Councillors of the Japanese Diet (LDP), interview by the author, 18 May 1998, Tokyo, tape recording, in author's personal possession, Tempe, Arizona, Hideo Usui, member of the House of Representatives of the Japanese Diet and former Defense Minister and Vice Defense Agency Minister (Career ministry appointment), interview by the author, 26 and 29 May 1998, Tokyo, tape recording, in author's personal possession, Tempe, Arizona, and Jiro Kodera, Director First International Economic Affairs Division of the Japanese Ministry of Foreign Affairs, interview by author, 20 May 1998, Tokyo, tape recording, in author's personal possession Tempe, Arizona.

⁵³ Sheldon W. Simon, *Multilateralism and Japan's Security Policy, The Korean Journal of Defense Analysis*, Vol. XI, No. 2, (Winter 1999): 81.

⁵⁴ This view was very explicitly expressed by Director General Ryozo Kato of MOFA. Ryozo Kato, Director General, Foreign Policy Bureau of the Japanese Ministry of Foreign Affairs, interview by author, 21 May 1998, Tokyo, tape recording, in author's personal possession Tempe, Arizona.

⁵⁵ Two examples of this opinion from academia are Kazuo Ota and Keichi Fujiwara. Several LDP Diet members also expressed this view off the record along with Tomoko Nakagawa and Hosaka Nobuto of the Socialist party. Kazuo Ota, Dean Rakuno Gakuen University, interview by author, 6 June 1998, Tokyo, tape recording, in author's personal possession Tempe, Arizona. Keichi Fujiwara, Professor Institute of Social Science Tokyo University, interview by author, 11 June 1998, Tokyo, tape recording, in author's personal possession Tempe, Arizona. Tomoko Nakagawa, Member of the House of Representatives of the Japanese Diet (SDP), interview by the author, 16 June 1998, Tokyo, tape recording, in author's personal possession, Tempe, Arizona. Hosaka Nobuto, Member of the House of Representatives of the Japanese Diet (SDP), interview by the author, 16 June 1998, Tokyo, tape recording, in author's personal possession, Tempe, Arizona.

⁵⁶ Field research interviews conducted May-June 1998 in Tokyo. Interviewees were asked to "How should Japan deal with its history in East Asia?" (N=49) Te young and old were classified as those older or younger than 50 years old. Diet members were classified the same way except if they had been in the Diet more than 15 years then they were classified as old. Alternatively if they were between 50 and 55 and had served less than 5 years in the Diet they were classified with the younger generation. For the Young N=24. For the old N=25.

57 The Japanese government is very aware of the problems of distinguishing between PKO missions and PKF missions. The primary difference being that a PKF mission would require SDF involvement in the *enforcement* of a U.N. brokered peace and the PKO mission requiring the SDF to support a U.N. brokered peace. Under U.N. command on a PKF mission the SDF would potentially be required to not only take defensive action, but also offensive action to support the U.N. brokered peace. Part of this discussion on the differences between the PKO and the PKF comes from an off the record interview with a government sponsored researcher working for the Japanese Defense Agency.
58 Colonel Yoshihisa Nakamura, Professor at the National Institute for Defense Studies, Japan Defense Agency, interview by the author, 28 May 1998, Tokyo, tape recording, in author's personal possession, Tempe, Arizona.
59 Colonel Noburo Yamaguchi, Colonel Ground self-Defense Forces, interview by the author, 2 June 1998, Tokyo, tape recording, in author's personal possession, Tempe, Arizona.
60 Nobuto Hosaka, Member of the House of Representatives of the Japanese Diet (SDP), interview by the author, 16 June 1998, Tokyo, tape recording, in author's personal possession, Tempe, Arizona.
61 Naoko Saiki, Director International Peace Cooperation Division, Ministry of Foreign Affairs, interview by author, 4 June 1998, Tokyo, tape recording, in author's personal possession Tempe, Arizona.
62 Keizo Takemi, Member of the House of Councillors of the Japanese Diet, current Cabinet Vice Foreign Minister and past House of Councillors Chair of Foreign Relations Committee and founding chair of the sub committee on Pacific Affairs. Interview by the author, 25 May 1998, Tokyo, tape recording, in author's personal possession, Tempe, Arizona.
63 Kuniko Nakajima interview.
64 French, Howard W. *An Upstart Governor Takes on Japan's Mandarins, The New York Times*, internet edition <http://www.nytimes.com/library/ world/asia/ 033000japan- ishihara.html>, March 30, 2000, 3.
65 Shigeru Ishiba, Member of the House of Representatives of the Japanese Diet (LDP), interview by the author, 4 June 1998, Tokyo, tape recording, in author's personal possession, Tempe, Arizona.
66 Hendrik Spruyt, *A New Architecture for Peace?: Reconfiguring Japan Among the Great Powers, The Pacific Review*, Vol. 11 No. 3 1998: 380.
67 Mulgan, 14.
68 Shozo Azuma, Member of the House of Representatives of the Japanese Diet (Liberal Party), interview by the author, 6 June 1998, Tokyo, tape recording, in author's personal possession, Tempe, Arizona.
69 T. J. Pempel, *Structural 'Gaiatsu': international Finance and Political Change in Japan, Comparative Political Studies*, Vol. 32 No. 8. (December 1999): 907–932.
70 Kiichi Fujiwara, Professor, Institute of Social Science, Tokyo University, interview by author, 11 June 1998, Tokyo, tape recording, in author's personal possession Tempe, Arizona.
71 Shin'ichi Ogawa, Professor, National Institute for Defense Studies, interview by author, 11 June 1998, Tokyo, tape recording, in author's personal possession Tempe, Arizona.

72 Joseph M. Grieco, *Anarchy and the Limits of Cooperation: A Realist Critique of the Newest Liberal Institutionalism*, in *Neorealism and Neoliberalism: The Contemporary Debate*, ed. David A Baldwin, 116–140, New York: Columbia University Press, 1993.

73 Sheldon W. Simon, *International Relations Theory and Southeast Asian Security*, *The Pacific Review*, Vol. 8, No. 1 (1995): 5–24.

74 Both of these "constants" have the *potential* to change but when one considers the changeability of other agents of change these two are fairly stable. For example leaders can change their opinions at any time but constitutional amendments are very rare.

POSTSCRIPT

The events of September 11, 2001 found Japan better prepared than it had been for the Gulf War, but still struggling under Article Nine to formulate an appropriate response in an international crisis. When the terrorists crashed their hijacked airplanes into the World Trade Center and the Pentagon the Japanese National Security Council was in session to deal with the aftermath of a typhoon (It was around midnight Japan time). The Security Council immediately issued a strong condemnation of the attack and offered Japan's support and assistance making Japan one of the first to do so. However this quick response was followed up by a much slower one when Prime Minister Koizumi waited several days to call President George W. Bush, thus becoming the last major world leader to do so.

Japan followed this up with a strong pledge of support for the American War on Terrorism. The Maritime Self Defense Forces (MSDF) were quickly dispatched to the Indian Ocean in support of the United States Navy's operations against Osama bin Laden's Al Qaeda and the Taliban in Afghanistan. Some ground support personnel were also sent to neighboring Pakistan for humanitarian purposes. The government's plans to send Aegis class destroyer to help protect the American fleet ran into problems when even some of the LDP's own coalition partners questioned the constitutionality of such a move. Japan also co-hosted a conference with the United States in which the various factions in Afghanistan met to plan for a post-Taliban government for Afganistan.

The Japanese Diet is currently debating a Bill that would authorize a reinterpretation of the constitution in order to permit the current SDF operations in support of the War on Terrorism. Passage is expected as of this writing but the level of new support for the United States is in question. The Aegis system is unlikely to gain Diet approval due to opposition from one of the ruling parties, *Koumeitou*.

It appears that Japan got one thing right this time around in that it responded quickly. Aside from the initial gaff of not calling President Bush for several days the Japanese government has responded quickly and as appropriately as it could given its constraints under Article Nine. It also appears that Japan has decided that the best way to normalize its foreign policy is to stick with the United States and to follow America's lead in world affairs. Japan recognizes its need to keep the United States as a close ally and the mutual treat of terrorism threatens the world wide stability that Japan so desperately needs in trying economic times.

It is important to remember that the Japan based cult *Aum Shin* committed several terrorist attacks in Japan in the 1990s. These attacks included an unsuccessful Anthrax attack in Tokyo and two successful Saren gas attacks in Tokyo, including one in the Tokyo subway that killed eight people. Rumors of Al Queda cells' operating it Japan understandably unnerve some Japanese officials. While Japan recognizes that it is currently an unlikely target of Al Queda's wrath it could be someday especially given its support for the United States in the current crisis. Japan choice to aid the United States in its War on Terrorism further invests Japan as a long term ally of the United States.

The problem however is that Japan appears not to have any clear or definitive plans as to its future foreign policy. This is most likely due to the current void in strong leadership at the highest levels of Japanese government and in MOFA. Prime Minister Koizumi, while popular, has yet to show vision as to how he intends to lead Japan in the 21st century. Foreign Minister Tanaka is currently in an ongoing feud with the MOFA bureaucracy over the direction and very operational policies of the ministry. This leads one to wonder if anyone is really in charge at MOFA. Japan still has a long way to go and many hurdles to overcome but it is making progress and moving forward to a much more "normal" foreign policy.

Kevin J. Cooney
November 17, 2001

GOVERNMENT/DIET MEMBER INTERVIEW QUESTIONS

Gov't/Diet Member Interview Questions   名前: _____
政府/国会職員用質問事項   役職: _____

<u>Foreign Policy Questions 外交政策に関する質問</u>

1. Why do you believe that the government felt it necessary to pass the PKO Law?
なぜ政府はPKO法案を可決する必要があったと思いますか?

   1a. Did you agree or disagree with the government at the time? Why?
   あなたは当時の政府の決断に賛成でしたか、或いは反対でしたか? またその理由を述べ
てください。

   1b. Do you still feel the same way now? If not, why do you feel different?
   今も当時の考えと同じですか? もし考えを変えた場合、その理由は何ですか?

2. What political groups pushed for the passage of the PKO Law and what were their motives or reasons for desiring its passage?
どの政治活動グループがPKO法案を可決に導くきっかけになったと思いますか、その動機や理由を述べてください。

   2a. What political groups opposed the PKO Law? Why?
   どの政治活動グループがPKO法案に反対しましたか? またそれはなぜですか?

3. What do you believe are the long term goals of Japanese foreign policy? (or Where do you feel that Japan is going in the future with its foreign policy?)
日本の外交政策の長期的目標（ゴール）は何だと思いますか?(また日本の外交政策は将来どのような方向に向かって行くと思いますか?)

   3a. Do you feel these are the right long term goals?
   では、今述べてくださったご意見が、最も正しい長期目標であると思いますか?

   3b. Why or why not? If not, where would you like to see it go in the future?
   はい：それは何故ですか?
   いいえ：では何故この方向ではよくないのですか。将来どの方向へ進んでいったらよい
と思いますか?

4. What in your opinion should the goals of Japanese security/foreign policy be?
日本の外交安全保証政策の目標（あり方）はどうあるべきだと思いますか?

    4a. What are the international and domestic obstacles to these goals?
    この目標を達成するにあたり、国内外においてなにか障害となるものはありますか?

    4b. How do domestic politics affect these foreign policy goals?
    国内政策はこの外交政策の目標にどのような影響を与えると思いますか?

    4c. How should Japan deal with these domestic political obstacles?
    日本はその障害となる国内政策にどう対応すべきだと思いますか?

    4d. How does this fit with Article 9?
    この目標は憲法第９条にどのように関わってきますか?

5. What role, if any, should Japan seek in international security fora (e.g. ARF, KEDO)?
日本は国際安全保証フォーラム（例.ARF,KEDO等）で、どのような役割を果たすべきだと思い
ますか? (ARF＝ASEAN (Association of Southeast Asian Nations) Regional Forum,
KEDO＝Korean Energy Development Organization)

6. What are Japan's top three security threats or concerns? Top three foreign policy concerns?
日本の最も懸念される安全保証問題と外交政策問題は何ですか?　３つずつあげてください。
    1.   1.

    2.   2.

    3.   3.

7. How does the September 1997 revision of the US/Japan Defense Guidelines affect Japanese foreign
policy?
(eg. SDF support for US forces, East Asia to area around Japan)
1997年9月に改正された日米防衛ガイドラインは日本の外交政策にどのように影響しますか?

    7a. What are the potential obstacles to the implementation of the new guidelines?
    この新しいガイドラインを取り入れることで障害となるものはなんですか?

8. What should be the role of the SDF in Japanese foreign policy?
日本の外交政策において自衛隊はどのような役割を果たすべきだと思いますか?

    8a. What limits, if any, should be placed on the SDF?
    自衛隊の役割に制限を設けるとしたら、どのような制限を設けたらよいですか?

9. How should Japan deal with its history in East Asia if it does take on a larger role in world affairs?
日本の対応が、世界情勢に、より大きな役割をになう場合、過去に東アジアで日本が行った行為に対し、どのように対処すべきだと思いますか?

    9a. What could or would be the domestic consequences of this larger role?
    このより大きな役割を担う結果生まれる、国内政策上の重要課題はなんですか?

10. Domestically who or what groups are pushing for foreign policy change?
国内において、だれがまたはどのグループが外交政策の改革促進を強く働きかけていますか?

    10a. Why are they pushing for this change?
    なぜこれらの人々はこの改革促進に積極的なのですか?

11. Internationally who or what groups are pushing for Japanese foreign policy change?
では国外においては、だれがまたはどのグループが日本政府の外交政策の改革促進を強く働きかけていますか?

    11a. Why are they pushing for this change?
    なぜこれらの人々はこの改革促進に積極的なのですか?

12. Do you think Article 9 should be revised in the future and what should the revisions be? How soon?
将来、憲法第9条を改正する必要があると思いますか、またどのように改正するべきですか?あると答えた場合、どの程度早く行うべきだと思いますか?

13. Countries that are seen as world leaders are seen as willing to bear the costs of world order. (For example the US keeping forces in East Asia and Europe) Is Japan prepared to undertake a world leadership role and what cost would it be willing to pay in order to take on that role? **(or to put it another way is Japan willing to sacrifice for the good of the world?)**

国際的リーダーといわれる国々は、世界つまり国際社会の秩序を保つために、その責任を担う意思がある、と見なされています（たとえば米国は東アジアとヨーロッパに軍を駐在させています）。日本は、リーダー国としての責任を担う準備ができていますか、またこの責任をまっとうするには、どのような代価を支払う意思がありますか。（つまり言い替えると、日本は、国際社会の秩序を保つために、犠牲を払ってでも世界のために貢献しようという意思はありますか？）

14. How are the new PKO Law revisions consistent with Japanese foreign policy goals and how are they in conflict?

新しく改正されたPKO法案は、日本の外交政策の目標とどのような点で一致しますか、また一致しない点はどのような点ですか？

    14a. Do you think the Bills that are noew before the Diet will pass?

    この議案（つまりPKO改正法案）は、国会で可決されると思いますか？

    14b. If I may ask, how do you plan to vote as of today?

    もしよければ、現在の時点では、どちらに投票する予定であるかを教えていただけませんか？

ACADEMIC/JOURNALIST INTERVIEW QUESTIONS

Academic/Journalist Questions

名前: _____

教育関係者/編集者用質問事項

役職:_____

<u>Foreign Policy Questions 外交政策に関する質問</u>

1. Why do you believe that the government felt it necessary to pass the PKO Law?
なぜ政府はPKO法案を可決する必要があったと思いますか?

    1a. Did you agree or disagree with the government at the time? Why?
あなたは当時の政府の決断に賛成でしたか、或いは反対でしたか? またその理由を述べてください。

    1b. Do you still feel the same way now? If not, why do you feel different?
今も当時の考えと同じですか? もし考えを変えた場合、その理由は何ですか?

2. What political groups pushed for the passage of the PKO Law and what were their motives or reasons for desiring its passage?
どの政治活動グループがPKO法案を可決に導くきっかけになったと思いますか、その動機や理由を述べてください。

    2a. What political groups opposed the PKO Law? Why?
どの政治活動グループがPKO法案に反対しましたか? またそれはなぜですか?

3. What do you believe are the long term goals of Japanese foreign policy? (or Where do you feel that Japan is going in the future with its foreign policy?)
日本の外交政策の長期的目標 (ゴール) は何だと思いますか? (また日本の外交政策は将来どのような方向に向かって行くと思いますか?)

    3a. Do you feel these are the right long term goals?
では、今述べてくださったご意見が、最も正しい長期目標であると思いますか?

    3b. Why or why not? If not, where would you like to see it go in the future?
はい : それは何故ですか?
いいえ : では何故この方向ではよくないのですか。将来どの方向へ進んでいったらよいと思いますか?

4. What in your opinion should the goals of Japanese security/foreign policy be?
日本の外交安全保証政策の目標（あり方）はどうあるべきだと思いますか？

    4a. What are the international and domestic obstacles to these goals?
    この目標を達成するにあたり、国内外においてなにか障害となるものはありますか？

    4b. How do domestic politics affect these foreign policy goals?
    国内政策はこの外交政策の目標にどのような影響を与えると思いますか？

    4c. How should Japan deal with these domestic political obstacles?
    日本はその障害となる国内政策にどう対応すべきだと思いますか？

    4d. How does this fit with Article 9?
    この目標は憲法第９条にどのように関わってきますか？

5. How are the new PKO Law revisions consistent with Japanese foreign policy goals and how are they in conflict?
新しく改正されたPKO法案は、日本の外交政策の目標とどのような点で一致しますか、また一致しない点はどのような点ですか？

    5a. Do you think the Bills that are now before the Diet will pass?
    この議案（つまりPKO改正法案）は、国会で可決されると思いますか？

6. What role, if any, should Japan seek in international security fora (e.g. ARF, KEDO)?
日本は国際安全保証フォーラム(例.ARF,KEDO等）で、どのような役割を果たすべきだと思いますか？ (ARF=ASEAN (Association of Southeast Asian Nations) Regional Forum,
KEDO=Korean Energy Development Organization)

7. What are Japan's top three security threats or concerns? Top three foreign policy concerns?
日本の最も懸念される安全保証問題と外交政策問題は何ですか？　3つずつあげてください。
    1.   1.

    2.   2.

    3.   3.

8. How does the September 1997 revision of the US/Japan Defense Guidelines affect Japanese foreign policy?
(eg. SDF support for US forces, East Asia to area around Japan)
1997年9月に改正された日米防衛ガイドラインは日本の外交政策にどのように影響しますか?

    8a. What are the potential obstacles to the implementation of the new guidelines?
    この新しいガイドラインを取り入れることで障害となるものはなんですか?

9. What should be the role of the SDF in Japanese foreign policy?
日本の外交政策において自衛隊はどのような役割を果たすべきだと思いますか?

    9a. What limits, if any, should be placed on the SDF?
    自衛隊の役割に制限を設けるとしたら、どのような制限を設けたらよいですか?

10. How should Japan deal with its history in East Asia if it does take on a larger role in world affairs?
日本の対応が、世界情勢に、より大きな役割をになう場合、過去に東アジアで日本が行った行為に対し、どのように対処すべきだと思いますか?

    10a. What could or would be the domestic consequences of this larger role?
    このより大きな役割を担う結果生まれる、国内政策上の重要課題はなんですか?

11. Domestically who or what groups are pushing for foreign policy change?
国内において、だれがまたはどのグループが外交政策の改革促進を強く働きかけていますか?

    11a. Why are they pushing for this change?
    なぜこれらの人々はこの改革促進に積極的なのですか?

12. Internationally who or what groups are pushing for Japanese foreign policy change?
では国外においては、だれがまたはどのグループが日本政府の外交政策の改革促進を強く働きかけていますか?

    12a. Why are they pushing for this change?
    なぜこれらの人々はこの改革促進に積極的なのですか?

13. Do you think Article 9 should be revised in the future and what should the revisions be? How soon?
将来、憲法第9条を改正する必要があると思いますか、またどのように改正するべきですか?
あると答えた場合、どの程度早く行うべきだと思いますか?

14. Countries that are seen as world leaders are seen as willing to bear the costs of world order. (For example the US keeping forces in East Asia and Europe) Is Japan prepared to undertake a world leadership role and what cost would it be willing to pay in order to take on that role? **(or to put it another way is Japan willing to sacrifice for the good of the world?)**

国際的リーダーといわれる国々は、世界つまり国際社会の秩序を保つために、その責任を担う意思がある、と見なされています（たとえば米国は東アジアとヨーロッパに軍を駐在させています）。日本は、リーダー国としての責任を担う準備ができていますか、またこの責任をまっとうするには、どのような代価を支払う意思がありますか。（つまり言い替えると、日本は、国際社会の秩序を保つために、犠牲を払ってでも世界のために貢献しようという意思はありますか？）

15. What theory of International Relations best describes Japanese Foreign Policy?

どの国際関係論に関する学説が、日本の外交政策について一番適切に述べていますか。

INTRODUCTION USED FOR THE FIELD INTERVIEWS

Thank you for agreeing to see me. Do you mind if I record our interview?

By way of introduction I would like to say that the research that I am conducting is academic in nature and that I am not a reporter and have no political agenda. The information from this interview will be used for academic purposes only. My research is focusing on foreign policy changes in Japan since the end of the Cold War. In particular, as a case study, I am examining the PKO Law as a significant symbol of that change. Furthermore I am examining the impetus and the sources driving changes in Japanese foreign policy. My first questions will deal with the original PKO passed in 1992 and then quickly move on to deal with the current foreign policy situation.

Many of my questions will seem at first to be very similar, but they contain subtle and critical differences for my research. The questions I will be asking you today will ask for **both** your opinions and perspectives (what you see happening) on Japanese foreign policy, both current foreign policy and future foreign policy goals. If you wish to say anything confidential by way of background information, opinion, or otherwise that you would not want to be attributed to you please let me know and I will not name you as the source of this information.

PARTIAL LIST OF ELITES INTERVIEWED

FOREIGN MINISTRY

Vice Minister Shunji Yanai
Ministry of Foreign Affairs

Director General Ukeru Magosaki
Intelligence and Analysis Bureau
Ministry of Foreign Affairs

Director General Ryozo Kato
Foreign Policy Bureau
Ministry of Foreign Affairs

Director Naoko Saiki
International Peace Cooperation
Division
Ministry of Foreign Affairs

Director Masafumi Iishi
Foreign Policy Planning Division
Ministry of Foreign Affairs

Tadahiko Yamaguchi, Official
General Coordination Division,
Minister's Secretariat
Ministry of Foreign Affairs

Director Jiro Kodera
First International Econonomic
Affairs Division
Ministry of Foreign Affairs

Deputy Director Tomiko Ichikawa
Northeast Asia Division
Ministry of Foreign Affairs

Director Toshio Kaitani
Human Rights and Refugee Division
Ministry of Foreign Affairs

DEFENSE AGENCY

Vice Minister Masahiro Akiyama
Japan Defense Agency

Mr. Kiyoshi Serizawa, Asst. Director
Defense Policy Division
Japan Defense Agency

Col. Noboru Yamaguchi
Deputy Chief, Defense Planning Div.
Ground Staff Office
Japan Defense Agency

Major Takashi Motomatsu
Planning Section
Plans & Operations Dept. GSO
Japan Defense Agency

Director Hideshi Tokuchi
Operations Division, Operations
Bureau
Japan Defense Agency

HOUSE OF COUNCILLORS (UPPER)

Councillor Tomoharu Yoda (LDP)

Councillor Yoshimasa Hayashi (LDP)

Councillor Keizo Takemi (LDP)

Councilor Kei Hata (LDP)

Councillor Ichita Yamamoto (LDP)

Councillor Hideki Tamura (LDP)

HOUSE OF REPRESENTATIVES
(LOWER)

Representative Hideo Usui (LDP)

Representative Tomoko Nakagawa
(SDP)

Representative Yoshinori Suematsu
(DPJ)

Representative Shingo Nishimura
(DPJ)

Representative Eiichi Nakao (LDP)
Representative Masaharu Nakagawa
(DPJ)

Representative Shigeru Ishiba
(Liberal Party)

Representative Yukihiko Ikeda (LDP)

Representative Hosaka Nobuto
(SDP)

Representative Mitsuo Higashinaka
(CP)

Representative Hajime Funada (LDP)

Representative Eisuke Mori (LDP)

Representative/Pastor Ryuichi Doi
(DPJ)

Representative Shozo Azuma
(Liberal Party)

PRIME MINISTER'S OFFICE

Director Teruaki Nagasaki
Secretariat of the International
Peace Cooperation Headquarters

Mr. Nobushige Takamizawa,
Cabinet Councillor
Cabinet National Security Affairs
Office

Mr. Kenjiro Monji, Cabinet
Councillor
Cabinet Councillors' Office on
External Affairs

Mr. Hiroshi Shigeta
Executive Secretary
International Peace Cooperation
Headquarters

GOVERNMENT EMPLOYED
RESEARCHERS

Professor Masashi Nishihara
National Defense Academy

Professor Shin'ichi Ogawa
National Institute for Defense
Studies

Professor (Col.)Yoshihisa Nakamura
The National Institute for Defense
Studies

Professor Yuzuru Kaneko
National Institute for Defense
Studies

Professor Takesada
The National Institute for Defense
Studies

ACADEMICS & OTHERS

Professor Akihiko Tanaka
Institute of Oriental Culture,
Tokyo University

Professor Hideo Sato
United Nations University

Professor Kazuo Ota, Dean
Rakuno Gakuen University

Professor Hajime Oshitani
Rakuno Gakuen University

Professor Akira Ogawa, Jr.
The Okazaki Institute,

Professor Kenichi Nakamura, Dean
Faculty of Law,
Hokkaido University

Professor Jun Morikawa
Rakuno Gakuen University

Professor Seiichi Kubota
Faculty of Modern Culture
(Former Journalist with Asahi
Shimbun)

Professor Osamu Iishi
Institute of Oriental Culture,
Tokyo University

Professor Takeshi Igarashi
Faculty of Law,
(co-author of LDP Foreign Policy
Platform)

Professor Toshiya Hoshino
Osaka School of International Public
Policy,
Osaka University

Professor Kiichi Fujiwara
Institute of Social Science,
Tokyo University

Ms. Kuniko Nakajima
The Okazaki Institute,
(former Official with Foreign
Ministry)

Professor Yoshihide Soeya
Faculty of Law,
Keio University
(co-author of LDP Foreign Policy
Platform)

Mr. Kenichi Mizuno
(LDP offical and son and adopted
son of two very senior party officials)

BIBLIOGRAPHY

Aikawa, Takaaki and Lynn Leavenworth. *The Mind of Japan: A Christian Perspective*. Valley Forge, Pennsylvania: The Judson Press, 1967.

Akaha, Tsuneo. Japan's Security Agenda in the Post-Cold War Era, The Pacific Review, Vol. 8, No. 1, 1995: 45–76.

———. *The Russian Far East as a Factor in Northeast Asia*, Peace Forum, Number 25/Winter 1997: 91–108.

———. *New Guidelines for U.S.-Japan Defense Cooperation: Its Background and Implications*. Monterey Institute of International Studies, 1997.

———. *The Impact of Foreign Governments: The Case of Japan*. Paper presented at the International Studies Association annual conference, Minneapolis, Minnesota, 17–21 March 1998.

———. *Japanese-Russian Relations: An Overview or Japanese Views of Russia: Through the Eyes of Others*. A paper presented at the International Symposium on Japan and Its Neighbors in the Global Village: Current and Emergent Issues. Nanzan University, Nagoya, Japan. 16–17 October 1999.

Akaha, Tsuneo and Frank Langdon, eds. *Japan in the Posthegemonic World*. Boulder, Colorado: Lynne Rienner Publishers, 1993.

Alagappa, Muthiah. *Comprehensive Security: Interpretations in ASEAN Countries, In Asian Security Issues: Regional and Global*. Edited by R.A. Scalapino, S. Sato, J. Wanandi, and S.-J. Han. Berkeley, California: Institute of East Asian Studies, University of California-Berkeley Press, 50–78.

Allinson, Gary D. and Yasunori Sone, eds. *Political Dynamics in Contemporary Japan*. Ithica, New York: Cornell University Press, 1993.

Arase, David. *Japan Needs Alliance-Plus in Northeast Asia*. Editorial from the

Nichibei Shimbun. Internet edition. 20 March 1999. <http://www.nichibei. org/je/arasemarch.html>.

Asada, Sadao. *Japan and the World 1853–1952: A Bibliographic Guide to Japanese Scholarship in Foreign Relations.* New York: Columbia University Press, 1989.

Asahi News, North Korea focus of defense white paper. Internet edition, 27 July 1999. <Http://www.asahi.com/english/enews.enews.html>.

Associated Press, *Japan, S. Korea Hold Naval Exercise, New York Times,* internet edition, <http://www.nytimes.com/apoline/i/AP-Koreas-Japan-Military. html>, 4 August 1999.

Auer, James E. *Article Nine of Japan's Constitution: from Renunciation of Armed Force "Forever" to the Third Largest Defense Budget in the World. Law and Contemporary Problems,* Spring 1990: 171–187.

Azuma, Shozo. Member of the House of Representatives of the Japanese Diet (Liberal Party). Interview by the author, 6 June 1998, Tokyo. Tape Recording. In author's personal possession, Tempe, Arizona.

Bamba, Nobuya and John F. Howes, eds. *Pacifism in Japan: The Christian and Socialist Tradition.* Vancouver, British Columbia: University of British Columbia Press, 1978.

Bandow, Doug. *Old Wine in New Bottles: The Pentagon's East Asia Security Strategy Report, International Journal of Korean Studies.* Vol. III, No. 1, Spring/Summer 1999: 60–93.

Barnhart, Michael A. *Japan and the World Since 1868.* New York: Edward Arnold, 1995.

Benfell, Steven T. *Profound Regrets: The Memory of World War II in Japan and International Relations in East Asia.* A paper presented at the 40th Annual Conference of the International Studies Association, Washington, D.C., February 17, 1999.

Berger, Mark. *Miracles of Modernization and Crisis of Capitalism: The United States- Japan-China Triangle and the Vicissitudes of the East Asian Model 1940s-1990s.* A paper presented at the International Symposium on Japan and Its Neighbors in the Global Village: Current and Emergent Issues. Nanzan University, Nagoya, Japan. 16–17 October 1999.

Bessho, Koro. *Identities and Security in East Asia.* New York: Oxford university Press, 1999.

Brooks, Stephen G. *Dueling Realisms, International Organization,* 52, 3, Summer 1997: 445–477.

Brzezinski, Zbigniew. *A Geostrategy for Eurasia, Foreign Affairs,* 76, 5. (September/October 1997), 62–63.

Bullens, Hendrik and Seiitsu Tachibana, eds. *Restructuring Security Concepts, Postures and Industrial Base.* Mosbach, Germany: Afes Press, 1997.

Buzan, Barry. *Japan's Defence Problematique, The Pacific Review,* Vol. 8, No. 1, 1995: 25–43.

Buzan, Barry, Ole Wœver, and Jaap de Wilde. *Security: A New Frame Work for Analysis*. Boulder, Colorado: Lynne Rienner Publishers, 1998.

Carlsnaes, Walter. *The Agency-Structure Problem in Foreign Policy Analysis, International Studies Quarterly*, 36, 1992: 245–270.

Carpenter,Ted Galen. *Roiling Asia: U.S. Coziness with China Upsets the Neighbors, Foreign Affairs*. Volume 77 No. 6 (November/December 1998), 2–6.

Carr, Edward Hallett. *Twenty Years' Crisis, 1919–1939: An Introduction to the Study of International Relations*. New York: Harper & Row, 1939.

Chai, Sun-Ki. *Entrenching the Yoshida Defense Doctrine: Three Techniques for Institutionalization, International Organization*, 51, 3, Summer 1997: 389–412.

Chan, Steve. *Asia Pacific Regionalism: Tentative Thoughts on Conceptual Basis and Empirical Linkages*. Paper presented at the International Studies Association Conference, Washington, D.C., February 16–20, 1999.

Chang, Iris. *The Rape of Nanking: The Forgotten Holocaust of World War II*. New York: Penguin Putnam Inc., 1997.

Chinworth, Michael W., ed. *Inside Japan's Defense: Technology, Economics & Strategy*. Washington: Brassey's (US), Inc., 1992.

———. Defense-Economic Linkages in U.S.-Japan Relations: An Overview of Policy Positions and Objectives. (Working Paper) 14 April 1999. <http://www.seas.gwu.edu/ nsarchive/japan/chinworth_wp.htm>.

Choi, Eunbong. *Balancing the past and the future: A Korean View of the Korea-Japan Relationship*. A paper presented at the International Symposium on Japan and Its Neighbors in the Global Village: Current and Emergent Issues, Nanzan University, Nagoya, Japan, 16–17 October 1999.

Christensen, Raymond V. and Paul E. Johnson. *Toward a Context-Rich Analysis of Electoral Systems: The Japanese Example, American Journal of Political Science*. August 1995, Vol. 39:3, 575–598.

Clesse, Armand, Takashi Inoguchi, E. B. Keehn, and J. A. A. Stockwin, eds. *The Vitality of Japan: Sources of National Strength and Weakness*. New York: St. Martin's Press, Inc., 1997.

Constitution of Japan, The. Law and Contemporary Problems, Spring, 1990: 200–214.

Collinwood, Dean W. *Japan and the Pacific Rim*, 5th ed. Guilford, Connecticut: Dushkin, 1999.

Cossa, Ralph A. ed. *Restructuring the U.S.-Japan Alliance: Toward a More Equal Partnership*. Washington, D.C.: Center for Strategic and International Studies, 1997.

———. Prospects for Northeast Asian Multilateral Security Cooperation, *International Journal of Korean Studies*. Vol. III, No. 1, Spring/Summer 1999: 35–59.

Cowhey, Peter F. *Domestic Institutions an the Credibility of International*

Commitments: Japan and the United States, International Organization 47, 2, Spring 1993: 299– 326.

Curtis, Gerald L., ed. *Japan's Foreign Policy After the Cold War: Coping with Change.* New York: M. E. Sharpe, 1993.

———. *The Japanese Way of Politics.* New York: Columbia University Press, 1988.

———. *The United States, Japan , and Asia.* New York: W. W. Norton and Company, 1994.

Daily Yomiuri. Defense Legislation Leaves Some Questions Unanswered. 27 May 1999. Internet edition. <http://www.yomiuri.co.jp/newse/0527po17.htm>.

de Kieffer, Donald. *Exercise of Force by the Japanese Self-Defense Force, North Carolina Journal of International Law & Commercial Regulation.* Winter 1991: v16, 69–77.

Dory, John T. and Richard D. Fisher, Jr. *U.S. and Asia Statistical Handbook 1998–1999 Edition.* Washington, D.C.: The Heritage Foundation, 1998.

Drifte, Reinhard. *Japan's Foreign Policy.* New York: Council on Foreign Relations Press, 1990.

———. *Japan's Foreign Policy for the 21st Century: From Economic Superpower to What Power?* Oxford: St. Antony's Press, 1998.

———. *The US-Japan-China Security Triangle and the future of East Asian Security,* to be published in: *Security in a Globalized World: Risks and Opportunities,* Laurent Goetschel, ed., Nomos Verlag: Baden-Baden, 1999.

Dupont, Alan. *Concepts of Security,* in *Unresolved Futures: Comprehensive Security in the Asia Pacific.* Edited by J. Rolfe. Wellington: Center for Strategic Studies, 1– 15.

Edström, Bert. *Japan's Quest for a Role in the World: Roles Ascribed to Japan Nationally and Internationally 1969–1982.* Ph.D. diss., Institute of Oriental Languages, University of Stockholm, 1988.

Embassy of Japan in Washington, D. C. (Reproduced from the unofficial translation provided by). *Japan: Law Concerning Cooperation for United Nations Peace- keeping Operations and Other Operations. International-Legal Materials,* v32, 3– 35, 215–216.

Ezrati, Milton. *Japan's Aging Economics, Foreign Affairs.* May/June 1997, Vol.76 No. 3, 96–104.

Feldman, Ofer. *The Political Personality of Japan: An Inquiry into the Belief Systems of Diet Members, Political Psychology,* Vol. 17, No. 4, 1996: 657–682.

Fic, Victor. *The Japanese PKO Bill, Asian Defense Journal,* Nov. 1992: 28–33.

———. *Geopolitical Implications of Japan's PKO Law, Asian Defense Journal,* Jan. 1993: 126–131.

Friedman, Edward. *The Politics of Democratization: Generalizing East Asian Experiences.* Boulder, Colorado: Westview Press, 1994.

Friedman, George and Meredith LeBard. *The Coming War with Japan*. New York: St. Martin's Press, 1991.

French, Howard W. *Japan's Cultural Bias Against Foreigners Comes Under Attack*, The New York Times, internet edition, <http://www.nytimes.com/library/world/asia/111599japan-discriminate.html>, November 15, 1999.

———. *Still Wary of Outsiders, Japan Expects Immigration Boom*, The New York Times, internet edition <http://www.nytimes.com/library/world/asia/031400japan-immigration.html> March 14, 2000.

———. *An Upstart Governor Takes on Japan's Mandarins*, The New York Times, internet edition <http://www.nytimes.com/library/world/asia/033000japan-ishihara.html>, March 30, 2000.

Fujiwara, Kiichi. Professor, Institute of Social Science, Tokyo University. Interview by author, 11 June 1998, Tokyo. Tape Recording. In author's personal possession Tempe, Arizona.

Fukui, Haruhiro. *Japan in the East Asian regional Order: An Historical Retrospective, Peace Forum*, Number 25/Winter 1997: 59–70.

Funada, Hajime. Member of the House of Representatives of the Japanese Diet (LDP), Chairman of the Sub-Committee on Asia and the Pacific. Interview by the author, 28 May 1998, Tokyo. Tape Recording. In author's personal possession, Tempe, Arizona.

Funibashi, Yoichi, ed. *Japan's International Agenda*. New York: New York University Press, 1994.

Funk, Robert B. *Japan's Constitution and U. N. Obligations in the Persian Gulf War: A Case for Non-Military Participation in U. N. Enforcement Actions. Cornell International Law Journal*, Vol. 25, 1992: 363–399.

Gallicchio, Marc. *Japan in American Security Policy: A Problem in Perspective*, (Working Paper #10) downloaded from: <http://www.seas.gwu.edu/nsaarchive/japan/gallicciowp.htm>, April 14,1999.

Ge, Tong. *Realism and Chinese Foreign Policy in East and Southeast Asia in the Post- Cold War Era*. Master's thesis/paper Arizona State University: Department of Political Science, 1999.

George, Alexander L. *Bridging the Gap: Theory and Practice in Foreign Policy*. Washington, D.C.: United States Institute of Peace Press, 1993.

Gibney, Alex. *The Pacific Century: Reinventing Japan (#5)*. Produced by the Pacific Basin Institute in association with KCTS/Seattle. 60 min. Jigsaw Productions, 1992. Videocassette.

———. *The Pacific Century*. Produced by the Pacific Basin Institute in association with KCTS/Seattle. Tapes 1–6. Jigsaw Productions, 1992. Videocassette.

Goldmann, Kjell. *Change and Stability in Foreign Policy: The Problems and Possibilities of Détente*. Princeton: Princeton University Press, 1988.

Goodman, Roger and Kirsten Refsing, eds. *Ideology and Practice in Modern Japan*. New York: Routledge, 1992.

Gorden, Raymond L. *Interviewing: Strategy, Techniques and Tactics.* Homewood, Illinois: The Dorsey Press, 1969.

Gourevitch, Peter, Takashi Inoguchi, and Courtney Purrington, eds. *United States-Japan Relations and International Institutions After the Cold War.* San Diego, California: Graduate School of International Relations and Pacific Studies, University of California, San Diego, 1995.

Grieco, Joseph M. *Anarchy and the Limits of Cooperation: A Realist Critique of the Newest Liberal Institutionalism.* In *Neorealism and Neoliberalism: The Contemporary Debate,* ed. David A Baldwin, 116–140. New York: Columbia University Press, 1993.

———. *China, Japan, and Germany in the New World Polity* (Chapter 8). To appear in John Mueller, ed., 1999. (Faxed copy of publisher's proof in possession of the author).

Guertner, Gary L. *Collective Security in Europe and Asia.* Carlisle Barracks, Pennsylvania: Strategic Studies Institute, 1992.

Hayao, Kenji. *The Japanese Prime Minister and Public Policy.* Pittsburgh, Pennsylvania: University of Pittsburgh Press, 1993.

Hata, Kei. *Urgent Recommendation Regarding Information Infrastructure Strategy.* Paper presented to Prime Minister Hashimoto, 8 December 1997 (English version, April 1998). Downloaded from: <http://www.k-hata.or.jp/itproe>.

———. Member of the House of Councillors of the Japanese Diet (LDP). Interview by the author, 18 May 1998, Tokyo. Tape Recording. In author's personal possession, Tempe, Arizona.

Higashinaka, Mitsuo. Member of the House of Representatives of the Japanese Diet (JCP). Interview by the author, 19 May 1998, Tokyo. Tape Recording. In author's personal possession, Tempe, Arizona.

Hermann, Charles F. *Changing Course: When Governments Choose to Redirect Foreign Policy, International Studies Quarterly.* 34, 1990: 3–21.

Hermann, Margaret G. and Charles F. Hermann. *Who Makes Foreign policy Decisions and How: An Empirical Inquiry, International Studies Quarterly,* 33, 1989: 361– 387.

Hokugo, Miyuki. *Japan, S. Korea, U.S. warn N. Korea against missile test, Asahi News.* Internet edition, 27 July 1999. <Http://www.asahi.com/english/enews.enews.html>.

Holsti, Kal J., ed. *Why Nations Realign: Foreign Policy Restructuring in the Postwar World.* London: George Allen and Unwin, 1982.

Hosaka, Nobuto. Member of the House of Representatives of the Japanese Diet (SDP). Interview by the author, 16 June 1998, Tokyo. Tape Recording. In author's personal possession, Tempe, Arizona.

Hoshino, Toshiya. Professor, Osaka School of International Policy, Osaka University. Interview by author. 10 June 1998, Tokyo. Tape recording. In author's personal possession Tempe, Arizona.

Hosokawa, Ryuichiro. *Japanese need a good dose of 'Pride'*, The Japan Times, Tuesday June 2, 1998, P. 18.

Hoye, Timothy. *Japanese Politics: Fixed and Floating Worlds.* New Jersey: Prentice Hall, 1999.

Hughes, Christopher W. *Japanese Policy and the North Korean 'Soft Landing'*, The Pacific Review, Vol. 11, No. 3, 1998: 389–415.

Hunsberger, Warren, ed. *Japan's Quest: The Search for International Role, Recognition, and Respect.* New York: M. E. Sharpe, Inc., 1997.

Igarashi, Takeshi. *Circumventing Japan-U. S. Conflict, Japan Quarterly,* Jan-March 1991: 15–22.

Iishi, Masafumi. Director Foreign Policy Planning Division of the Japanese Ministry of Foreign Affairs. Interview by author, 1 June 1998, Tokyo. Tape Recording. In author's personal possession Tempe, Arizona.

Iishi, Osamu. Professor Institute of Oriental Culture, Tokyo University. Interview by author, 29 May 1998, Tokyo. Tape Recording. In author's personal possession Tempe, Arizona.

Ike, Nobutaka. The Beginnings of Political Democracy in Japan. Baltimore, Maryland: The John Hopkins University Press, 1952.

———. *Japanese Politics: Patron-Client Democracy,* 2nd ed. New York: Alfred A. Knopf, 1972.

Ikeda, Yukihiko. Member of the House of Representatives of the Japanese Diet (LDP), Former Foreign and Defense Minister. Interview by the author. 16 June 1998, Tokyo. Tape Recording. In author's personal possession, Tempe, Arizona.

Inoguchi, Takashi. *Japan's Response to the Gulf Crisis: An Analytic Overview,* Journal of Japanese Studies, 17:2, 1991: 257–290.

———. *Japan's International Relations.* London: Pinter Publishers, 1990.

Iseri, Hirofumi. *Clearing the Mist from the Peace-keeping Debate, Japan Echo.* Volume XIX, Number 3, Autumn 1992: 44–49.

Ishiba, Shigeru. Member of the House of Representatives of the Japanese Diet (LDP). Interview by the author, 4 June 1998, Tokyo. Tape Recording. In author's personal possession, Tempe, Arizona.

Ishihara, Shintaro. *The Japan that Can say "No" (No to Ieru Nihon).* Translated and edited by Frank Baldwin. New York: Simon and Schuster, 1991.

Ito, Mayumi. *Globalization of Japan: Japanese 'Sakoku' Mentality and U.S. Eforts to Open Japan.* New York: St. Martin's Press, 1998.

Izumura, Fusakazu. *Should Japan Get a Permanent Seat on the U. N. Security Council?, Tokyo Business Today,* (March 1993): 54.

Johnson, Chalmers. *Japan: Who Governs?* New York: W. W. Norton & Company, 1995.

Johnson, Chalmers and E. B. Keehn. *The Pentagon's Ossified Strategy, Foreign Affairs.* 74, 4 (July/August 1995): 103–114.

JPOLL, Roper Center for Public Opinion Research, University of Connecticut.

"The data used in this book were originally collected by the *Asahi Shimbun, Jiji Press, Yomiuri Shimbun, Nihon Keizai Shimbun,* and the Prime Minister's Office. The data was obtained from the Japan Public Opinion Location Library, JPOLL, Roper Center for Public Opinion Research, University of Connecticut. Neither the original collectors of the data, nor the Roper Center, bear any responsibility for the analysis or interpretations presented here." <http://roper1.ropercenter.uconn.edu>.

Kades, Charles L. *The American Role in Revising Japan's Imperial Constitution, Political Science Quarterly,* Vol. 104, Nov. 2, 1989: 217.

Kamiya, Setsuko and Kanako Takahara. *Tojo film opens to applause, criticism, The Japan Times.* Sunday May 24, 1998, P. 2.

Kang, C. S. *Korea and Japanese Security, International Journal of Korean Studies.* Vol. III, No. 1, Spring/Summer 1999: 94–115.

Kataoka, Tetsuya. *The Price of a Constitution: The Origin of Japan's Postwar Politics.* New York: Crane Russak, 1991.

Kato, Ryozo. Director General, Foreign Policy Bureau of the Japanese Ministry of Foreign Affairs. Interview by author, 21 May 1998, Tokyo. Tape Recording. In author's personal possession Tempe, Arizona.

Kennan, George F. *Memoirs 1925–1950.* New York: Bantam Books, 1967.

Kennedy, John W. *Tokyo: Indifferent to the Risen Son. Pentecostal Evangel.* (5 December 1999): 10.

Kennedy, Paul. *The Rise and Fall of the Great Powers: Economic Change and Military conflict from 1500–2000.* New York: Random House, 1987.

Kim, Lieutenant Colonel Andrew H. N. *Japan and Peace-keeping Operations, Military Review,* (April 1994): 22–33.

Kissinger, Henry. *Diplomacy.* New York: Simon and Schuster, 1994.

Kitaoka, Shinichi. *A Green Light for Japanese Peace-keepers, Japan Echo,* Volume XIX, Number 3, (Autumn 1992): 42.

Kristof, Nicholas D. *A Big Exception for a Nation of Apologizers. The New York Times.* 12 June 1995, A1 and A4.

———. *The Problem of Memory, Foreign Affairs.* Volume 77 No. 6 (November/December 1998): 37–49.

———. *Seeking to Be Tokyo's Governor, Politician Attacks U.S. Presence. The New York Times.* 26 March 1999, A12.

———. *A Tojo Battles History, for Grandpa and for Japan. The New York Times.* Internet edition. 22 April 1999. <http://www.nytimes.com/library/world/asia/042299japan-tojo.html>.

Kodama, Katsuya. *Non-Provocative Defense as a New Japanese Defense Policy.* Paper presented at the International Studies Association Conference, Washington, D.C. February 17–20, 1999.

Kodera, Jiro. Director First International Economic Affairs Division of the Japanese Ministry of Foreign Affairs. Interview by author, 20 May 1998, Tokyo. Tape Recording. In author's personal possession Tempe, Arizona.

Koh, B. C. *Japan's Administrative Elite.* Berkeley, California: University of California Press, 1989.

———. *U.S.-Japan Security Cooperation and the Two Koreas.* A paper presented at the International Studies Association 41st Annual Convention, Los Angeles, California, 17 March 2000, 1.

Kubota, Seiichi. Professor, Faculty of Modern Culture, Tokyo Junshin Women's College (former Journalist with the Asahi Shimbun). Interview by the author, 1 June 1998, Tokyo. Tape Recording. In author's personal possession Tempe, Arizona.

Langdon, Frank. *Japan's Regional and Global Coalition participation: Political and Economic Aspects.* Vancouver, British Columbia: Institute of International Relations, the University of British Columbia, 1997.

Leitch, Richard D., Akira Kato, and Martin E. Weinstein, eds. *Japan's Role in the Post- Cold War World.* Westport, Connecticut: Greenwood Press, 1995.

Luney, Percy R. Jr., and Takahashi, Kazuyuki, ed. *Japanese Constitutional Law.* Tokyo: University of Tokyo Press, 1993.

Madsen, Sandra. *The Japanese Constitution and Self-Defense Forces: Prospects for a New Japanese Military Role. Transnational Law & Contemporary Problems,* Fall 1993: v3, 549–579.

Magosaki, Ukeru. *New Diplomatic Challenges in East Asia.* Unpublished paper. Japanese Ministry of Foreign Affairs, 1998.

Markman, Robert. *A Whole Lot of Bull $\mathcal{S}*\#\%!, Worth.* February 2000, 116–125.

Masaki, Hisane. *Japan, China consider upgrading security forum, The Japan Times,* internet edition, 14 September 1999. <http://www.japantimes.co.jp/news/news 9–99/ news.html>.

Mastanduno, Michael. *Preserving the Unipolar Moment: Realist Theories and U.S. Grand Strategy after the Cold War, International Security,* Vol. 21, No. 4, Spring 1997, 49–88.

McDonough, Peter, Samuel H. Barnes, and Antonio Lòpez Pina. *The Cultural Dynamics of Democratization in Spain.* Ithica, New York: Cornell University Press, 1998.

Mendel, Jr., Douglas H. *The Japanese People and Foreign Policy: A Study of Public Opinion in Post-Treaty Japan.* Berkeley, California: University of California Press, 1961.

Mensing, John. Email comment on how Japan embraced defeat, 13 October 1999, H- Net/KIAPS List for United States and Japanese Relations, <H-US-Japan@H-Net.msu.edu>.

Midford, Paul. *From Reactive State to Cautious Leader: The Nakayama Proposal and Japan's Role in Promoting the Creation of the ASEAN Regional Forum (ARF).* Unpublished Paper, Columbia University: Department of Political Science, 1998.

———. The US-Japan Defense Guidelines: Balance of Power, Balance of

Threat and Asian Reactions. Paper presented at the International Studies Association Conference, Washington, D.C. February 17–20, 1999.

Ministry of Foreign Affairs (Japan). Japan and the United States: Teamwork Today and Tomorrow. Ministry of Foreign Affairs (Japan) publication, February 1993.

———. Japan's ODA: Annual Report 1997. Tokyo: Association for Promotion of International Cooperation, 1998.

Miyashita, Akitoshi. Consensus or Compliance?: 'Gaiatsu' and Japan's Foreign aid to China and Russia. Paper presented at the International Studies Association Annual Conference, Los Angeles, California, 14–18 March 2000.

Mochizuki, Mike M. Japan: Domestic Change and Foreign Policy. Santa Monica, California: RAND, 1995.

Monji, Kenjiro. Councillor, Cabinet Office of the Prime Minister, Office on External Affairs, Office of the Prime Minister of Japan. Interview by the author. 11 June 1998, Tokyo. Tape Recording. In author's personal possession, Tempe, Arizona.

Morganthau, Hans J. Politics Among Nations. Revised by Kenneth W. Thompson. New York: Knopf, 1985.

Mori, Eisuke. Member of the House of Representatives of the Japanese Diet (LDP). Interview by the author, 22 May 1998, Tokyo. Tape Recording. In author's personal possession, Tempe, Arizona.

Morikawa, Jun. Professor Rakuno Gakuen University. Interview by author, 22 June 1998, Tokyo. Tape Recording. In author's personal possession Tempe, Arizona.

Motomatsu, Takashi. Major in the Japanese Ground Self Defense Forces and former commander of a SDF PKO mission to the Golan Heights, current station Planning Section of the Plans and Operations Department Japan Defense Agency. Interview by the author, 5 June 1998, Tokyo. Author's notes. In author's personal possession, Tempe, Arizona.

Mulgan, Aurelia George. Strategic Update - Japan. School of Politics, University of New South Wales, Australian Defence Force Academy. Conference paper, 1999.

Nakagawa, Tomoko. Member of the House of Representatives of the Japanese Diet (SDP). Interview by the author, 16 June 1998, Tokyo. Tape Recording. In author's personal possession, Tempe, Arizona.

Nakajima, Kuniko. Former career diplomat with the Japanese Ministry of Foreign Affairs and currently a researcher with the Okazaki Institute. Interview by the author, 18 June 1998, Tokyo. Tape recording. In author's personal possession, Tempe, Arizona.

Nakamura, Kenichi. Dean of Law, Hokkaido University (Top Japanese Researcher on the PKO Law). Interview by author, 20 June 1998, Tokyo. Tape Recording. In author's personal possession Tempe, Arizona.

Nakamura, Yoshihisa. Colonel in the GSDF and Professor at the National Institute for Defense Studies, Japan Defense Agency. Interview by the author, 28 May 1998, Tokyo. Tape Recording. In author's personal possession, Tempe, Arizona.

Nakanishi, Terumasa. *Japan's Place in the World, Japan Echo*. Volume XIX, Special Issue, 1992: 2–5.

Nakano, Minoru. *The Policy-Making Process in Contemporary Japan*. Jeremy Scott, trans. New York: St. Martin's Press, Inc., 1997.

National Institute of Population and Social Security Research. *Selected Demographic indicators for Japan*. Internet web page: <http://www.ipss.go.jp/English/S_D_I/ Indip.html>.

Newland, Kathleen, ed. *The International Relations of Japan*. London: MacMillan, 1990.

New York Times. Japan Discovers Defense. 26 August 1999. Internet edition. <http://www.nytimes.com/yr/mo/day/editorial/26thu1.html>.

Nishihara, Masashi. Professor at the National Defense Academy, Japan Defense Agency. Interview by the author, 31 May 1998, Tokyo. Tape Recording. In author's personal possession, Tempe, Arizona.

———. *Japanese Defense Policy: Issues and Options*. A paper presented at the International Symposium on Japan and Its Neighbors in the Global Village: Current and Emergent Issues. Nanzan University, Nagoya, Japan. 16–17 October 1999.

Nishimura, Mutsuyoshi. *Peace-keeping Operations: Setting the Record Straight. Japan Echo*. Volume XIX, Number 3, Autumn 1992: 50–56.

Nishimura, Shingo. Member of the House of Representatives of the Japanese Diet (Liberal Party). Interview by the author. 17 June 1998, Tokyo. Tape Recording. In author's personal possession, Tempe, Arizona.

Oberdorfer, Don and Hajime Izumi. The United States, Japan and the Korean Peninsula: Coordinating Policies and Objectives. (Working Paper) 14 April 1999, <http:// www.seas.gwu.edu/nsaarchive/japan/donizumi-wp.htm>.

Odawara, Atsushi. *The Kaifu Bungle. Japan Quarterly*, Jan- March 1991: 6–14.

Ogata, Sadako. *The Changing Role of Japan in the United Nations. Journal of International Affairs*, Summer 1983: n27, 29–42.

Ogawa, Akira. Professor, Okazaki Research Institute, Tokyo, Japan. Interview by author, 18 June 1998, Tokyo. Tape Recording. In author's personal possession Tempe, Arizona.

Ogawa, Shin'ichi. Professor, National Institute for Defense Studies. Interview by author. 11 June 1998, Tokyo. Tape Recording. In author's personal possession Tempe, Arizona.

Oshiba, Ryo. *Japan's U.N. Policy in the 1990s*. Paper presented at the International Studies Association annual conference, Washington, D.C., February 16–20, 1999.

Oshitani, Hajime. Professor at Rakuno Gakuen University. Interview by author, 25 June 1998, Tokyo. Tape Recording. In author's personal possession Tempe, Arizona.

Ota, Kazuo. *The Place and Role of Political Parties in Contemporary Societies in Connection with the HASTIC Production System: An Analysis of Japanese Political Parties, Journal of Rakuno Gakuen University*, Vol. 21, No. 2, 1997: 205–214.

———. Dean Rakuno Gakuen University. Interview by author, 6 June 1998, Tokyo. Tape Recording. In author's personal possession Tempe, Arizona.

Overby, Charles M. *A Call for Peace: The Implications of Japan's War-Renouncing Constitution* (Bilingual Edition). Kunihiro Masao, trans. Tokyo: Kodansha International, 1997.

Oxford American Dictionary. New York: Avon Books, 1982.

Ozawa, Ichiro. *Blueprint for a New Japan: The Rethinking of a Nation (Nihon Kaizo Keikaku)*. Translated by Louisa Rubinfien and edited by Eric Grower. New York: Kodansha International, 1994.

Paris, Gilles. *Le Japonais Kochiro Matsuura da succeder a Federico Mayor a la tete de l'Unesco, Le Monde*, 22 October 1999 as cited by H-Japan <H-JAPAN@H- NET.MSU.EDU> #1999–91 5–7 November 1999.

Parker, Jay M. *The U.S.-Japan Defense Guidelines and the Future East Asian Security Environment*. Paper presented at the International Studies Association annual conference, Washington, D.C., February 16–20, 1999.

Pempel, T. J. *Structural 'Gaiatsu': international Finance and Political Change in Japan, Comparative Political Studies*. Vol. 32 No. 8. (December 1999): 907–932.

———. *Regime Shift: Comparative Dynamics of the Japanese Political Economy*. Ithaca, New York: Cornell University Press, 1998.

Powell, Robert. *Absolute and Relative Gains in International Relations Theory, American Political Science Review*, Vol. 85, No. 4, December 1991: 1303–1320.

———. *Anarchy in International Relations Theory: The Neorealist-Neoliberal Debate, International Organization*, 48, 2, Spring 1994: 313–344.

Putnam, Robert. *Diplomacy and domestic politics: the logic of two-level games, International Organization*, 42, 3, Summer 1988, 427–460.

Ramsdell, Daniel B. *The Japanese Diet: Stability and Change in the Japanese House of Representatives 1890–1990*. Lanham, Maryland: University Press of America, 1992.

Reischauer, Edwin O. *The United States and Japan*, 3rd Ed. New York: Viking Press, 1969.

———. *Japan: The Story of a Nation*, 4th ed. New York: McGraw-Hill Publishing Company, 1990.

Rosenau, James N. *The Study of Political Adaptation: Essays on the Analysis of World Politics*. New York: Nichols Publishing, 1981.

Rhodes, John. Former Republican Congressman and Minority Whip from Arizona. Conversation between the author and the Congressman during the Spring 1996 at the University Club, Arizona State University, Tempe, Arizona. Author's notes. In author's personal possession, Tempe, Arizona.

Ross, Robert S. *Managing a Changing Relationship: China's Japan Policy in the 1990s.* Paper presented at the Strategic Studies Institute, Unted States Army War College, Carlisle Barracks, 23–25 April 1996.

Rostati, Jerel A., Joe D. Hagan, and Martin W. Sampson III, eds. *Foreign Policy Restructuring: How Governments Respond to Global Change.* Columbia, South Carolina: University of South Carolina Press, 1994.

Royer, Kendrick F. *The Demise of the World's First Pacifist Constitution: Japanese Constitutional Interpretation and the Growth of Executive Power to Make War. Vanderbilt Journal of Transnational Law,* 1993: v26, 749–801.

Sackton, Frank, Major General United States Army (Ret.) and former aid to General Douglas MacArthur during the occupation of Japan. Interviews by author, 19 and 24 September 1997, Tempe, Arizona. Tape Recording. In author's personal possession Tempe, Arizona.

Saiki, Naoko. Director International Peace Cooperation Division, Ministry of Foreign Affairs. Interview by author, 4 June 1998, Tokyo. Tape Recording. In author's personal possession Tempe, Arizona.

Saito, Shiro. *Japan at the Summit: Its Role in the Western Alliance and Asian Pacific Co-operation.* New York: Routledge, 1990.

Sakamoto, Masahiro. *PAX Americana II and Japan.* Paper presented at the International Studies Association Conference, Washington, D.C. February 17–20, 1999.

Sampson III, Martin W. and Steven G. Walker, *Cultural Norms and National Roles: A Comparison of Japan and France,* in Stephen G. Walker, ed., *Role Theory and Foreign Policy Analysis.* (Durham: Duke University Press, 1987), Chapter 7, 105–122.

Sanger, David E. *U.S. and Japanese Told to Resolve Dispute on Trade-Blunt Warning to Both—New World Trade Chief Calls Conflict a 'Delicate Matter'—Nationalism is Cited, The New York Times,* 14 June 1995, A1.

Sasaki, Yoshitaka. *Japan's Undue International Contribution. Japan Quarterly,* July- Sep. 1993: 259–265.

Sato, Yoichiro. *Toward a Non-Threatening US-Japan Alliance.* Paper presented at the International Studies Association Conference, Washington, D.C. February 17–20, 1999.

Scalapino, Robert, ed. *The Foreign Policy of Modern Japan.* Berkeley, California: University of California Press, 1977.

Scheiner, Irwin. *Modern Japan: An Interpretive Anthology.* New York: MacMillan Publishering, 1974.

Schmiegelow, Hendrik and Michèle Schmiegelow. *How Japan Affects the International System, International Organization,* 44, 4, Autumn 1990: 553–584.

Schoppa, Leonard J. *Two level games and bargaining outcomes: why 'gaiatsu'
    succeeds in Japan in some cases but not in others*, International
    Organization, 47, 3, Summer 1993, 353–386.
Selin, Shannon. *Asia Pacific Arms Buildups Part One: Scope, Causes and
    Problems*. Vancouver, British Columbia: Institute of International
    Relations, the University of British Columbia, 1994.
Shibata, Akiho. *Japanese Peacekeeping Legislation and Recent Developments in
    U.N. Operations*. The Yale Journal of International Law, 1994: v19,
    307–348.
Simon, Sheldon W. *East Asian Security in the Post-Cold War Era*. New York: M.
    E. Sharpe, Inc., 1993.
———. *International Relations Theory and Southeast Asian Security*. The Pacific
    Review. Vol. 8, No. 1 (1995): 5–24.
———. *Multilateralism and Japan's Security Policy*, The Korean Journal of
    Defense Analysis, Vol. XI, No. 2, (Winter 1999): 79–96.
Sims, Calvin. *U.S. Resists Cut in Funds by Japan for G.I.'s*. The New York Times.
    Internet edition. 17 February 2000. <http://www.nytimes.com/yr/mo/day/
    news/world/japan-us-troops.html>.
———. *Tokyo Chief Starts New Furror, on Immigrants*, The New York Times,
    internet   edition
    <http://www.nytimes.com/library/world/asia/041100japan-immigrants
    .html>, April 11, 2000.
Smith, Geoffrey. *Japan Expanding Defense Role*, The Washington Times. 7
    March 2000, 11 as cited by Northeast Asia Peace and Security Network
    Daily Report for Tuesday March 7, 2000, from Berkeley, California, USA,
    <NAPSNet@nautilus .org (NAPSNet)>.
Snow, Donald. *National Security: Defense Policy in a Changed International
    Order*, 4th ed. New York: St. Martin's Press, 1998.
Soeya, Yoshihide. *Japan's Duel Identity and the U.S.-Japan Alliance*. Institute for
    International Studies, Stanford University, May 1998.
Spruyt, Hendrik. *A New Architecture for Peace?: Reconfiguring Japan Among the
    Great Powers*, The Pacific Review, Vol. 11 No. 3 1998: 364–388.
Stevenson, Matthew. *Re-Reading Rosecrance: International Norms and the
    Trading State*. Paper presented at the International Studies Association
    Annual Conference, Los Angeles, California, 14–18 March 2000.
Storry, Richard. *A History of Modern Japan*. Baltimore, Maryland: Penguin
    Books, 1969.
Takagi, Yoko. *Japan's Foreign Policy: Japan's decision making of the foreign pol-
    icy and the PKO Law* (sic). Research Paper for Dr. Linda Rawles, Grand
    Canyon University, 1998.
Takayanagi, Sakio and Katsuya Kodama, eds. *Japan and Peace*. Mie, Japan:
    Mie Academic Press, 1994.
Takemi, Keizo. Member of the House of Councillors of the Japanese Diet.

Current Cabinet Vice Foreign Minister and past House of Councillors Chair of Foreign Relations Committee and founding chair of the sub committee on Pacific Affairs. Interview by the author, 25 May 1998, Tokyo. Tape Recording. In author's personal possession, Tempe, Arizona.

Takesada, Professor. National Institute for Defense Studies. Interview by the author. 5 June 1998, Tokyo. Tape Recording. In author's personal possession, Tempe, Arizona.

Tan, See Seng. *Constituting Asia-Pacific (In)Security: A Radical Constructivist Study in "Track II" Security Dialogues.* Ph.D. diss., Arizona State University, May 1999.

Tanaka, Akihiko. Professor, Institute of Oriental Culture, Tokyo University. Interview by author. 16 June 1998, Tokyo. Tape Recording. In author's personal possession Tempe, Arizona.

———. *Japan and Regional Integration in Asia-Pacific.* A paper presented at the 40th Annual Conference of the International Studies Association, Washington, D.C. February 17, 1999.

Taylor, Trevor and Seizaburo Sato, eds. Vol. 4, *Future Sources of Global Conflict: The Security Challenges for Japan and Europe in a Post-Cold War World.* London: Royal Institute of International Affairs and Institute for International Policy Studies, 1995.

Terada, Takashi. *The origins of Japan's APEC policy: Foreign Minister Takeo Miki's Asia-Pacific policy and current implications, The Pacific Review,* Vol. 11 No. 3, 1999: 337–363.

Tow, William, Russell Trood, and Toshiya Hoshino, eds. *Bilateralism in a Multilateral Era: The Future of the San Francisco Alliance System in the Asia-Pacific.* Tokyo: The Japan Institute of International Affairs, 1997.

Tucker, Robert W. *The Inequality of Nations.* New York: Basic Books, Inc., 1977.

Urata, Kenji. *The Peace and Security of Japan, National Lawyers Guild Practitioner,* Summer 1987: v44, n3 and 75–86.

Usui, Hideo. Member of the House of Representatives of the Japanese Diet and former Defense Minister and Vice Defense Agency Minister (Career ministry appointment). Interview by the author, 26 and 29 May 1998, Tokyo. Tape Recording. In author's personal possession, Tempe, Arizona.

van Wolferen, Karel. *The Enigma of Japanese Power.* Tokyo: Charles E. Tuttle Co., 1993.

Vogel, Ezra F. *Japan as Number One: Lessons for America.* Cambridge, Mass.: Harvard University Press, 1979.

Walker, Stephen G., ed. *Role Theory and Foreign Policy Analysis.* Durham: Duke University Press, 1987.

Waltz, Kenneth N. *Man, the State, and War: A Theoretical Analysis.* New York: Columbia University Press, 1954, 1959.

———. Conference comment January 1999 Scottsdale, Arizona. Author's personal notes. In the author's personal possession, Tempe, Arizona, January 1999

Wan, Ming. *Spending Strategies in World Politics: How Japan used Its Economic Power in the Past Decade, International Studies Quarterly*, 39, (1995): 85–108.

Ward, Michael D., David R. Davis, and Corey L. Lofdahl. *A Century of Tradeoffs: Defense and Growth in Japan and the United States, International Studies Quarterly*, 39, (1995): 27–50.

Watts, William. *The United States and Japan: A Troubled Partnership*. Cambridge, Massachusetts: Ballinger Publishing Company, 1984.

Welfield, John, ed. *An Empire in Eclipse: Japan in the Postwar American Alliance System: A Study in the Interaction of Domestic Politics and Foreign Policy*. New Jersey: The Athlone Press, 1988.

Wittkopf, Eugene R. and James M. McCormick, eds. *The Domestic Sources of American Foreign Policy: Insights and Evidence*, 3rd ed. New York: Rowman and Littlefield Publishers, Inc., 1999.

WuDunn, Sheryl and Nicholas D. Kristof. *Japan as No. 1? In Debt, Maybe, at the Rate Things Have Been Going. New York Times.* 1 September 1999. Internet   edition. <http://www.nytimes.com/yr/mo/day/news/financial/japan-debt.html>.

Yamaguchi, Jiro. *The Gulf War and the Transformation of Japanese Constitutional Politics, Journal of Japanese Studies.* 18:1, 1992: 155–172.

Yamaguchi, Noboru. Colonel Ground Self Defense Forces, Deputy Chief of Defense Planning Division, Ground Staff Office, Japan Defense Agency. Interview by author 2 June 1998, Tokyo, Japan, Tape Recording. In author's personal possession, Tempe, Arizona.

Yamamoto, Ichiro. Member of the House of Councillors of the Japanese Diet. Interview by the author, 18 June 1998, Tokyo. Tape Recording. In author's personal possession, Tempe, Arizona.

Yamauchi, Toshihiro. *Gunning for Japan's Peace Constitution, Japan Quarterly*. April- June 1992: 159–167.

Yanai, Shunji. *Law Concerning Cooperation for United Nations Peace-Keeping Operations and Other Operations: the Japanese PKO Experience, The Japanese Journal of International Law.* 36 (Tokyo: The International Law Association of Japan, 1993): 33–75.

———. Vice Minister Japanese Ministry of Foreign Affairs (Currently Ambassador to the U.S.). Interview by author, 20 May 1998, Tokyo. Tape Recording. In author's personal possession Tempe, Arizona.

Yomiuri Shimbun. Appropriation Sought for Refueling Aircraft. 21 July 1999. Internet edition. <http://www.yomiyuri.co.jp/newse/ 0722po01.htm>.

———. *Law on Constitutional Poll Needed.* 9 August 1999. Internet edition. <http://www.yomiuri.co.jp/newse/0809ed16.htm>.

Zhao, Quansheng, ed. *Japanese Policymaking: The Politics Behind Politics:*

Informal Mechanisms and the Making of China Policy. Westport: Praeger Publishers, 1993.

Zinberg, Yakov. *In Search for Alternative National Interests: Russo-Japanese Territorial Disputes After the Cold War.* A paper presented at the 40th Annual Conference of the International Studies Association, Washington, D.C. February 17, 1999.

INDEX

Abandoned 45, 103–104, 108, 110, 112–113, 118, 122
Abandonment 67, 70, 104–105, 108, 115, 117, 145–146
Abnormal 23
Absolute gains 62, 64–66, 174–175
Academics 14, 77–78, 82–84
Adjusting to the post-Cold War world 136
Aegis 185
Agriculture 112
Air Self Defense Forces (ASDF)
See also ASDF
Alliance 19, 34, 41, 44, 62, 64, 81, 103, 105, 107–108, 110–113, 115–117, 119, 121–122, 137–138, 146, 150, 162
Allied leaders 25, 28
Ally 7, 31, 34, 47, 67, 104, 107, 113, 115–119, 136, 141, 143, 147, 149–150, 171–172, 177
America 60–62, 67, 69–70, 88, 93
American foreign policy 108, 121, 143
Americans 34, 41, 67, 110, 139–140, 163
Anglo-American relationship 60
Anti-Nationalist 34

APEC 8, 67
Apology 31, 46–47
ARF 8, 64, 67, 115–116, 121, 147
Article Nine 4–6, 8, 15, 17, 23–39, 57, 60, 63, 65–68, 70–71, 76–77, 80–82, 84, 91, 111, 118, 136, 143– 145, 161, 163–168, 170, 172, 174–175, 177
ASDF 91
ASEAN 8, 12, 67, 113, 115–116
ASEAN Regional Forum (ARF)
See also ARF
Ashida Amendment 30
Asia-Pacific Economic Cooperation forum (APEC)
See also APEC
Association of Southeast Asian Nations (ASEAN)
See also ASEAN

Bilateral 88, 110–111, 114–116, 146, 149
British 58, 60
Bully 25, 140, 143
Bureaucratic Decision making 11, 72
Bureaucrats 19, 57, 65, 72, 83, 87, 112, 160
Bush, George H.W. 36

Cabinet 13, 23, 26–27, 29–30, 32–33, 38, 114, 165
Cambodia 40, 42
Cambodia, Mozambique, and the Golan Heights 42
Capitalist 61, 117, 121–122, 176
Catalyst for change, the 4
Change agents 15, 18, 75–76, 79, 171–172
China 8, 12, 18, 24–25, 39, 45–46, 81, 89, 104–111, 113–117, 119, 121, 123–124, 137–138, 145–147, 150, 162, 167–170
Clean government 41
Clinton, William J. 62, 104, 111
Cold War 3–7, 10, 12, 16, 19, 24–25, 28, 31, 33–35, 44–45, 57, 59, 66–71, 73, 75, 88, 104–106, 111–112, 114, 136, 140, 143, 159, 168, 171, 174–175
Colonial 113, 117
Colonizing 114
Communist bloc 31
Concluding remarks 175
Conclusion 119, 151
Consensus 15, 17, 24, 28, 41, 57–58, 62, 77
Conservative 29, 33, 38–39, 46, 89, 124, 147, 164
Constitution 3–6, 15, 18, 23–40, 57, 59–60, 66, 82, 91, 105, 107, 111, 119, 121, 136, 142, 144, 149, 160– 164, 166, 168–170
Constitutional Limitations 3, 63, 71, 107, 136, 143, 145, 151, 174
Constitutional reform 26, 34, 82, 163
Cooperation 6, 8, 23, 36, 41, 63–64, 66–67, 70, 105, 108, 114, 116, 120–121, 146–147, 174
Crisis 6, 16, 35–36, 40, 45, 73, 87–88, 91, 106, 111–112, 116, 136, 149–150, 163, 165–167, 170–171, 178

Cultural politics 43
Curtis, Gerald L. 11–12
Cybernetics 11, 72–73

Decision making 69–70, 72–77, 79, 81, 83, 86–87, 91, 139, 172, 175–176, 178
Defense agency 14, 31, 61, 72, 83, 144
Demilitarized Zone (DMZ)
    See also DMZ
Democratic 12–13, 24, 26, 32, 41, 48, 58, 61, 78, 87, 110, 117, 121–122, 141, 160, 176
Democratic Socialist Party (DSP)
    See also DSP
Democratization 26
Dètente 9
Diet 3, 6, 13–16, 18, 23–24, 29–30, 36–37, 40–43, 47–48, 61, 68–69, 73–75, 77–87, 89, 91, 103, 112–113, 136–139, 151, 159–162, 164, 166–167, 169, 171, 175–176
Diplomatic 12, 27, 61, 77, 105, 148, 150
DMZ 117
Domestic
Economy 107, 112
Political systems 11, 72
Drifte, Reinhard 12, 111, 139
DSP 41

East Asia 7–8, 15, 19, 30, 45–46, 48, 60, 61, 67, 81, 89, 92, 103–104, 110, 113–114, 119, 121, 123–124, 135, 145, 147, 163, 167, 169, 174, 177
East Asian security 67, 116, 121
Economic
Conflicts 104
Power 43, 67, 73, 80, 90, 104, 106–107, 135, 139
Slump 18–19

Strength 3, 59, 165, 175, 177
Economy 7, 19, 62, 71, 80, 106–107,
  111–112, 115, 117, 140, 143, 165,
  167
Emperor 27–29, 44
Expansionism 35

Field research, the 83
Fora 15, 64, 67, 80, 116, 121, 147,
  174
Foreign ministry 13–15, 41
Foreign policy
Normalization 167
Restructuring 8–10, 57, 62, 69–70,
  73, 84, 86, 89, 91–92
Foreign pressure 75, 139, 141–144,
  172, 174–176
Further research 175
Future sources of foreign policy 159

Gaiatsu 19, 34, 36, 40, 75, 81, 87–88,
  92, 124, 135, 139, 172, 174, 177
Gaijin 16
GDP 34, 140
Generation 7, 144, 166, 169–171,
  175–177
Geo-strategic 135–136
Germans 40
GNP 5, 106
Golan Heights 42–43, 68
Goldmann, Kjell 8–10
Goodwill 66, 143–144, 148, 174
Government officials 14, 78
Great power 3, 48, 59, 87, 145, 152,
  159
Ground Self Defense Force (GSDF)
See also GSDF
GSDF 105
Guidelines 16, 61, 80, 145, 149–150,
  162, 176
Gulf War 5–6, 8, 16, 18, 25, 35–38,
  43, 68–70, 72–73, 75, 79, 88, 104,
  136, 141, 148, 152, 161, 165,
  168, 171, 175
Gulf War and Japanese foreign policy,
  the 35

Hasagawa, Genkichi 29
Hatoyama, Ichiro 32
Hegemon 18–19
Hermann, Charles 8, 10–11, 13, 15,
  18–19, 57, 68–77, 86, 89, 92, 139,
  142, 159, 171–172, 175
Hermannís model 11, 172
Historical background 25
Holsti, Kal 8–10
Hosokawa, Morihiro 37, 105, 113
House of Counselors 14, 32, 41
House of Representatives 14, 30, 41
How Japan views its place in the world
  and the ìmythî of gaiatsu 135

ICBM 113
Ideologues 161
Imperial 28, 35
Implications for Hermannís model -
  What have we learned? 171
Independence 60, 62, 88, 136, 143
India 15, 105, 115, 138, 162, 176
Influence 7, 18, 25, 35, 43, 45, 63,
  66–68, 70, 72, 74, 76, 80, 87, 89,
  104–105, 124, 139, 143, 159–160,
  162, 168, 171–172, 174–176
Intercontinental Ballistic Missiles
  (ICBM)
See also ICBM
International community 36, 38–39,
  73, 112, 160, 174
International economy 107, 112
International politics and the PKO 39
International relations 19, 57, 63–64,
  66, 68, 174
International system 7, 19, 92, 139
Internationalization 169
Introduction 3
Iran 107

Iraq 5, 35–37
Ishihara, Shintaro 44, 61–62, 170

Japan Communist Party (JCP)
See also JCP
Japan Defense Agency (JDA)
See also JDA
Japanís
Limitations 166
National security 105
Options 111
Passing 104, 111
Security options 103
Japanís future 168
Japanese
Foreign policy 4–8, 10–20, 24–25, 31,
    34–35, 47, 57, 60–61, 63, 66–68,
    73, 75–83, 86–87, 89, 92, 105,
    107–108, 110–111, 116, 124,
    136–137, 139, 141–142, 159–162,
    166, 168, 170–171, 174–177
Hegemony 19, 159, 166
Imperialism 46
Limitations 58
Power 13, 27, 87, 139
Japanese foreign and security policy
    1952-1990 31
Japanese foreign policy 17, 144, 148
Japanese National Security Council
    185
JCP 59, 116, 141, 164
JDA 72–73, 83–84, 160

Kades, Charles 27
Kaifu bill and why it failed, the 40
Kaifu, Toshiki 36–37, 40–41, 74
Kato, Ryozo 47, 88, 143, 148, 165
KEDO 116
Kenpou 26–27, 29, 31–32, 37, 57,
    67, 83, 136, 147, 160–161,
    163–164, 166
Koizumi, Junichiro 185
Komeito 41

Korean Energy Development
    Organization (KEDO)
See also KEDO
Korean peninsula 16, 47, 108, 110,
    117–118, 150
Korean War 28, 31, 117
Koreas 145, 150
Kuril Islands 115
Kuwait 5, 35–36

Law concerning cooperation in U.N.
    peacekeeping and other opera-
    tions, the 6, 23
LDP 12, 24, 33–34, 38–39, 41, 44,
    58, 61–62, 70, 72, 74, 82,
    163–164, 170
Leadership 3–4, 7, 13, 18, 28, 47–48,
    61–62, 68, 70, 73–75, 80, 87, 89,
    91, 105, 135–136, 142, 144, 147,
    150–152, 159, 164–172
Lee Kwan Yew 40
Left wing 24, 33–34, 39, 147
Legal issues 37
Liberal Democratic Party (LDP)
See also LDP
Limitations 3, 28, 34, 58, 63, 65–66,
    71, 76, 107, 136, 143, 145–146,
    149, 151, 166, 172, 174–175, 177
Literature, the 8

MacArthur, Douglas 5, 23, 26–29, 31,
    164
Manga 45
Mass culture 169
Maturation 3, 7–8, 16, 87
Meiji 26, 33, 39
Middle East 35, 106, 108
Military power 18, 24, 39, 59, 80–81,
    86, 88, 90, 106, 113
Ministry of Foreign Affairs (MOFA)
See also MOFA
Miyazawa PKO bill, the 41
Miyazawa, Kiichi 37, 39–41, 74

MOFA 13, 18, 47–48, 61–62, 72–74,
79–81, 83–84, 86–88, 106,
112–113, 115, 136, 143–144, 146,
148– 149, 159–160, 164–166,
169–171, 175–176
Mozambique 42–43
Multilateral 12, 64, 80, 91, 110–111,
115–116, 121, 138, 145–148, 161,
174, 177
Multilateral efforts 146
Multilateral options including
ASEAN/ARF 115
Multinational 36, 165
Murayama, Tomiichi 37, 47
Myth 19, 90, 135, 140, 142, 144, 172
Myth of gaiatsu, the 140

National Police Reserve (NPR)
See also NPR
National Safety Forces (NSF)
See also NSF
National security 5, 15, 19, 43, 45,
59, 103, 105–107, 110, 117, 121,
143, 147, 165, 176
Nationalist 34, 44–45
Natural resources 58
Nemawashi 24
Neoinstitutionalists 66
Neorealism 7
Neutral 42, 44, 59, 116, 119
New world order 4–5, 71, 175
Normal 4–5, 7–8, 43, 45, 138, 142,
144–145, 149, 152, 169
Normal nation 4, 7–8, 16, 25, 46, 81,
142, 144–145, 164, 166–169, 175
North Korea 15, 25, 47, 75, 91–92,
106, 108, 110, 117–119, 150–151,
162
Northeast Asia 108–111, 115–116,
118, 121, 174
NPR 31
NSF 31
Nuclear umbrella 33, 112, 115, 119,

162
Nuclear weapons 24, 32, 105, 118,
138

Objectives and expected significance
of the book 18
Obuchi, Keizo 39, 117
Occupation forces 28, 31
Occupation government 5, 23, 28
ODA 82, 160
Official Development Assistance
(ODA)
See also ODA
Oil 35–36, 41, 45
Old verses new 88
Older generation 7, 47, 58, 88–89,
166, 177
OPEC 35
Options 12, 19, 60–61, 63, 66–67,
70, 91–92, 103, 105–106,
111–113, 115, 117–119, 123–124,
145, 147, 150, 167, 174, 176–177
Ota, Kazuo 24, 61
Outline of the book 19
Overview of the results of the field
research 86
Oxwalk 58

Píyongyang 118
Pacific Rim 34, 39, 114, 116
Pacifism 4, 29, 31–32, 44, 150, 152,
161, 165–166, 168, 175–176
Pakistani 15
Pax Americana 4, 45, 112, 135, 159
Peace constitution 23, 164
Peace Keeping Forces (PKF)
See also PKF
Peacekeeping Operations (PKO)
See also PKO
Peacekeeping operations law
See also PKO Law
Peacetime 88
Philippines 40, 135, 167

PKF 148–149, 169
PKO 6, 8, 13–14
PKO Law 6, 8, 13–18, 23–25, 37–38,
  40, 43, 48, 58, 68, 71–74, 77–79,
  82, 136, 142, 148–149, 161–162,
  165, 175
PKO law 37
Political debate, the 40
Population 40, 58–59, 76, 107, 162
Post-Cold War 18, 61, 64, 68, 70, 74,
  77, 87, 92, 104, 111–112,
  135–136, 145, 147, 162, 170–171,
  175
Potsdam declaration 25
Power politics 143, 172
Power projection 60, 146, 151
Pragmatic realism 172
Prime Minister 27, 30–33, 36–37,
  39–42, 47
Prime Ministerís Office 13, 83–84,
  141, 149, 159, 161, 170
Public opinion 19, 44, 108, 149,
  160–161
Public support 57–58, 92, 149

Raw materials 45, 58, 107
Realism 57, 62–66, 70, 91, 105, 172,
  174
Realists 7, 64, 70, 91, 108, 121, 147
Regional 7–8, 12, 19, 25, 67, 106,
  110, 113–121, 135, 145–148, 150,
  168–169, 174, 177
Reinterpretation 34, 57, 91, 174
Relative gains 62, 64–67, 70, 108,
  174–176
Reliability and validity 15
Research
Elite interviewing 13
Model 68
Question 6
Tool 77
Right wing 17, 114, 124, 152
Rise 7, 18, 35, 107

Rogue 47
Roh Tae Woo 40
ROK 118
Rosenau, James N. 3, 8–10, 69
Russia 106, 108, 113, 115, 119, 121,
  137–138, 162

Sackton, Frank 27–28
Safety Ministry 32
Saikosaibansho 33
San Francisco Peace Treaty 31
SCAP 27–31
SDF 5–6, 8, 16, 23–25, 30–31, 33–44,
  46, 68, 81, 84, 88, 103, 117, 139,
  141, 144–145, 148–149, 151,
  159– 166, 168–169, 171, 174, 176
SDF in Japanese foreign policy, the
  162
SDP 24, 37, 59
SDPJ 58, 72
Sea Lanes of Communication (SLOC)
See also SLOC
Second World War
See World War II 3, 5, 7, 23, 34, 43,
  46, 78, 81, 113, 145
Security 5, 7–8, 12, 19, 23, 25, 31,
  37–38, 43, 45, 58–60, 63–64,
  66–67, 80, 92, 103–113, 116–118,
  120– 121, 123, 137–139, 143,
  145–148, 150, 163, 169–170, 174,
  176–177
Security Council 24–25, 38, 43, 46,
  61, 67, 137–138, 148
Security policy 16, 34, 37, 60–61, 64,
  66, 80, 88, 111, 115, 119, 139,
  147, 149–150, 160, 176
Security Treaty 5–6, 12, 24, 33–34,
  43, 45, 59, 61–63, 66–67, 71, 81,
  103, 105–106, 110–111, 114,
  116– 117, 135, 141, 145, 162, 170
Self Defense Forces (SDF)
See also SDF
Self-defense 16, 43, 146, 149, 151,

161
September 11 185
Simon, Sheldon 63–64, 116,
    145–147, 169, 174
Singapore 40
Sino-American 115
SLOC 45, 66, 105, 107, 116
Social Democratic Party of Japan
    (SDPJ)
See also SDPJ
Socialist Party 17, 30, 32, 41
South Korea 24, 40, 47, 80, 89, 105,
    113, 116–119, 121, 124, 135, 151,
    177
Sovereignty 25–26, 29, 34–35, 47,
    135, 139, 141–142, 175, 177
Stagnation 160
Statesmanship 78
Story of Japanís ìabnormalî foreign
    policy under Article Nine, the 23
Story to be told and the puzzle to be
    solved, the 3
Suggestions for foreign policy normal-
    ization 170
Supreme Commander for the Allied
    Powers (SCAP)
See also SCAP
Supreme Court 33

Taiwan 105, 108, 116, 123, 138, 150,
    163, 170
Technology 24, 58, 113, 137, 146
Theater Missile Defense (TMD)
See also TMD
Threat 5, 9, 15, 23–24, 26, 29, 59,
    66, 80, 91, 103, 105–108, 110,
    114–121, 137–138, 145–146, 151,
    162– 163, 168, 170
Tiananmen Square 123
TMD 91
Towards a Security
Council seat and beyond 43
Trade 45, 59, 66, 104, 107–108, 112,

138–139, 141
Trilateral 111, 121

U.N. peacekeeping mission 15–16, 68
U.S. forces 16, 110, 117, 135, 176
U.S. military 59, 61, 105, 118, 135
U.S./Japan Security Treaty 5, 12, 34,
    59, 66–67, 103, 105–106,
    110–111, 114, 116–117, 135, 141,
    145, 162, 170
U.S./Soviet 4
UN
See also United Nations
Unconstitutional 121, 151, 169
UNESCO 67
Unilateral 118
Unilateral Options or go it alone 118
United Nations 6, 24–25, 31, 35–40,
    42–43, 45, 66, 119, 148–149
Educational, Scientific, and Cultural
    Organization (UNESCO)
See also UNESCO
See also Security Council
Transitional Authority-Cambodia
    (UNTAC)
See also UNTAC
United States 103, 105–106,
    108–111, 114, 139–141, 145,
    148–150, 165, 174
United States in terms of gross nation-
    al product 5
UNTAC 40, 42
US/Japanese relations 6

Variables 16

Wa 24, 57, 107
War on terrorism 185
What is Japan doing? 145
Where is Japan going? 159
Whitney, Courtney 29
World
Community 3, 59, 104, 168, 171, 177

Leadership 151, 159, 165–168
World Trade Organization (WTO)
See also WTO
World War II 4, 16–17, 24–25, 28, 32,
    35, 37, 40, 45–47, 58–59, 61, 89,
    113–115, 124, 135, 143, 161, 165,
    167–170, 175, 177
WTO 107

Yoshida Doctrine 5–7, 33, 35, 59–62,
    70–71, 112, 135, 143, 171
Younger generation 7, 48, 58, 68, 75,
    87, 89, 144, 166, 169–170, 175,
    177

Zemin, Jiang 39